THE EAGLE AND THE LOTUS

THE EAGLE
AND THE LOTUS

Western intervention in Vietnam
1847-1968

J. F. CAIRNS

LANSDOWNE PRESS

First published 1969 by
LANSDOWNE PRESS PTY LTD
346 St Kilda Road Melbourne
Copyright © 1969 J. F. Cairns

SBN 70180160 3

Printed and bound in Australia by
Wilke and Company Limited
37-49 Browns Road
Clayton Victoria

CONTENTS

INTRODUCTION

Mourn not the dead
But rather mourn the apathetic throng,
  The cowed and meek
Who see the world's great anguish and its wrong
  And do not speak.
Anon.

By 1963 I thought that the war in Vietnam would escalate (greatly intensify and extend), that it could not be won and that American and allied troops would eventually have to be withdrawn with a very uncomfortable loss of face.

I thought that most of the 'Viet Cong' were South Vietnamese and most of their arms and supplies had *not* been brought in from North Vietnam or anywhere else. I thought their dynamic for action was not imported but was the dynamic of a national revolution.

I expected that as the American attack escalated, more North Vietnamese would become involved, and more arms and supplies for the Viet Cong would come from China, the Soviet Union and European Communist countries.

But I believed that the war would eventually stop because of the strength of the resistance in Vietnam and because a sufficiently large number of Americans would object either to the use of their impersonal, overwhelming war *machine* against *people,* or would reject the cost and risks of escalation towards a war against China.

I believed that the war was not justified as a defence of America or her allies, nor was it in the interests of the Vietnamese people, whose interests were really served by the emergence of those 'transformations and innovations' of the national revolution, which had really created the 'Viet Cong', and which the American military intervention was impeding and suppressing.

I put forward these views at hundreds of meetings all round Australia in a plea against militarisation of the intervention in Vietnam as Diem faced the Buddhists in 1963 and after his overthrow and assassination by our 'friends'.

Some of my critics have said that I came to my conclusions about Vietnam and then looked at the facts.

In reaching them I was influenced by a theory of history, but from 1962 I devoted many hours of study to the facts. I first remember thinking of Indochina soon after World War II. I thought of it in vague contrast to Indonesia, Singapore and Malaya, which countries I studied and later lectured on, in the University of Melbourne.

During the years 1948 to 1950 I gave five or six lectures on Indochina for the Victorian Adult Education Council. These lectures covered a brief twentieth-century history and comments on current events since 1945. Indochina was then in the news because of fighting in Tonking for which the Communists were blamed.

In 1948-50, I tried to sum up the current position in a way that was not altogether accurate. I said it appeared the French were again well established in Indochina; that the fighting in Tonking would not become a problem for them, let alone for the world, and it was hardly likely that there would be much change in the constitutional relationship between the French and Indochina; and finally, although the people in Indochina had suffered great injustice at the hands of the French, there was so much conflict between the peoples of Tonking, Annam and Cochinchina that they would not be strong enough to embarrass the French much.

Between 1950 and 1954 I did not keep up with events in Indochina and the defeat of the French at Dien Bien Phu came as a surprise. As time went on I thought the settlement at Geneva was reasonable, but I was surprised that the British and Australian governments had not supported the American attempt to continue the war. The establishment of the Diem government appeared to me to be nationalist and effective, and it seemed the Americans were now following a line—as compared to continuing the war—that was better for the people of South Vietnam and one that might work. I saw and listened to Ngo Dinh Diem when he came to Australia in 1957. I was impressed by his physical fitness and confidence, but alarmed by his assumptions of god-like purposes. I was dismayed at the uninformed and superficial attitudes of the Australian authorities.

It was not until 1959 that enough reports were available to suggest that things were far from well in South Vietnam. Invariably these reports were that Diem had done all he could to round up or destroy what was left of the Communists in South Vietnam and that the Communist-led rebels were few in number, mostly local, poorly armed and supplied only by captured weapons.

The despatch of Australian 'advisers' to Vietnam to aid Diem in 1962 passed almost unnoticed. I did no more than watch the position much more closely. It was not until early in 1963 that I began to fear what seemed likely to happen in Vietnam.

By then it appeared that the Diem Government was a reactionary dictatorship and in June 1963 I predicted its overthrow. When that happened, and after the assassination of John Kennedy, I thought that Vietnam would extend into a world crisis. It seemed to me then that America, under the influence of Cardinal Spellman and many of his bishops and priests, was committed to a holy war in Vietnam; that Australia would be drawn in, and, as the American sponsored government in Saigon proved incapable of maintaining itself, American (and Australian forces) would take over more and more of the fighting. Because of failure in South Vietnam, I thought fighting would extend to the North and later turn against China.

I did say late in 1963 that Australia would have more than a hundred thousand troops in Vietnam within a couple of years. I said that to justify it and make it possible, the government, relying on the Santamaria-led Catholics, would stir up a holy war atmosphere in Australia in which people who dissented would be ostracised and gaoled. I was too pessimistic. Democratic sentiment, or perhaps apathy in Australia, was too strong.

The American military escalation in Vietnam was more gradual than I expected and I had not realised how much involvement in Vietnam, for the Australian government, was merely a political or propaganda exercise. It was not that the Australian government really feared, or cared, about what was happening in Vietnam. It sent troops there to please America in the hope that sending them would impose a moral obligation on the Americans to defend us whatever happened. For the Australian government, and most of its supporters on this matter, it was security on the cheap and it was to remain that way.

When I first spoke in Parliament about Vietnam in 1963 I emphasised the error and evil of the military escalation. I said nothing about the 'Viet Cong' except that they had a lot of internal support and that they were being killed. I noted one report that said 'of the approximately 400 "Viet Cong" killed each month it is inevitable many should be innocent bystanders' and 'many can be killed in error'.

Statements like this have led some of my belligerent opponents to conclude that I wanted the 'Viet Cong' to win. The people who were killed like this in Vietnam certainly had my sympathy but I was doing no more than stating facts. I asked Parliament in September 1963: 'How many innocent bystanders can be "killed in error" and how long can such killings continue?'

Knowing human behaviour as I do I thought *that* was the crucial question about the war in Vietnam.

During 1964, 1965 and 1966 I spoke at over 600 meetings about Vietnam and wrote innumerable articles and notes. I appeared at most of the 'teach-ins' and TV programs on the subject and I think I can claim to have maintained a standard as academic and objective as anyone.

The Eagle and the Lotus is the story of Vietnam as it grew in my mind during those years.

Many of its conclusions have changed and grown with the growth of the subject. They will continue to do so. But, now in 1969, I would like to state a few things about the war in Vietnam, for which, if the world ignores them, I think it will pay heavily. Perhaps no events in history more than those in Vietnam have proved how difficult it is for a social revolution to work its way out and how difficult it is to stop.

A social revolution is a shift in basic power in a society and, later, in the way things are done. The 'developing world' consists of countries that must have a social revolution if they are to develop.

In no two of these countries is the situation the same and Vietnam is a special case of acute development and conflict. In most of these countries the social revolution is far more slow-acting and less intense. But it is present in all.

It depends for its nature and strength (or lack of it) upon conditions *within* the country concerned. In most places there is sufficient strength in it to threaten the colonial or semi-colonial system within which it operates. Western capitalism, led by the United States, will always intervene against it and at best on the side of its most progressive opponents. China and the Soviet Union will vie with one another to give the social revolution the strongest imprimatur but will be cautious in giving it material aid. They will be delighted to see it cause trouble for America. They will be more likely to want that result than to be keen to work for its success. They will always put their own security well ahead of the revolutionary movement. America is much more counter-revolutionary than China or the Soviet Union is revolutionary.

But American experience in Vietnam will change some of this.

Her intervention has failed to achieve its objectives; so much so that a Communist government for South Vietnam is more likely now than it was in 1955. Consequently it is most unlikely that America will intervene again with mass military forces in any other country in Asia. There will be a return to the bias against American troops doing the fighting. There may be no place at all for American troops in Asian countries. America will be unable *not* to negotiate herself out of Vietnam although that inevitable result will be postponed as long as possible. Having done that she is not likely to go back in again. The Dulles doctrine *is* dead.

The significance of this for Australia is that it is a turning point in our relations with other countries. Our foreign and defence policy has always been to send our troops along with those of our powerful friends, Britain and then the United States, in the belief that this would guarantee that our powerful friend would always defend us.

This meant a policy of putting our troops into someone else's country. But first Britain, in her policy of independence for her colonies and her final withdrawal from Malaysia and Singapore, and now America in the case of Vietnam, are removing the foundations of this policy. One consequence of the old policy was that we saw things as Britain or America saw them—correctly or incorrectly. It seemed impossible for us to tolerate a different or a more objective view. (That this was true for the Menzies-Holt-Gorton governments in the case of Vietnam should cause no surprise, but that it was also the case for all in the Department of External Affairs except three or four is most disquieting.)

It is high time that we made a searching re-examination of all our foreign relations and particularly those with the United States. This book does not attempt to do that. It merely makes out the case that it must be done.

We in Australia may not have handed over our future fully to others. We may still be able to govern ourselves so that our large productive potential may develop under the power of individual enterprise and in accord with the priorities of public interest, here and abroad, and in a free and open society. However, it seems more likely that we will accept at best the dull mediocrity of public and private bureaucracies for the security it is expected to give. But the die may not be cast.

The significant point here is not whether it is or not, but that we must free ourselves from conventional submissiveness in foreign policy—we must cease to be military camp followers—if we are to have a chance of building a better society in Australia.

Because of its political motivation and ignorance the Australian establishment has confused dissent with subversion and enthroned dullness and conformity. This has come about only because it has been possible to exaggerate the red and yellow peril and convince people that to be safe we must fully submerge our independence to a powerful friend and his local spokesmen.

Before we can really progress we must win back our independence. We must use our own brains to decide what threatens us and to decide what we will do about that threat. Although the threat is not nearly as great as it has ever been made out to be, and although we have wasted millions reacting to it, we ourselves will need to do more to establish national security. But it may cost us much less.

There is an America of the military-industrial complex. There is an America that overmilitarises every situation. There is an America that would force the world back to the stone age rather than lose face and money. But these are not the only Americas. The struggle for human progress is more acute in America than anywhere in the world. This is because there are powerful forces in America for human progress. If we are to take sides in this matter we cannot take sides for or against America. We must take part in the American struggle.

The end of the war in Vietnam, and the American withdrawal, will leave the war drive in America little blunted. But it will *not reduce* the area of co-operation between Australia and the United States. It can mean a reduction in the military aspects of that co-operation and an increase in all the elements that go to make up economic progress in South East Asia and normal diplomatic and trading relations with China. It is in these circumstances that Australia may be able to work out a new foreign policy and thereby a way to produce here a much freer, more open, more humane and rational society, and one more committed to moral values. Vietnam could prove a turning point in our history. It could make us into a grown-up nation.

For us, this will be the only compensation for the unnecessary loss of hundreds of thousands of Vietnamese lives.

CHAPTER ONE

NINETEENTH CENTURY PACIFICATION

This much can be said of the 20th century so far: its wars have been more soaked in human blood and misery than any others in history. And no other war in this century has lasted so long, or been so complex, or created so much argument or disagreement as the Vietnam war.

No one can be sure that he possesses the ultimate truth about Vietnam. Certainly, simplistic views of the war must be rejected. Such views are based on errors of fact and judgment. But until a clearer understanding of what has happened and what is happening in Vietnam can be grasped, and until government policy is based on more accurate assessments, havoc and destruction will continue. For a long time there was the very grave risk of war between America and China because of the conflict in and around Vietnam, although the danger seems less at the moment. As for us in Australia, we have seen our nation torn and divided by bitter disputes about the war—without doubt the most unpopular this country has ever been engaged in.

But, thankfully, the war in Vietnam has been de-escalated. After the world was taken to the brink of catastrophe, it now sees peace talks instead. Three American administrations, those of Eisenhower, Kennedy and Johnson, were committed to the principle of a political solution to the war. But each continued a military escalation. Nixon, apparently more military than his predecessors, has now ruled out a military solution.

How did this come about? What caused America's 'agonising re-appraisal' that ended escalation and turned the world's most powerful military nation instead towards negotiation? What is so extraordinary about the Vietnam war? How did it begin? How can it really be ended?

The war in Vietnam did not begin in 1959 or 1960 or in 1945. A leading Vietnamese historian, Hoang Van Chi, wrote in 1964: 'Throughout the whole period of French colonial rule armed revolts rarely ceased, and even intermittent intervals in the fighting were marked by non-violent agitations. Even before the French came there had been a long struggle for independence of foreign powers and against others.'

For about a thousand years after the birth of Christ, Vietnam was occupied by the Chinese. For as many centuries, Indian influences penetrated into Vietnam. During this millenium, there was both resistance and assimilation, but the Vietnamese were able to retain their identity and did not become Chinese or Indian. Not only did they acquire a remarkable cultural unity with an inherent resistance to the Chinese, but an aggressiveness towards all who were not Vietnamese. This experience made them, perhaps, the most disliked and feared people of South East Asia.

Although they drove out their Chinese conquerors and won their freedom in 939 A.D., they were hardly ever free of Chinese attempts to take over. The Vietnamese, however, were able to withstand all attempts at foreign domination till the French succeeded in imposing it in the 19th century.

But it still remains true that the most unifying factor among the Vietnamese is their universal eagerness to resist China. Joseph Buttinger believes[1] that 'Between 940 and 1400, Vietnam, after a painful beginning marred by civil wars and conditions close to chaos, developed a stable and efficient political regime. The central power of the State, built around a hereditary monarchy, was normally supreme, and medieval Vietnam, even in times of crisis, always was united under one government.' And again, 'the unity of the country, which as a oneness of language, culture and national feelings has existed even during long periods of political separation, was one of the most striking features of 19th century pre-colonial Vietnam.'

Vietnam is not just a geographical area. It is a nation, a people, a language and a political identity whose strength and aggression is the result of foreign attacks and invasions for a thousand years. But Vietnam is Buddhist too and Buddhism in Vietnam is 18 centuries old.

At first and for a long time there was competition between two popular sects of Buddhism—the A-Ham or Agama and the Thien or Dhyana—until Thien became the most important. Thien, called 'Southern Buddhism', one of the many varieties of Mahayana Buddhism of China, Japan, Korea and Vietnam, spread to a minority in southern and central Vietnam. For the first time in history it achieved unification at the Buddhist National Congress, late in 1963 just after the overthrow of Ngo Dinh Diem.

Characteristics of Thien Buddhism are its lack of doctrine and its adaptability. It claims to reject anything which might hinder man's progressive reaching after knowledge and applying it in his daily life.[2] Thien is said to be an attitude or method for arriving at knowledge *and* action. Nhat Hanh writes: 'A person who practises Zen Meditation does not have to rely on beliefs in hell, nirvana or causality; he has only to rely on the reality of his body, his psychology, biology and his own past experiences or the instructions of Zen Masters who have preceded him. His aim is to *attain,* to *see*; once he has attained Satori (insight) his action will conform by itself to reality.'

But this is not all. The village pagoda does not often have a 'well-qualified Zen Master' and, 'for this reason' popular Buddhism in Vietnam is a 'mixture of some basic Zen elements and many practices of the Pure-Land sect.' The practice of the Pure-Land sect is to achieve concentration of mind through self-absorption and reciting the name of the Buddha. The practitioner keeps five precepts; abstention from killing, from acts of banditry and theft, from wrong sexual practices, from lying and from wrong speech and intoxicants. He is also expected to perform right actions. From all this he accumulates merit which will make his present life joyful and deliver him to the land of absolute joy or 'Pure-Land' after his death. In Saigon there is a large pagoda called Temple of the Zen-Pure Land School, and it is said that most of the village pagodas and their attendant monks belong to this school. The beliefs of the typical peasant are, in fact, a mixture of Buddhism, Taoism and Confucianism with other elements left from earlier native creeds. But these beliefs play a significant part in the spiritual make-up of the Vietnamese.

This cultural inheritance, in particular Buddhism and Confucianism, as we will see, was at 'the very core of the Royalist and Mandarinal Resistance against the French.'

In later years there has been what is called a 'renaissance of Buddhism' in South East Asia and it has coincided with the struggle for independence from white, European, Western powers. Equally there has been a Buddhist resistance against Communism, although this is little more than a decade old.

In Vietnam the revival of Buddhism began about 1930. In South Vietnam perhaps it reached its peak about 1963. The manifest desire of the Buddhists, in this revival, seems to be to reconstruct their country from top to bottom (or perhaps more accurately the other way round) and to '. . . mobilise the potential force of their religion to rebuild their society and consequently (to carry) Buddhism into every domain of life, culture, economics, politics, social welfare.'[3]

This Buddhist development, the Lotus, the 'third force' in South East Asia, or part of it, has of course come under attack both from American capitalism and from Communism. Of what is the Lotus capable? It is difficult to say. The weaknesses of Asia's progressive forces lay in this: that the established orders, whose very survival depended on resisting progress, were backed in their resistance by European intervention. The most recent example in Vietnam is the American intervention, the Eagle.

We will later see the nature and effects of this partnership. It is true that the Asian philosophy proved to be mystical and withdrawing. It was logical that it should be so. How could one be expected to believe that anything could be achieved when people were dying everywhere? Was it not inevitable that *fate* should be the dominating factor? But modern Buddhism apparently has begun to accept ideas of rational analysis, and to conceive that things on earth can be changed for the better.

So, indeed, has Communism, and perhaps this attitude is its dominant quality, and therefore chief interest for Asians. The Communists, too, do not accept submissiveness to fate and personal withdrawal. They believe that man can achieve everything through effort.

But there were other sources for this belief. The entire generation of Asians who looked to Sun Yat Sen, Tagore, and in Vietnam to Phan Boi Chau, Tang Bat Ho, Bui Quang Chieu and Phan Chau Trinh, whose work we will look at later, saw in these leaders a combination of the power of reason and a belief in human progress.

But the steps from belief to actual progress required severe social upheaval, since any progress challenged the very existence of the established orders. In Vietnam, of all places, the struggle, as we shall see, was the worst.

Certainly many of those who led the enlightenment in Asia were killed by the Communists, some of whom had learned their dogmatism in Russia and China. But the impact of the Eagle may have been the force that did more in Vietnam to help to re-establish belief in fate and in the powerlessness of man. It may be that the destruction of Vietnamese villages and cities, invariably by American bombs, napalm and firepower, destroyed the possibility of an 'enlightened lotus'. If it has, what it will have installed in its place is Communism. It is no answer to all this to say that Communism was inevitable, because the basic assumption of American intervention in Vietnam was that it was not inevitable.

If Asia is to progress she must change her old submission to the idea of an all-governing fate. She must change to an acceptance of reason and of humanly-initiated progress.

We may legitimately ask: how much has America's Vietnamese intervention contributed to such a change?

The Eagle may never have had any chance to do more than carry off the Lotus crushed in its talons. Well, if that is so, it would have been better if the Eagle had never flown in Vietnamese skies at all and the Lotus had been left to fight, with its own weapons, the dogmatism and inhumanity in Communism.

At any rate, it is false and misleading to believe that Vietnam had no indigenous strength for this struggle. Vietnam was always much more than a bunch of semi-feudal landlords and officials on the one hand and a bunch of dogmatic Communists on the other. This was the assumption behind American intervention, and it may well be that action based upon this assumption did most to give these very features to the actual situation.

It is false and misleading to give the impression, as is so often done, that Vietnam is a recent creation possessing very little feeling for unity. Her urge for unity is matched by her urge to resist foreign encroachment.

The only thing dividing the Vietnamese is the question of who should control the united Vietnam, the Vietnamese in the North or those in the South, and that conflict goes back, not to Geneva in 1954, but a thousand years.

The French conquest of Vietnam began quietly enough when French Jesuit missionaries arrived in Annam in 1662-3.[4] What these missionaries did was to provide the chief sanction for the intervention of Europeans in Vietnam, and the pressing cause of their maintaining and extending that intervention. This was so even when the intervention cost French and American governments and capitalists a staggering amount in money and material goods.

The spiritual link with Vietnam was always to remain critical in determining European intervention. It was finally able to outweigh for a long time a material cost to the United States of some $30,000 million a year. French conquest of Vietnam and Roman Catholicism were always inseparable. The link between the two provided for many Americans, and powerful Americans, an effective justification for the war until, finally, it was to be out-weighed by material factors and by a different spiritual factor. But this is to move too far ahead. France's intervention in Vietnam (Indochina) grew under the influence of the missionary Pigneau de Behaine who entered into a treaty with Nguyen Anh, a Vietnamese prince in exile, to help him regain the throne. With a little help from Frenchmen and arms, Nguyen Anh took Saigon by force, was crowned Emperor Gia Long, and conquered the whole of Annam.

The French revolution and its aftermath reduced French attention to Vietnam. The next Emperor, Ming Mang, a fervent believer in Confucianism, hated the French and banished or killed the missionaries in increasing numbers. He also dealt sternly with Vietnamese who had become Christian converts. These converts have a long record in Vietnam of identification as traitors and foreign collaborators. The French missionaries urged the French government to help the Vietnamese converts and to support Le, the pretender to the throne.

In April 1847, two French naval vessels appeared in the harbour of Tourane (Danang), the port of Hue, the royal capital, and bombarded the port in the classical European Christian style. Buttinger records that 'In 70 minutes French guns had taken a hundred times more lives than all the Vietnamese governments in two centuries of religious persecution.'[5] The French demanded that persecution of

missionaries must stop. But little was gained, and both under Thieu
Tri, who had succeeded Gia Long, and Tu-Duc, who followed Thieu
Tri, the Vietnamese attitude to missionaries and Vietnamese converts
did not change.

In France meanwhile, the practice of free elections was out of
fashion, and in December 1851 Louis Napoleon needed Roman Catholic help to bring off his coup d'etat. He received it, was successful, and
emerged subject to 'clerical pressure on behalf of the missionary interests in the Far East.' France was also anxious to keep up with
British expansion into China—the opium war had preceded Louis'
coup by two years.

The French expedition that went to Tourane in August 1857,
was unsuccessful. It was ravaged by disease and heat, and it turned
south to Saigon where, without resistance, it was able to capture the
city, whose total population could not have been beyond a few hundreds of thousands. With Saigon as their base, the French were able to
control the communications out of the Mekong delta and consequently
the supply of rice to the centre and north of Vietnam. Rice control was
the lever the French used to force an arrangement—the Treaty of
Saigon in 1861—upon the Emperor Tu-Duc. Furthermore, the French
gained a footing in Tonking (north Vietnam) through a pro-Christian
pretender from the Le dynasty. And in 1863, they negotiated a treaty
with King Norodom of Cambodia giving France complete control
over Cambodia's foreign affairs and consulates within the country.
Cambodian collaboration with the French was, from the start, for
protection against the Thais, and often against the Vietnamese.

But these arrangements did not give the French much power,
nor did they go deep in Vietnamese life, nor geographically into the
countryside. Vietnamese resistance never ceased and soon began to
take on a coordinated form. Historian Harold Isaacs saw it as 'The
line of French priests, conquerors and governors (which) is matched
by a line no less long of Indochinese fighters and martyrs and
leaders of the people.'[6]

Foreign intervention in Vietnam has been mainly, or even wholly,
military. But it became evident as long ago as the early 1890's that 'A
country is not conquered and pacified after military operations have
bent all heads by terror; when the first fear is overcome, ferments of
revolt will grow among the masses, which the accumulated bitterness
caused by . . . force will multiply and steadily increase.'[7]

There has been endless debate about 'how to win the war' in
Vietnam. The debate began about 1860. There is nothing new that
can now come into it. From 1847 to 1892, mostly under governors who
were admirals, the French relied upon force. But the 1890's brought to
Vietnam four young French colonels, one of whom was Gallieni. While
they too relied upon force and considered, as it would now be stated,

that 'security had to be established before you could win the support of
the people', they talked about other things. They asserted there must
be a broad program of civic action: roads, schools, markets and medical
posts had to be provided; in some cases there should be resettlement of
farmers and small loans for them should be provided. There is nothing
new about the idea that guerrillas often 'had the broadest popular
support'.[8]

The southern part of Vietnam, Cochinchina, was occupied by the
French between 1860 and 1867. Vietnamese resistance was, first, a
conventional war of two years' duration and then, after the Vietnamese
defeat, it became a long drawn out guerrilla campaign. There were,
under French navy administrations, many years of 'war winning'
experimentation which finally allowed 1883 to be accepted by the
French as the date of their conquest of Indochina.

By this time, Cochinchina was such that most large towns were
French controlled, but much of the delta and the provinces near
Cambodia were not. Tonkin and Annam were protectorates, with Hue
and Hanoi still open to guerrilla attacks. It was not until the end of
the 19th century that this, the first phase of Vietnamese resistance, can
be said to have ended. Till then, the resistance had been led by the
mandarins—those, who in the name of the Emperor, had been in
charge of all civil, military and judicial affairs, from the royal court
down to the village level, ever since Vietnam regained independence
from China in 939. At first, there was a general refusal to work for a
French-controlled administration, then followed the organisation of a
guerrilla campaign by the mandarins to harass the French, and insurrections to oust them. Guerrilla attacks and insurrections occurred
in all those very places which today fill the news about Vietnam.

Thus French rule, between 1870 and 1900, succeeded in uniting
mandarins and people, formerly separated, in a common fight against
foreign rule. 'Terror' was common on both sides. Vietnamese 'terror'
consisted of assassinations and kidnappings, which were frequent;
many villages, often Catholic, because they generally co-operated with
the French, were burnt down, both as a punishment and as a deterrent.
French 'terror' consisted of burning and blasting villages and a common example was the practice of beheading in a formal kind of
ceremony every man, woman and child in a village suspected of
helping the guerrillas.[9]

As a rule the guerrilla war was fought by small and constantly
moving bands of 20 or 25 soldiers. They captured their weapons and
ammunition from the enemy, attacked by night, retreated when they
met a superior force and merged into villages in the daytime. Today's
students of the protracted war 1870-1900, could logically conclude that
the guerrillas must have read Mao and Giap and must have been
controlled from some Communist headquarters outside the country.

Then, as now, Vietnam was divided—with one difference—there
was no talk of negotiations. It appears that the official French history
of Indochina shows not only all these familiar modern features over
and over again, but shows too, how French troops, numerically strong,
well equipped with overwhelming fire power, and well led, missed their
objectives; were subject to frequent ambush and received little aid or
information from the villagers, who, at the same time, provided 'the
sea' in which the guerrillas could swim.[10]

And so the debate about winning the war went on. Why was it so?
What had to be done? Everything was tried. French policy tacked
into the wind of Vietnamese resistance; first towards violence to establish order and then towards civic action to satisfy French conscience and because violence had failed. Massacres and ambushes
happened in exactly the same places where they have happened in
recent years. Areas were cleared and held. Security spread out like
an oil stain. Guerrillas were searched for and destroyed, and often,
as now, the same ones over and over again. Guerrillas were killed,
thousands of them; civilians were killed, and the claimed casualties
were far greater than the actual. The history of the war today could
have been written then.

But the 1870-1900 war appeared to be won. In a significant way
it was won. The mandarinal phase of resistance was defeated by 1893.
Its basis had been the leadership of the mandarins who were defending
their own positions. Although French intervention brought the people
to the side of the mandarins there was nothing in it for the people. The
mandarins wanted change even less than did the French. They organised resistance mainly because they wanted to stop change.
Buttinger concludes of this period: 'The death of the entire movement
was primarily due to the absence of meaningful political aims.' If there
was to be further resistance, clearly it would have to be led by *new*
men, inspired by *new* ideas, carried forward by *new* social forces and
organised in different ways. It would need 'meaningful political aims.'
Many of these new men and new social forces were to be activated by
the French intervention itself. But none of the new ideas could be
invented, none of the new men could come from outside, none of the
new organisation could be imposed like a conspiracy. They all had to
grow out of Vietnamese soil. And grow they did.

The mandarinal guerrilla campaign left its mark. Perhaps in no
other country in the world has the traditional system of government
given itself to the organisation of such a task. But the defeat of the
mandarinal resistance left its mark too.[11] It has been said, often
enough, that this defeat meant the destruction of the old system of
administration, and the destruction, as well, of the village as a social
and economic unit. This took away almost everything from the poor,
but it took away much from everyone. However, it seems, the end of

the mandarinal insurrection brought no substantial change. One of the pro-French mandarins summed it up in 1905:

'There is no piracy as formerly, but discontent reigns in every class of the Vietnamese population. The King has no longer any authority; the mandarins (are) deprived of moral direction (and) have no power . . . while the people are impoverished by taxes which mount ceaselessly and very rapidly. . . In my opinion, the actual situation is much more difficult than it was formerly. Then there were only a few bandits who ravaged the country, the rest of the population favouring France, but now the discontent is general.'[12]

Throughout this period the advocates of force had always, in the end, prevailed. Their object was order and control, force was the only means of achieving this. They recognised the need for support from the people, but no one was ever able to get it by 'civic action', or by the 'policy of association' (the policy of using collaborators), any more than by the policy of direct French rule. Very few ever took it seriously.

There were two main reasons for this. First, it was always the French people in Vietnam, the colony, who prevailed. They wanted full freedom to exploit the natives for excessive and untaxed profits, and if they suffered losses, they demanded that the taxpayers of France 'rush to their aid'. But the costs of colonial development, the railways, roads, buildings, had to be met, as far as possible, in the colony itself. And, since Frenchmen in the colony could escape taxation, it had to fall on the natives. Exports had to increase so the French could make money. Little could be manufactured in Vietnam because if much were, there would be fewer imports from France. Only a few Vietnamese were Western-educated and these were able to find only subsidiary positions even after their return from France.

But for Frenchmen at home, colonisation was not a hard-headed economic activity. It certainly was for the colons, but for France Vietnam was always expensive. By 1895, this 'imperialist adventure' was said to have cost France 750 million gold francs. It was the dominance of the French colons which explained many of the French failures. A second important reason was France's inability to get support from any Vietnamese who counted. Buttinger quotes a French historian, seriously worried about the problem: 'Those who collaborate with us succumb to the lure of money, or even worse, to unrestrained and unscrupulous ambition. Nobility of soul, disinterestedness, and courage are to be found in the opposition. Against this coalition of forces nothing can be done'.[13] Buttinger put it: 'A few Christians or crooks were the only ones whom the French managed to enlist.'[14]

People have wondered why 'corruption' among 'our' Vietnamese has prevailed through to 1969. They imagine that it can be removed somehow, and new, clean methods of government by 'our' Vietnamese established. They fail to realise that 'corruption' is endemic and inevitable. For those who collaborate with a foreign power there is no honour; there is only money and ambition. Why, then, did France persist with her resolute action to 'win the war in Vietnam'? For most of the time she did so not really for money or power, but for spiritual reasons.

No action of the kind sustained by the French in Indochina could have been maintained so long for purely pragmatic reasons. One can only sustain prolonged defeat and failure if the action is taken for spiritual reasons.

Frenchmen were convinced beyond doubt, even up to the point of their terrible retreat as prisoners from Dien Bien Phu, that they were in Vietnam for a 'higher purpose'. It was when things, from a practical view, looked the worst and hopeless, that France was the most determined to stay in Vietnam. What was called Pierre Leroy-Beaulieu's 'battle cry' of 1882—'Colonisation is for France a question of life or death'—was the spirit that always emerged when things looked blackest in real terms. France was in Vietnam for *civilisation* and because this was part of her own spiritual identity.

One *must* find spiritual motivation for an activity that strives after the impossible or which is otherwise unforgivably cruel and heartless. Among the cruel and heartless men France brought to Vietnam were others whose spirit, integrity and courage were magnificent. It could not have been otherwise. But the good men also were often enough involved in cruelty to the Vietnamese. Their spiritual beliefs justified that cruelty in their own eyes. The ends did justify the means, and this is the only way cruelty and barbarity can for long be justified.

CHAPTER TWO

MAKING A REVOLUTION

The second phase of the Vietnamese resistance began about 1900. It differed in many ways from the first phase, and the differences seem to have obscured some of the basic characteristics of the struggle which emerged again after the Second World War. The inspiration and leadership of the second phase was the 'national elite'—intellectuals and students of Vietnamese history who found the nature and results of foreign occupation intellectually repulsive. Perhaps the most important of them was Phan Boi Chau who began his work in 1900 and died in 1940. Chau looked to China and Japan for aid. It is probably fair to say that he assumed that Vietnamese liberation could come only from external aid and intervention. In a sense, he sought a revolution both from above and from outside. Chau was encouraged to look towards Japan rather than to China by another famous Vietnamese nationalist, Tang Bat Ho. They both found that China's Dr. Sun Yet Sen was inclined to see Tonking as an aid to revolution in China rather than a means of Chinese help for Vietnam. Yet another Vietnamese nationalist, Phan Chau Trinh, unwilling to regard Japan as a source of strength for the liberation of Vietnam, designed a plan which looked to the Vietnamese people themselves as the means of liberation. In a sense the rival leader to this view was Bui Quang Chieu, who, educated in France, worked for collaboration with the French. But his view also meant more Vietnamese say in affairs.

But Chau remained the most influential leader of them all, and it is said that, at least between 1907 and 1919, no act of resistance was committed in Vietnam, that was not directly instigated by Chau's agents or inspired by his teachings. This is said to be true for the movement to modernise education, for peasant demonstrations in Annam in 1908, and Cholon in 1913, for bombs exploded in Saigon and Hanoi and Hue, for the killing of collaborators all over the country, for insurrections in Tonking, for invasions by Vietnamese from China in 1914 and 1915, and for the widespread uprising led by the young Emperor Duy Tan in 1916.

Chau became convinced that the French had to be driven out of Vietnam by force. In 1907 he became disillusioned with Japan, who, badly in need of money following the 1905 war against Russia, recognised all French possessions in Asia in exchange for a loan of 300 million francs from France. Japan's victory over Russia may have strengthened Asian national movements by its very clear determination that Asians could defeat white people, but it turned the Vietnamese nationalist leaders to other sources for inspiration. In 1908, all Vietnamese students were required to leave Japan. Even Chau himself, and the Vietnamese nationalist Prince Cuong De, were excluded from Japan. After the 1911 revolutionary triumph in China, Chau and his friends turned to China and in that country they formed a Vietnamese government in exile. But Chau only too painfully discovered one of the features of the Chinese national movement—he was arrested in south China in 1913 and offered to the French for a large ransom. He was later freed as a result of intervention by Sun Yat Sen.

The high points of the 'national elite' resistance in Vietnam were in the years 1908, 1913, 1914, 1915, 1916 and 1918. One cannot escape the significance of the First World War in these dates, but it is by no means certain that the war changed the Vietnamese resistance significantly during those years. However, the return of more than 100,000 Vietnamese from Europe, where they had worked for the French Army, as well as the impact of the 1917 Russian revolution, must have had some meaning for later years. Certainly by 1930, or even by 1925, all the national elite and constitutional opponents of the French were either moribund or impotent. Formation of a unified Communist Party for Vietnam in 1930 coincided with, rather than caused, in 1930-32, the most general and significant uprising of the century up to that date. It may well be that Communists influenced the timing and nature of the uprising, but the materials for uprising were already present, and highly explosive.

Many writers have concluded, or agreed, that there is 'no darker year in the entire period of French rule in Vietnam than 1931'. Discontent was universal, resistance was general but organisation was almost non-existent. Thousands of Vietnamese were killed by the French 'not in the heat of any battles, because there were no battles,' but in the chase—the chase of human beings as if they were the quarry in a hunt.

Men, women and children were shot down as they fled, prisoners were taken and shot on written orders, only one in 10 being kept for interrogation. Suspects were condemned en masse, often without trial and mostly without evidence. The 'courts' sent hundreds to the guillotine. In 1933, after 'peace' had been established, there were still more than 10,000 prisoners in gaols and concentration camps and on the infamous island of Poulo Condore. By now, of course, Communism had come to the fore in both French claims and explanations, but Governor-General Pasquier on December 17, 1932, claimed that 'Communism has disappeared'. The French were convinced that the value of resolute action against the 'pirates' and 'Communists' had been proved along with the stupidity of those who had continued to argue that concessions should be made to the natives. The war in Vietnam had been won once more.

But it is obvious now that the uprising of 1930-32 and the ease with which it was destroyed proves much about the resistance between 1900 and that date. It is not easy to sum up the second phase in the Vietnamese resistance. The probability is that it caused more disruption than had resistance in the latter decades of the 19th century. More people were worse off both economically and socially. Discontent was far more widespread, and far more of its causes were results of the French occupation. Certainly for its leaders there was available a more complete and rational ideology—an understanding of what was wrong and what was needed to put things right—although the remedy was, in a sense, a general and negative one, that is, to oust the French.

Notwithstanding the existence of these stronger and more relevant causes for action, the resistance in the second phase does not appear to have been as great as the guerrilla campaign of the 1870-1900 period. What can have been the reasons for this? It cannot have been that the need for national independence was not sufficiently related to the need for economic and social reform, because this had been no better related in the earlier period. The most apparent difference is in leadership and organisation. The first phase of the resistance had been led by the mandarins and it was organised by their traditional governing system. The second phase was led by the national elite, but it was a leadership of ideas. To say this is not to deprive men like Chau of their significance, but merely to indicate what the needs of the Vietnamese resistance were in 1932—how it was important to show the intimate and vital connection between ousting the French and securing economic, political and social changes in Vietnam, and to organise for this purpose. The significance of the mandarinal government system, and what it was able to do in its guerrilla campaign of the 19th century, cannot have escaped the Vietnamese nationalists who were to lead the recovery from the debacle of 1932. But revolution from the top, that of the nationalist elite, was insufficient.

Organisation and leadership are vital for any change large enough to be called national, but unless there is deep-seated need for national change, organisation and leadership alone are not enough. Revolution requires material conditions, deep-seated national causes. It is no superficial thing. Change can be superficial or revolutionary. If change is to be revolutionary there must be deep-seated and long-operating causes. But both revolutionary and superficial change can be violent, and revolutionary change is almost certain to be violent.

Revolutionary change in Vietnam seems to be the outcome of two conditions, sometimes operating separately, but mostly together. The first conditions is the desire for national independence—to oust some foreign occupation or control. When this condition operates alone, as it did in America before 1776, it produces nothing but national independence. It brings about no internal economic or social change of much significance. Revolution, in this case, is the action taken against foreign occupation or control. Most of the history of Vietnam since 1858 has been that of a revolution against foreign occupation or control. Why has it never been possible for, first the French, and then the Americans, to find a way to 'win the war'? As Buttinger[15] puts it: 'The reason is simple. Foreign rule, no matter how enlightened, has always been irreconcilable with the moral needs of any civilised people'. The second condition which induces revolution is economic and social. It occurs when the economic and social system breaks down or imposes severe economic and social exploitation upon many people—perhaps a majority. In this case, revolution is the action taken to oust those who control the economic and social system. A severe breakdown of the system, or severe exploitation by it, may be modified by superficial changes and a potential revolution thereby can be prevented. Probably no great concessions are needed to have this effect, but ruling classes generally are not prepared to concede enough. It has been possible in the industrial countries in the 19th and 20th centuries—mainly because of the productive power of industry—to prevent violent revolutions.

But the operation of the system in Vietnam has produced a revolution. It must be emphasised that this situation is rare and has occurred only in countries that have not been industrialised. The Vietnamese revolution is rare indeed for other reasons—because of its intensity and because of its limitations. But it is a result alone of Vietnamese conditions; it has grown out of Vietnamese soil and it is fixed to that soil. One can draw lines on the map of Vietnam itself and the revolution is intense upon one side and almost non-existent on the other.

The unique intensity of the Vietnamese revolution and its fixity in Vietnam condemn the domino theory for the nonsense it really is. Revolutions are not exported; they are home-produced.

What accounts for the fact that there is a revolution in Vietnam? First of all, as we have seen, the revolution in Vietnam has taken over a century to mature. Its primary cause, again as we have seen, was the peculiar and lasting nature of foreign control—mainly that of the French. Not all foreign occupations have produced such an intense and general revolutionary reaction. In all probability none has done so—not the British, the German, the Portuguese, the Dutch or the Spanish. Each produced a resistance but none so intense as that in Vietnam. This is not because the French were morally one bit worse than the others; it seems to be because they were more efficient in creating a socially and economically more thorough colony. It was the French occupation that changed Vietnam fundamentally. In this sense, the French occupation produced the revolution, both as a national reaction to oust the foreigners and as a reaction against social and economic conditions, for it was the French occupation which produced these very conditions./

We have already seen something of the effect of the French presence on Vietnamese national feelings. What were the social and economic forces which combined with nationalism to produce the Vietnamese revolution? Buttinger[16] points out the direction in which we will find them when he wrote: 'These new forces, with their fresh concepts of action and sources of thought, *were only incidentally the result of political experience. They were primarily the result of the transformation of Vietnamese society.*' [Emphasis supplied.] These forces which produced the revolution were *not* imported into Vietnam, nor *invented* there, by Communists or others. They were produced in Vietnam and they in turn produced not only the revolution but the revolutionaries.

Pre-French Vietnam had been ruled by a professional, trained governing class—the mandarins. The basis of their power was the tradition that gave power to those who passed through prescribed study. It was not inherited privilege or wealth that gave power to the mandarins. Mandarins not infrequently became rich by the use of their political power, but they did not gain political power by first becoming rich. This system was destroyed, as we have seen, not by native developments, but by the economic changes produced by the French occupation.

Let us now sum up these changes which created the national revolution existing in Vietnam in the form it took by 1932. The French produced a semi-feudal class of big landowners who were able to exercise power over the resulting class of small landowners, tenants and landless labourers. Not only was there less land for people to own, and more division of what they did own, but there were more people trying to get access to land. Population increased,[17] doubtless both because of the upheaval itself and because of the greater use of medicines and medical techniques, limited as they were. Before this rural transformation, rice growing in Vietnam had been mainly for village consumption. People grew as much rice as they needed. Export of rice from Vietnam was prohibited. But under French rule rice exports became a main concern. Rice exports from Saigon in 1860 were 57,000 tons, in 1887, 320,000 tons and in 1937 had reached 1,500,000 tons. Rice growing therefore became a commercial activity and its economics were such that land holdings would be combined and farmers transformed into tenants and labourers. A large and increasing proportion of the crop would have to be paid to the landlords in rent so that more and more could be sold for exports. This rice is what the landlords made money from and what the French exporters needed.

By 1938, 2.5 per cent of all the landowners in Cochinchina owned almost half the land, and about 600,000 hectares of the 2,500,000 hectares of rice-growing land was owned by Europeans. Many people were employed as labourers on these large farms. Furthermore, by 1938 in Cochinchina, 72 per cent of the landowners had been sandwiched into 15 per cent of the land. In Tonking and Annam the result was not so extreme. In Tonking, the large landowners held 20 per cent of the land, and in Annam 10 per cent. In both areas small landowners made up about 98 per cent of all landowners, and held in Tonking 40 per cent, and in Annam 50 per cent of the land.

But associated with this concentration of land there was harsh exploitation of labourers, tenants and small landowners. Labourers were exploited by low wages, tenants by excessive rents and small landowners by high cost of land and high interest charges. Tenants and small landowners had to borrow to obtain rice seed. Rural debt in Cochinchina increased from 31 million piastres in 1900 to 134 million piastres in 1930. The tenant or farmer had little rice left after he paid rent and interest and the small landowner was not much better off. In fact it was mainly the debt and interest process that brought small farms under the control of the landlords who were also the lenders.

'This drive for change in the countryside is rooted in the agrarian system of South Vietnam. That system was characterised, on one hand, by a great concentration of land in the hands of a few, on the other, by a great mass of peasants who were either entirely landless or whose plots were too small to support them. Added to this was the fact that rents in kind were crushing (40-50 per cent of the crop). Investigations by French geographers and agronomists on the eve of the Second World War enable us to bring the picture into sharper focus. In the Annam coast strip, 30 per cent of the peasants had no land, 65 per cent had less than half a hectare, while 0.058 per cent of the population held ten per cent of the land. In the provinces south and west of Saigon the geographer Pierre Gourou states that two out of three peasant families were landless; almost 50 per cent of the land in this area was held by one-fiftieth of the population.'[18]

Another factor conducive to revolution was that the semi-feudal class of Vietnamese landlords was able to exercise powers of life and death over labourers, tenants and small farmers, but had little power in national affairs—this power was exercised by the French. This factor made the landowners into poor collaborators although not into revolutionaries. Buttinger records:[19] 'The largest group (of non-revolutionary nationalists), despite deep political discontent, who consistently worked for a modus vivendi with the colonial regime, were the big landowners'. But, 'When the large uprisings of 1930 and 1931 occurred in Tonking and Annam, the leaders of the Constitutionalist Party, by siding with the French and applauding the brutal suppression of the revolutionary movements, no doubt assured the continued existence of their party, if only as a political corpse.'

Yet another factor inducing revolution, and a significant one, was that the wealthy Vietnamese could not invest in industry, and little in commerce, in Vietnam. Industry in Vietnam was discouraged because the French wanted to import from France and would brook little competition. There was no tariff party in Vietnam. Commercial investment was supplied and controlled very largely by the Bank of Indochina and its few associates. The wealthy Vietnamese never became a bourgeois class as the French often claimed. Instead they remained outside both the economic system and 'society' and were frustrated and humiliated by their experience. The native rich remained landowners, and landowning gave them little honourable status. They severely exploited their own people and accumulated wealth but remained unable to contribute to economic progress. Buttinger believes that: 'The absence of true independence enabled the French to cut the purchasing power of the Vietnamese almost in half.'[20]

In essence, the land question in Vietnam changed from an overall shortage to unequal distribution—social and economic inequality came with it and added further to the revolutionary dynamic. Ever larger quantities of rice were produced in the country as a whole, more and more were exported while the peasants' share declined until they could meet their rent and interest obligations only by eating less. At the same time the accumulated wealth could not supply the process of industrialisation. Once it began, this process was never halted or modified. Like the war being fought (which preserved it) the process had an inexorable tendency to 'escalate'.

There were even more extremes in other fields of French economic activity. Rubber became second to rice in exports, followed by coal, tea and coffee. Tungsten and tin were to come later. On the rubber, tea and coffee plantations, and in the coal mines, exploitation was more extreme than on the rice paddies. The corvée, or forced labour, which used also to build railways and provide men for service in France's wars, was the rule till as recently as about 1935. The system of employment was virtual slavery.

Time and time again French administrations tried by laws and regulations to reduce the burden of rent and interest, to make land easier to get, to protect native labour on the plantations and in the mines, and to provide 'civic action'—schools, medical posts and markets. What is being tried now in Vietnam under the heading of 'civic action' has been tried many times before and often more realistically and consistently. But this kind of reform and 'civic action' does not touch the causes of poverty and social frustration for the mass of the

Vietnamese people, because poverty and frustration are caused by the *structure* of economic and social systems. In Vietnam, reform and civic action amount only to patches on the surface of a structure that causes revolution. If poverty and frustration—the way in which the causes of revolution are actually felt by the people—are to be removed so that the people will not act in a revolutionary way then there must be *structural* changes in the social and economic system. This is what the revolution, and in turn, the war in Vietnam, is really about.

At this point it is worth mentioning that 'economic aid' from wealthy countries to developing countries, justifiable on humanitarian grounds, is similar to reform and civic action in Vietnam. It can have little effect in producing economic progress unless structural economic and social changes take place. Indeed it can delay them.

Now the question arises, why have structural changes never taken place in Vietnam sufficient to ward off revolution? The answer lies in the fact that neither the French before 1954, nor the Americans afterwards, could even permit, let alone compel these structural changes. If they took place it would mean an end to the sources of wealth of the landlords and merchants and an end to the power of the officials and generals. What was left for the landlords, merchants, officials and generals, and for the French and Americans who stood behind them? Surely not a policy that could win the support of the people, and thereby outflank the Communists or rebels or pirates, who were so much feared, but only the 'lure of money' and 'unrestrained and unscrupulous ambition'. This was hardly the basis for a social revolution. Added to all these conditions tending to produce revolution, were the absence of political rights for the Vietnamese, the effects of the poor education system, the inability of the educated to obtain recognition, and finally, the burden of taxation.

There has never been an election in Vietnam in which those who voted have had the slightest effect in determining who would exercise power. This is equally as true of the 1967 election as of any previous election in any part of Vietnam. As late as the 1920s only about 200,000 children of a potential of 2,000,000 received any education at all, and that in crowded and understaffed schools. Sons of the wealthy could go to a university in France, and some did, but few of them grew to like the system any better for that. Virginia Thompson[21] described the kind of society they were educated for: 'This unhappy attitude (the 'esprit colon') is an aggressive composite of smugness, laziness, fear and racial prejudice. Though colonial society is less class-bound than in France, it is an aristocracy in its relations with the natives. According to this philosophy the most miserable white man is above the best native.' It is necessary to realise that those attitudes are present in every class system but are much more pronounced in a colony, where 'apartheid' attitudes towards coloured people are similar to those practised in South Africa and in the United States. If the ruling class consistently maintains them, a revolutionary attitude by the class which has no say in its own affairs is inevitable.[22]

Europeans and wealthy Vietnamese were able to prevent the application of taxes to themselves or, if they were applied, to make others pay them. Early in the 19th century in Tonking, tax statistics show, Vietnamese paid 5,000,000 piastres in taxes while Europeans paid only 9,000 piastres. In 1897, 100 kilos of salt cost about one-half piastre but in 1907, taxes had increased the cost fivefold.

These then were the conditions out of which the Vietnamese revolution grew. France had made a revolution in Vietnam.

CHAPTER THREE

THE REVOLUTION EMERGES

On June 17, 1930, Nguyen Thai Hoc and 12 of his friends were guillotined in Hanoi, each one after shouting, two yards from the guillotine: 'Vietnam! Vietnam!' Since then the same defiance and determination has spread over Vietnam until today there can be no room for doubt: it is stronger and more specific than ever before. How did this movement acquire its determination and strength?

The strength of this movement is not merely its nationalism, important as that is, not merely hatred of foreigners for what they have done and the urge to expel them and everything associated with foreigners. That surely can be understood by everybody. But it is more than that. The significance of what grew after 1931 lies in the way every economic and social grievance in Vietnam was linked to 'imperialism' —to occupation and control of Vietnam by the French and the Americans. It was true that the French had created in Vietnam the economic and social structure which, in turn, caused these grievances. If the French had never come, Vietnam would have suffered exploitation and injustice, but its history would have been far different. Both the French and the Americans could not avoid protecting the social structure (which they frequently disliked) because to interfere with it would have destroyed the only means they had for maintaining security and keeping the Communists and the other revolutionaries at bay. To have changed the *structure* would have been to do the work of the revolutionaries.

The fact that the main causes of Vietnamese grievances were, or could be shown to be, alien, gave the entire nationalist movement, even the leaders of the Constitutional Party, and conservatives like Ngo Dinh Diem, an anti-capitalist attitude. An author, recognised as the best authority on this aspect of Vietnamese nationalism, Pierre Dabezies,[23] has concluded that 'virtually all anti-French nationalist groups in Vietnam at one time or another tended toward socialist ideas.'

There were few supporters of capitalism because the colonial regimes had prevented the development of native capitalism and anything like mass prosperity. With all nationalists tending to be anti-capitalist and socialist in outlook it is easy to see how the Communists derived their unusual strength in Vietnam. It was easy and logical to link socialism to nationalism and to link anti-capitalist and anti-

French feelings. It was easy for those who had a strong case about economic and social grievances to gain a following when these grievances could be blamed so easily on the foreigners. What was needed was not merely nationalism as an anti-foreign emotion (which the nationalists had relied upon until then) but nationalism that made every social and economic grievance part and parcel of the same ideology. Only the Communists in Vietnam were able to achieve this, or were able to achieve it far better than anyone else. Everyone else held back at some point in the attack on the French or the Americans, and at some point of attack on the social and economic structure. As the situation became more and more intense the complete revolutionary was more and more able to lead the movement for national independence. There was poverty and suppression but so many others merely co-operated or were mild in their opposition.

When Christians will do nothing to resist oppression, indeed, when they accept it and thereby co-operate with it, have they any right to complain when Communists obtain the leadership of those who will no longer tolerate it?

The task of the Communists was made easier too by the growing practice of the French to identify all their opponents as Communists. They did this because it helped them to gain assistance in their war. The French defended their colonial position, knowing the Americans, in particular, were anti-colonial, by claiming that anyone who was prepared to see it go would have no alternative but to accept Communism in its place. In recent years the Americans have done much the same thing—they have established the argument that the Viet Cong and the National Liberation Front are wholly Communist, and therefore, the only alternative to one or other of the Saigon governments is Communism. Those non-Communists who were not prepared to accept the miserable and outrageous conditions of colonialism under the French, or the complete dependence upon America of any of the Saigon governments, have no alternative but to become more and more 'Communist' as time goes by. For all these reasons, as Buttinger[24] concludes, 'the Communist Party of Vietnam had regained much of the strength it possessed before the catastrophe of 1931'.

However, the Communist Party of Vietnam had to await the developments which followed 1941, to obtain, by 1954, that position in Vietnam which is probably unique in the world's revolutionary movements. The Party had by then almost complete and undisputed leadership of the country's movement for national independence and for economic and social reform. But the war that soon followed was destined to break down and complicate that situation too. The Communists were, however, able to provide one thing better than any of their competitors. The mandarinal guerrilla war of 1870-1900 had demonstrated the value of organisation, when it existed, just as the national elite resistance of 1900-1919 had, by the absence of effective organisation, proved the same thing. The Communists after 1931 gave the Vietnamese national-socio-economic revolution that kind of organisation which linked it to the people. Without this opportunity, which the Communists were able to take because it suited them ideally, they would have been left in a position no stronger than the ones they hold in most other countries.

The Communists in Vietnam were not able to follow Moscow or Peking. They had to have a significant measure of independence of Moscow or Peking because what they did was determined by conditions in Vietnam. They, just as was the revolution, were created by those conditions and were linked to them. It is only Communist parties which are superficial to their own societies which can easily follow every turn of the Moscow or Peking line. The national character of Vietnamese Communism was yet another feature which demonstrated the uniqueness of the movement in that country.

As a result of its catastrophe in 1931, the national resistance movement involved itself in another of its great debates about tactics. Communists were forced to go underground, or chose to do so, and the election in 1936 of the French Popular Front government induced even the convinced revolutionaries in France to adopt a 'legal honeymoon' with the authorities in Vietnam. This was as short lived as was the Popular Front in France, and yet a rather naive confidence in the French 'Left' remained among the Vietnamese revolutionaries.

Next came events which changed, first the French attitude in Vietnam and then that of the Vietnamese resistance toward the French. The Hitler-Stalin Pact meant that the French Communist Party immediately responded by opposing the war against Hitler and, as a result, it was outlawed in France. Simultaneously, drastic action was taken in Vietnam against all people known or suspected of being Communists. The Vietnamese resistance then began a most militant phase which carried it over into the period of the German defeat of France and the first Japanese arrivals in Vietnam.

The Vietnamese resistance in December 1940 was able to overthrow the French authorities in several districts, but the French reaction against it was sudden and effective. Many Vietnamese, as usual, were killed. More than 6,000 were killed or wounded and thousands more arrested, and the Communist Party, again, was said to have been 'virtually destroyed'. Tran Trung Lap, described as 'the soul (of this revolution)' was taken prisoner and on 18 December, 1940, executed. A French writer, Rene Bauchar, concluded, 'We may truly claim that even with numerically superior forces the illustrious Colonel Gallieni of 1895 did not reach the dizzy heights of success achieved by our leaders of 1940.' No doubt the war in Vietnam had been won again.

But in the 1940s, Japan was able to turn Indochina into a base for her military operations. After 30 years of weighing up the question, the French had refused 'to arm the Vietnamese people for the defence of Indochina' and, of course, when the Japanese came there was no real resistance at all. What French resistance remained, had been finally ended in July 1940, when Admiral Darlan of Vichy fame replaced General Catroux in Indochina with Admiral Decoux. After leaving his appointment Catroux joined the Free French.

It became Japanese policy not to take over civil administration in Indochina but to use the available French administration. The arrangement not only destroyed what was left of French soul and spirit, but imposed great burdens on the Vietnamese and not a little on French De Gaullists in Vietnam. The French historian, De-villiers, believes that the Vichy persecution of De Gaullists was more intense in Vietnam than it was in France.

Admiral Decoux, described as 'much too conservative to become a real fascist', was powerless against the Japanese but was a strong man in dealing with the Vietnamese. He suspended all elective bodies, calling them 'demagogues' tribunals'. But, of course, none of them ever had any powers to make decisions. They were merely advisory bodies. Between 1940 and 1943, 17 newspapers and periodicals were suppressed and administrative internment without trial was instituted.

The threat of Thailand and the presence of Japan were enough to cause the French to show how tough they were. This they did by using aircraft and artillery to destroy entire villages and towns in which there were some men who fought against the French or Japanese, but more who were not involved at all, and even some who were loyal to the French. Strangely, prisoners were actually taken by the French and it is recorded that they could be seen in Saigon standing in long rows under glaring searchlights, strung together by wires pushed through the palms of their hands. And the effect of all this must have been greatly increased human suffering.

The Japanese, like the French, turned the screw even tighter to maximise exports from Vietnam. The Japanese were more desperate and ruthless. The result was that starvation gradually spread throughout Vietnam. When it was revealed that between 1.5 and two million people had died in Tonking in 1945, it was Admiral Decoux who explained it, by blaming the 'cruel destruction of the Allied bombing' in the Axis ports and lines of communication.

In May 1941, the Vietminh, or the Vietnam Independence League, was formed, taking the form of a multi-party or multi-group organisation, under Communist leadership. What was needed to give the anti-French and anti-Japanese forces in Vietnam their best prospects of success was not a single party Communist organisation but an organisation which would draw closely together all sections of the nationalist movement. This was the aim, and therefore the structure, of the Vietminh.

Most anti-Communists argue that the adoption of this structure by the Vietminh, and later by the National Liberation Front in South Vietnam, was a result of Communist deceit; the decision to hide their own presence or leadership and to manipulate those who would not otherwise co-operate. This is certainly one reason influencing Communists in 'united front' activities, but the main reason is quite practical. It is to design an organisation most likely to be effective and successful. Sometimes the anti-Communists, like Diem later on, recognising the use of deceit by Communists, justify their own use of similar methods. Frequently they have no better reason for it, and often what they do, unlike the Communists, is not influenced at all by practical considerations. Thus they are left with nothing but deceit.

While the strength of the Vietminh grew between 1941 and 1945, it is clear that it did not much waste its strength in opposition to the French or Japanese. One of the most significant causes of its growth in strength and support was its ability, after June 1941, when Hitler attacked the Soviet Union, to be able to identify itself with the allied cause against Hitler, Japan and, of course, against Vichy France. Again this was not basically deception. There was much substance in the identification. The allies helped the Vietminh and the Vietminh helped the allies. Ho Chi Minh came to believe in this identification, and was perhaps naive enough to think that the allies would support both independence for Vietnam and the Vietminh after the war. Perhaps the Atlantic Charter, the Roosevelt spirit and the democratic nature of the war were sufficient to justify such a belief for most people. But it is surprising to find it in a life-long revolutionary—if it was there.

The Vietminh policy was not directed at getting rid of the Japanese, although it was anti-Japanese; it remained directed at the French and at building up its own strength. Like Ngo Dinh Diem in Saigon in 1955-56, Ho Chi Minh turned first to deal with his *Vietnamese* rivals. Just as Diem first bought out or attacked the Binh Xuen, Cao Dai and Hoa Hao, so Ho Chi Minh eliminated his Vietnamese nationalist rivals by acts of war, by assassination, intimidation and double dealing. This, neither the French nor Japanese seemed to object to—and often assisted. The end result was that, by 1946, the Vietminh had no effective rivals at all.

In 1945, with the writing on the wall for Japan, the French began to debate their future policy. French parachutists, dropped into Vietnam, like Paul Mus, believed that the only way to save France in Vietnam was for the French to resist the Japanese. Admiral Decoux, like the colonel at the Kwai river bridge, firmly opposed this policy. The Japanese, of course, became fully aware of the French intentions and plans. They decided to forestall any possible action. They took action in March 1945, and within 24 hours most French units were disarmed and interned, but some French forces resisted and about 1,700 were killed.

The elimination of the French, coupled with Japan's new found hope that she could find friends in Vietnam for the future, led her to adopt there the same policy adopted in some other areas in South East Asia. She began to look for some Vietnamese to whom she could grant 'national independence' and who could form a government. It seems that Ngo Dinh Diem was Japan's first choice. He was a 'stout nationalist untainted by a propensity for radical reforms'. According to Buttinger,[25] 'Ngo Dinh Diem, who had a score to settle with the French, eagerly agreed to head a government that, in spite of its dependence on the Japanese, would probably be able to do a great deal toward the establishment of true independence.'

The Japanese and Diem worked closely together for a few weeks and many details of the new government were worked out. Slogans, victory arches and street decorations with the name Ngo Dinh Diem were prepared—yet this government was never formed. Doubtless the decision not to go ahead was made by the Japanese—Diem proved too difficult to handle and the Japanese found the leader of their government in the more pliable Tran Trong Kim.

While these activities, at a high but powerless level, were going on, the Vietminh was working at the 'grass roots'. By June 1945, six provinces, some say five, between China and Hanoi, were firmly won over by the Vietminh against the full scale opposition of the Japanese 21st Division. Two days after the Japanese capitulation, Ho Chi Minh gave the order for a general insurrection, '. . . which, in the absence of opposition, achieved its first great victory on August 19 in Hanoi'. It must not be assumed from this that the Vietminh was strong enough to dominate Tonking let alone the rest of Vietnam. It must not be assumed either that Communism amounted to much at this point. Apart from a small group of intellectuals no one knew anything of Communism and few were attracted to it or influenced by it. Communism was riding on the steed of nationalism and could do no more than go where nationalism took it. While the Vietminh were by far the strongest party or group in Vietnam they possessed nothing like the strength needed to resist a foreign power. They had achieved an important victory, due more to circumstances than their own ability or strength, and it was little more than just one more step in a century-long struggle.

It would have been better for the Vietminh if they had been able to go further. The Japanese had given them formal powers of government but, of course, their powers were only formal—the Japanese had not given themselves up to the Vietminh to be handed over to the allied forces on their arrival. But the Vietminh had achieved much. Buttinger[26] records that: 'Even sober men were swept off their feet during those exhilarating days.' Vietnam had never been so united. The French appointed Bao Dai as Emperor, and declared their willingness to have Ho Chi Minh form a government, but popular activity was far stronger and demanded much more. As a result of it Bao Dai resigned altogether and Vietnam was a republic. Buttinger goes on: 'There is no more convincing testimony to the strength of the popular support the Vietminh enjoyed at the time than that Bao Dai gave up his throne and expressed his support of a Vietminh regime'. The Soviet Union and all Communist parties abroad, of course, had taken the Stalinist line: the Vietminh should have accepted much less—a Bao Dai constitutional monarchy.

It seemed in Hanoi and Saigon on August 25, 1945, that the French would never come back and that Vietnamese national independence was secure. Ho Chi Minh formed his government on August 29 with all the Vietnamese constitutional requirements mainly derived from the action of the former Emperor. On September 2, independence was proclaimed in Hanoi before a rally of 500,000. Few people anywhere in the world, except some in France and on the way to Vietnam, ever thought that things would change. The Japanese merely looked on while the Vietnamese triumph ran its course. Within two weeks the Vietminh was in full control in the north and centre and near enough to it in the south. Not only in control, but Ho Chi Minh was welcomed everywhere, in Catholic as well as in other areas, as a national hero.

But Vietnamese government seems destined never to be a matter alone for Vietnamese. The allied leaders had met at Potsdam in July 1945 and reached an agreement which included the stipulation that, following the defeat of the Japanese, the British were to occupy the southern half of Vietnam up to the 16th Parallel, and Chiang Kai Shek's Chinese forces were to take over the country north of that parallel.

This agreement was specific about what they should do: the British and Chinese forces were restricted to 'the round-up and disarming of the Japanese and the recovery of allied prisoners of war and internees.'[27] Stalin, of course, agreed to this. What was to happen after that? Potsdam was silent. But the allied leaders had, at Potsdam, completed their dividing up of the world. Why shouldn't the Soviet Union, having won a sphere of influence in Eastern Europe by consent of the other great powers, be prepared to hand Vietnam over to the Chinese in the north and to the British in the south? At least it meant that China and Britain were the de facto powers and they

would have to make the deals with the returning colonial power—
France. And this might cause conflict among the imperialists.

For Vietnam, the supreme irony of Potsdam, was that in an
international agreement made to end a war—a war fought for self-
government and determination and which resulted in national independence for Vietnam—it was provided that foreign troops should
have authority to re-enter the country. Yet this Second World War
had generated the idea, in the Atlantic Charter and elsewhere, that
there should be no more interference with small countries. Churchill
and Roosevelt, in August 1941, had announced, in accord, the second
and third points of the Charter which stated the rights of self-determin-
ation and self-government. The two world leaders sent their words
ringing round the world when they spoke of respect for '. . . the right
of all people to choose the form of government under which they will
live', and that they wished to see '. . . sovereign rights and self-
government restored to those who have been forcibly deprived of
them'. There was hardly any reason why the Vietnamese should not
have expected that these words applied to them.

Although the French had themselves, by 1945, been engaged for
years in a war of national liberation complete with an occupation,
an underground, collaborators and terror, it is true to say that no
Frenchman, De Gaullist or anyone else, was able to see that liberation
from foreign rule was as attractive to the Vietnamese as it had been
to him, or was prepared to concede independence to Vietnam.

The French were amazingly quick in returning to Indochina.
Major General Gracey arrived in Saigon with British forces on September 13, 1945. Some of the French had parachuted into Vietnam before
that, some were in Kunming in China, others were in Calcutta, others
came with General Gracey, but the main force units were still in
France. The French in Kunming were appalled at the Potsdam provision that China should take over North Vietnam and were aware of the
strength of the Vietminh. The French in Calcutta and in France saw
no reason to expect much trouble on their return. But North Vietnam
was firmly controlled by the Vietminh although they had only a
tenuous hold in the south. Their strength however, allowed Buttinger[28]
to conclude that September, 1945, began '. . . the bloodiest period in
the entire history of French Indochina.' The revolution had emerged.

CHAPTER FOUR

THE REVOLUTION BECOMES A WAR

The expected arrival of the French created an excruciating problem for the Vietminh and for all the nationalists, and even for the Vietnamese opportunists like the religious sects Cao Dai and Hoa Hao. Should they resist the French, and this would probably mean having to resist the British too, or should they not oppose the French entry and then negotiate with them? The debate on this question racked and divided the Vietminh. Resisting the French was the most natural thing to do. It was supported by most non-Communist nationalists and consistently advocated by the Trotskyists. It seems certain that resistance was the course which the mass of the Vietminh wanted.

But acceptance of the French return and negotiation with them was the course chosen by Ho Chi Minh and his party. The decision was denounced by the Trotskyists, the Cao Dai, Hoa Hao and many others as a betrayal both of the revolution and of Vietnamese independence. They argued that it was the aim of the French to regain Vietnam—all Vietnamese leaders conceded that—that the French would use force to deal with any resistance—this too was conceded by all—and, therefore, it would be wrong to allow the French to come back and firmly re-establish themselves.

Although popular feeling backed this position and no one gave much credence to the official Vietminh line that the allies would urge the French to grant independence to Vietnam, the national movement ended up by accepting the course proposed by the Communist leadership of the Vietminh. But within four weeks the Vietminh government had been thrown out of Saigon and the 10-year war had begun.

This was one of the earliest of many occasions when Ho Chi Minh was faced with inevitable force and chose to avoid it. It was one of the many occasions when the Vietnamese national liberation movement has accepted that course. Each alternative in August 1945: trying to stop the French from landing, or allowing them in then bargaining with them, was unattractive. Each held risks of death and suffering for many people. But the Vietminh decision of August 1945 revealed a motivation which had operated on many occasions before and was to operate again many times in the next few years. The tendency to try to prevent the development of violence was common in Vietnam. It would be surprising if it were not so. The Vietnamese nationalist movement had suffered so much from violence over a century that it

naturally wanted to avoid violence or, at some critical point, even
to submit to it. Perhaps the Trotskyists foresaw more vividly than
everyone else what the French would do, but it may well be that the
breathing space gained for the revolution increased its prospects of
success.

There can be little doubt that the course adopted helped Hanoi,
but it can have given Saigon no advantage. But, of course, war would
quickly have come to Saigon in any case.

Then, and for another year, the Communists in Vietnam followed
a moderate course, ready to compromise with the French, and ready
to discourage violence against the French and the British. What is
surprising was that they received as much co-operation as they did
from the impatient, angry and confident mass of their supporters. It
is difficult to evaluate their strategy but Buttinger[29] is satisfied that
'. . . the gamble of the Communists was perfectly sensible, even if they
themselves knew an armed conflict with the French was inevitable'.

It helps to understand the Communist choice in Vietnam in 1945
if we realise that they stood alone. The Soviet Union was not only not
interested but had been prepared to see the future of Asia in the hands
of Chiang Kai Shek. The French Communist Party was firmly in the
Stalinist groove and counselled moderation. The Vietnamese Communists knew that Chiang Kai Shek was against them and could not
be trusted to help anything in Vietnam which was the slightest bit
revolutionary. They had nothing to hold on to from outside except
their much criticised faith in Britain and America. The real problem
was that the policy of compromise meant that the revolution in the
south had to come to a halt. As changes were brought about in land
ownership in the country and in administration in the cities, opposition was provoked as well as support won. The British and French
claimed there was disorder and intervened to put it down.

Major General Gracey, in charge in Saigon, had refused to recognise the Vietminh government. Later Gracey said: 'They came to see
me and said "welcome" and all that sort of thing. It was an un-
pleasant situation and I promptly kicked them out.' Gracey pursued
an aggressive policy.

Harold Isaacson, a distinguished historian and an eye witness of
many of the events he describes, put it this way: 'The British had
come to "restore" order, and they began by promptly disrupting the
order they found prevailing throughout their zone. They declared
martial law. They suppressed Annamite newspapers. They re-armed
the bulk of the 5,000 French troops who had been under Japanese
internment. They ordered the disarming of Vietminh militia and
police. As their own troops—almost all Indian—began arriving on
September 12, they moved even more directly against the local regime.
They evicted it from the Cochinchina government building and sent

troops to take over from Vietminh police most of the important police stations in the city. Vietminh representatives were evicted from the Bank of Indochina and the Treasury. Annamites in general were excluded from arrangements made for bank withdrawals and rationing scarce commodities. Each of these acts was formally protested against by the Vietminh Committee.'

By releasing and re-arming the French troops, Gracey provoked those very disturbances which he then used to justify his exceeding his instructions from Admiral Louis Mountbatten to confine operations of British and Indian troops to the limited tasks set down under the Potsdam Agreement. Furthermore, he reprimanded Marshal Terauchi, Commander of the Japanese forces in Indochina, for not using his troops to maintain order, and he permitted the French coup d'etat on September 23, 1945, in which they seized control of the machinery of government in Saigon.

The Vietminh's aim of negotiating with the French was doomed if order was not maintained. But natural Vietnamese anger and fear of the French, coupled with the vested French interest in disorder, were together so great that good order had no chance from the start. The French Commander, General Leclerc, had met General Douglas MacArthur who encouraged his mission to Indochina and advised him: 'Bring in troops, more troops, as many as you can'.

So successful were the French that by September 23 they felt ready for action. On that date they had a victory celebration in Saigon. Of it, Ellen Hammer writes: 'French civilians insulted and attacked any Vietnamese who dared appear on the streets, while French and British soldiers looked on. Correspondents both French and foreign who happened to be on the scene were shocked by the outrage.'[30]

It was the French intention to 'teach the natives a lesson' and by September 23, they felt able to do it. But Gracey thought they had gone too far, or perhaps he thought Mountbatten would think they had gone too far. He ordered the French soldiers back into their barracks and advised the French to negotiate. Mountbatten refrained from replacing Gracey only on the plea of General Leclerc. But all this was too late. The war, which French intransigence made inevitable, began on September 24, 1945, when the Vietnamese struck back at their tormentors. Within a few weeks the fighting spread from Saigon to most areas of the south. There was a crippling general strike in Saigon and the city went dead except for the sounds of gunfire and explosions of grenades. The familiar sounds of Saigon had begun again. Hostages were taken by the Vietnamese and, of course, atrocities were committed by them.

General Gracey now had to call in the Japanese again because the French were not able to handle the situation and he doubtless did not want British and Indian casualties. Marshal Terauchi was told that he would be charged as a war criminal if he did not use his troops properly. Now with Japanese help, the French were able to capture and kill the more militant Vietnamese elements who opposed them. British pressure on the French produced a truce and negotiations began between the French and a Committee of the South—the first postwar, essentially South Vietnamese, revolutionary group.

Leclerc knew that the French still lacked enough strength to defeat their opponents and was wise enough to welcome the truce. It gave him time, not for negotiations, but to bring in more troops. As more and more French troops poured into Saigon after October 5, the more tenuous became the truce and less real became the negotiations. It all seemed to be coming to an end on October 8, but perhaps the French needed a few more troops, for they accepted a continuation of the truce until October 11. On that date the truce ended and the fighting began. The main force of the Vietnamese was ejected from Saigon but the native population left with them and the city was blockaded. It took the French some weeks to break the blockade.

The Indian Congress Party protested the use of Indian troops for this colonial adventure. British Liberal and Labour papers, and a few Labour members of parliament, attacked the use of British troops in Vietnam. But soon Gracey had no need to fear Mountbatten. The British Labour Foreign Minister, Ernest Bevin, perhaps to save time, concluded an accord with the French Ambassador in London which recognised the French as '. . . the only authorised civil administration south of the 16th parallel' and defended the 'close and friendly co-operation between British and French Commanders.' Some explain this accord by Bevin's unfamiliarity with conditions in Vietnam (and perhaps the Foreign Office was unfamiliar too), but the British Government, like the Chinese in the north, may have gained something tangible out of the agreement with the French. Not only were the French now aided by the British, but the Japanese troops were used in combat, to patrol highways and bases and to carry supplies all over South Vietnam.

Leclerc saw his campaign in South Vietnam as nothing more than a simple mopping up operation. Thus began the mistaken military evaluations of the war that have persisted to the present day. French forces did not reach Long Xuen until January 9, 1946; Chaudoc and Hatien until January 20, and Bah Gia until January 30. Bien Hoa and Phuoc Tuy, for instance, remained contested areas. Progress south of the Mekong delta was more difficult and French troops did not reach Camau until the middle of February. Scorched earth and guerrillas met the French in their penetration from town to town. At no time and place were the French troops safe from guerrilla attacks and it was four months before they had occupied the main cities of the south. By then the French commanders concluded once more that the war had been won.

But neither the French superiority in tanks, aircraft and firepower could now permanently threaten Vietnamese control of the country. The situation led the French historian of the period, Paul Devilliers, who was with Leclerc's army, to conclude: 'From this time on the work of pacifying the country revealed an aspect which it would never lose again: to be forever put in question. . . If we departed believing a region pacified they would arrive on our heels and the terror would start again . . . we needed . . . fortified posts, enlightened self-defence . . . a thorough job of information and policing . . . not 53,000 men but 100,000 and Cochinchina was not the only problem.'[31]

But the war in the south was not won any more in the middle of 1946 than it was in 1954. Although the long-term causes of revolution were stronger in the south the revolution itself was going further in the north. The Chinese in occupation of the north had an attitude very different from that of the British in the south. By the time the French had accomplished in the south what they considered was complete reconquest they did not have even one soldier in the north, and to get one there, they had first to come to terms with the Chinese. In the north the French had a myth that their handicaps were caused by American hostility and Chinese support for the Vietnamese revolution. The slight American hostility there, derived from Roosevelt, soon changed under Foreign Secretary James Byrnes to open sympathy and assistance for the French. The Chinese did little that was calculated to help the Vietnamese. Their aims were to help themselves to whatever they could get in Tonking and to force the French to concede in China as much as possible in exchange for an open door back into Tonking.

Ho Chi Minh was stronger in the north than in the south, partly because of the difference between the Chinese and the British, and partly because of the absence in the north of the religious sects. But he was not nearly strong enough to resist either the Chinese or the French. There was more general support for the Vietminh in the north. Many rich men supported the Vietminh. The most influential Catholic leader, Nguyen Manh Ha, became Ho Chi Minh's first Minister of Economics, and a mass meeting of Catholic priests on September 23, 1945, proclaimed support for the Vietminh. Four Catholic bishops, on November 4, 1945, asked Catholics of the world to come to the aid of their 'invaded country and its children, animated by pure patriotism and decimated on the battlefield.'[32] In the north, more than in the south, the Vietminh used political methods to win widespread support. This was not for reasons of deceit but because widespread support was needed and could be obtained. The spirit of national revolution carried many people into action, action which determined what was done. The result was not something that was merely designed by Communists or caused by them. In a real sense the result was the act of the people.

This great upsurge of activity was very marked in the north. By spring of 1946, 120 newspapers were registered in Hanoi, where under the French there had been but twenty. When the Vietminh took power, there had been a two-year famine, and now floods brought further disasters; but a national work campaign at least ensured that the people no longer starved to death. Further troubles arose from the Chinese army. The rank-and-file lived on the land and the officers made fortunes. The Chinese army command was involved in a network of corruption and formed many companies to acquire both French and Vietnamese interests, while thousands of military and civil profiteers hoped that the Chinese occupation would be permanent. Yet the Kuomintang was in Tonking not chiefly to make money but to hold a bargaining counter against the French. They had no sympathy for the Vietminh. They tried to find Vietnamese of standing whom they could put into power against the Vietminh. But the Vietminh commanded such widespread support that the Chinese could find none of sufficient standing to take effective action against it. The Chinese plan required the French back in Tonking, and a strong and growing Vietminh would make the return more urgent for the French and would cause them to concede more to the Chinese to get back. It was on this slender tightrope that Ho Chi Minh maintained his balance.

The Vietminh could gain nothing from fighting the Chinese. They took the opportunity to begin to deal with their opponents and rivals. With Chinese help the VNQDD and the Dong Minh Hoi, rival national organisations, succeeded in capturing Vietminh leaders including Vo Nguyen Giap. Elections had been proposed and the Chinese, knowing that the other groups would receive little support, asserted that the opposition to the Vietminh should have 70 seats of a total of 380 irrespective of the election results. This was agreed, but the elections proved a fiasco for the opposition and a triumph for the Vietminh. Most of their candidates received 80 per cent and more of the votes. An elected candidate, friendly to the Vietminh, was citizen Vinh Thuy—the former Emperor Bao Dai.

But the French were coming and nothing could stop them. On February 28, 1946, they concluded an agreement with the Chinese. France gave up her old concessions in Shanghai, Tientsin, Hankow and Canton and a few other holdings she had possessed before the Second World War, and in exchange she gained one thing only—French troops were to relieve the Chinese armies of occupation in north Indochina between March 1 and 15, 1946.[33]

Up to this point the Soviet Union had not recognised Ho Chi Minh's government and showed no interest in what was happening in Indochina.[34] The Chinese occupation, harmful though it had been, had protected for a while the independence of North Vietnam, but now the Vietminh, deprived of all outside support, military or diplomatic, had to face alone what has been called 'the true challenge to the cause of their national independence'—the return of the French to the north. As in the case of the south, there was never any doubt in the mind of Ho Chi Minh about what policy should be adopted. He would negotiate and compromise with the French. This is proved by a hundred things that Ho said and did. He and his lieutenants had been meeting with French representatives in Hanoi since August 27, 1945. Devilliers records that Ho now combined an offer to compromise with them with a warning that was 'both honest and prophetic'. He told the French when he made his offer of compromise to '. . . keep in mind that we are determined to fight to the end if forced to.'[35] But there were powerful French leaders who believed that the Vietminh would not fight or, if they did, that they could easily be beaten. That the French would always win was a belief held even by those Frenchmen who were most prepared to compromise. French defeat was for Frenchmen inconceivable.

Ho Chi Minh then, as at so many other times, sought to avoid war, but sought Vietnamese independence even by war, if there was no other way. He knew that a 'war of liberation' would be long and terrible and there seemed good reason to believe that it might be avoided. At the time, General Leclerc did not, with any pleasure, contemplate the extension of war into north Indochina. Hammer records Leclerc's view:[36] 'We never intended to launch an armed conquest of North Indochina. The Cochinchinese experience demonstrated that to accomplish this, we would need forces much stronger than those we have now.'

Ho Chi Minh and the French representative in Hanoi, Jean Sainteny, were busy working out both political and military provisions on which there would be agreement. On February 24, 1946, a new government was formed in Hanoi which reflected these provisions. Four Ministers were of the Vietminh, four of the opposition and the crucial portfolios of defence and interior (army and police) went to neutrals. Dong Minh Ho and VNQDD leaders were included. The Vietminh complied with the opposition demand that Giap (elected by 97 per cent of the vote while a prisoner of the French) should not be in the government. But these arrangements did not mean any shift of power—there was little support among the people for any of the opposition groups, and several of the new ministers were supporters of the Vietminh. However, a very important agreement between the government and the French soon followed. On March 6, the day

Leclerc's army arrived in Haiphong, this agreement was signed. The main provision was French recognition not of North Vietnam but of Vietnam, 'as a free state with its own government, parliament, army and finances.' In return, the Vietnamese agreed that Vietnam was to form 'part of the Indochinese Federation and the French Union'. In the appendix to the agreement the French troops that could be stationed in Vietnam were fixed at 25,000, and the French promised to withdraw their troops in five annual instalments to be completed in 1952.

But Sainteny and Leclerc, even if they were sincere and did not intend to use the agreement as the door through which the French troops could re-enter north Indochina, soon lost whatever modifying influence they may have had. On arrival, Leclerc said that he would have come whether an agreement had been reached or not. The French High Commissioner, Admiral d'Argenlieu, immediately attacked the policy of Sainteny and Leclerc and began to destroy its effects. He said he was 'convinced that the French would quickly destroy the Vietminh'; and he expressed his 'amazement that France had such a fine expeditionary corps in Indochina and yet its leaders prefer to negotiate rather than to fight.'

Perhaps Sainteny and Leclerc had difficulty in defending their position, but Ho Chi Minh could not have found his any easier to defend. The national revolutionary movement had an enormous momentum and there was no movement for any talks with the French, let alone any deal. There was also a grave risk that if the policy of compromise failed the fighting spirit of the masses might be lost and with it the whole revolution for Vietnamese independence and political power in Vietnam. It seems that everyone who took part in supporting the policy of negotiations, including Ho Chi Minh, really believed that failure would result. But the leadership persisted with the policy and it was finally accepted by the great majority. Joseph Buttinger[37] draws a conclusion that is no more than fair: 'In facing this test after March 6, 1946, Ho Chi Minh and his more prominent colleagues proved that they were eminently qualified to lead the national revolution, in days of strain as well as in days of triumph'. On March 7, Giap, in a speech in which passion was perfectly blended with cold political logic, convincingly defended the Franco-Vietnamese agreement before an estimated crowd of 100,000 gathered in front of the Hanoi Municipal Theatre. Ho Chi Minh also addressed the meeting. In his short speech, he solemnly swore to his followers that he had not sold them out. He concluded by saying: "You know that I would rather die than sell our country".'

Even as the agreement was reached it seemed that the French would not tolerate Vietnamese independence, and the Vietnamese would not surrender their independence. How could there be any-

thing but war? Why did both sides sign the agreement? The French
had strong and clear motives—summed up, they are that the agreement
would give them time to bring in more troops. The motives of the
Vietminh are not so clear. While it is certain that Ho Chi Minh hoped
that the French socialists would modify French demands, at times it
seems that his own reason for continuing to seek compromise with the
French was a desire to postpone war. It may, of course be, that the
Vietminh was able to profit from the time gained by improving and
strengthening their military organisation for the conflict that everyone
must have been sure would sooner or later come. But the initiative,
and the aggression, had to come from the French. The Vietminh had
to hold on to what they had, to maintain the status quo, whereas the
French had to break it. Hence, it was the French who started the war
when it came soon after.

First of all, Admiral d'Argenlieu publicly denounced the March
6 agreement, then moved to separate Cochinchina from Tonking.
None of the provisions that were to apply to Cochinchina were ever
applied. Troops were moved into Annam, the totals provided for in
the agreement were exceeded and further talks that were to come were
continuously postponed. These talks sought by Ho Chi Minh in France
were at last consented to at Dalat and the French representatives were
colonial administrators without authority to speak on anything of
importance. The talks soon ended in what has been called 'profound
disagreement'. As a result Ho Chi Minh decided to go to Paris. Within
24 hours of his departure, d'Argenlieu announced that Cochinchina
had become a separate republic. On his arrival in France Ho Chi Minh
found that he could have no early conference with anyone. Finally he
was able to reach agreement about a conference, delegates arrived
from Vietnam, and the conference opened on July 26 in Fontainbleu.
But no member of the French government was in attendance.

In Vietnam, d'Argenlieu announced that relations between France
and the Vietnamese people could not be settled at a conference of
delegates only from Hanoi. Failure of the French government to dis-
avow what clearly contradicted the March 6 agreement, and refusal
of the French to make any concession at all at Fontainbleu, brought
the conference to an end on September 10 and the Vietnamese delegates left for home three days later. But Ho Chi Minh stayed on
and continued to work for some means of preventing a complete
breakdown. He emerged with a modus vivendi signed by the Minister
for Overseas Territories, Marius Moutet, which was full of concessions
to the French but contained nothing for the Vietnamese. But it had
prevented a breakdown.

On their arrival home the Vietnamese delegates received a tumul-
tuous reception for their uncompromising stand and Ho Chi Minh
must have been surprised and relieved when he too received a great

welcome on his arrival soon after. But he was still left with the problem of reconciling his modus vivendi with the national determination to resist the French. It seems astonishing that he survived, let alone was acclaimed. He soon found that the French had taken good advantage of the time they had gained. Displays of heavy military equipment were put on by the French and they were regarded with anger and resentment by the people. General Valluy, in Saigon, proposed a plan, rejected by Leclerc, for a land attack on Haiphong and a parachute descent on Hanoi. It seems the French were not yet ready for that kind of action. During these times the Vietminh were seeking allies and disposing of enemies—ruthlessly. In this conflict there was bad faith on both sides and bitterness among the Vietnamese bred of the desperation felt by all. The Vietminh's policy of physical extermination of their enemies may have gained something for them but it drove thousands into the French camp. Buttinger[38] drew a conclusion about this period which remains true to the present day: 'In . . . clashes of religious and political fanatics, it is the born butchers, no matter how small a minority, who determine how the captured enemy will be treated.' The 'canals were literally obstructed by Vietminh corpses', whose fate was 'one of the many bitter fruits of Communist terror.'

But all this seems not to have come strangely to the Vietnamese who had known terror for a century. Buttinger[39] points out what was true in 1946, and remained true for a long time: 'Whatever truthful accusation the French might produce against the Communists in the Vietminh weighed little against the fact that the Vietminh had established national independence and was engaged in a war for its preservation.' Not even the crimes committed by the Communists during the revolution and the subsequent war could possibly make much impression on the people. Everybody engaged in this struggle committed crimes, and the French, at least in the eyes of the suffering Vietnamese, more than anyone else. Besides, the cry of Communism had been raised by the colonial regime for more than 20 years, whenever the Vietnamese voiced demands that the national movement considered the very opposite of Communism: democratic freedoms, social justice, respect for human beings, and enough to eat. 'Anti-Communism' as Devilliers put it, 'was once again merely a pretext', and 'was recognised as such by the Vietnamese, this time as a pretext for the denial of national freedom.' French anti-Communist propaganda had quite unintended results. As Buttinger put it, 'It strengthened the notion that the Communists were the most determined and most efficient enemies of the French, which was reason enough for most people to lend their sympathy if not their active support.'

I have quoted Buttinger at length in this section because of what I believe to be the compelling accuracy of his observation. The war in Vietnam can never be understood, and it is not understood for instance by the American government or by the Australian government, unless it is realised that what the Vietnamese are fighting for is not something imposed upon them against their will. What they are fighting for is something that meets their needs—their needs for national identity and human dignity. Their response is not much modified or changed by anything that the Communists have done. 'Everybody engaged in this struggle has committed crimes', as Buttinger points out, and the crimes that appear to the Vietnamese far the worst are the crimes of the foreigners and their collaborators.

One is appalled at the ease and matter-of-factness with which crimes are committed in Vietnam. Nor are they always committed by 'religious and political fanatics', and by no means is it always the 'born butchers' who are responsible. Members of the Communist Party in Vietnam have been guilty of terrible crimes but no one can prove that they exceed the crimes of members of Christian Churches. The idea that these crimes are Asian must also be rejected. Asians do not treat human life and dignity any more lightly than Europeans: if anything, they appear to value them as highly. They are not more inclined to corruption. The repulsive thing about European behaviour in Vietnam is that crimes and corruption committed and supported by Europeans are committed without an apparent twinge of conscience—a condition that is possible only on the assumption that this behaviour is justified because of the venality of the other side and the superiority of ours. But the venality of the other side is understandable—it is a product of a hundred years of murder and depravity brought to Vietnam by Europeans. One cannot resist the impression that the reaction of the Vietnamese against their foreign tormentors and their collaborators is not so great as one would expect. One cannot reject the evidence that the behaviour of many Communists, however bad, is almost irrelevant to the overwhelming evil of foreign intervention and its consequences.

It was because of these circumstances that French intransigence and cynical preparation for war in north Indochina began to polarise the people. Buttinger[40] records the opinion, 'This intransigent attitude of the French was something in the nature of a secret weapon for the triumph of Communism. It greatly facilitated the application of purely Communist methods, which in a sense were only a replica of the policies pursued by the French.' The victory of the Vietminh in early September 1945 had not been a matter of organisation or control or deep committal. It was a whirlwind of enthusiasm. Red flags shot up all over Vietnam and they were improvised from all kinds of material. The Vietminh set up the call. 'This is independence' and people all over Vietnam ran and cheered. But there was very little that was politics in this and far less that was ideology. This reaction of the people has properly been called 'instinctive wisdom' and had it not been resisted it would have meant the most national, the most independent, Vietnam in centuries. But what changed it?

It was the intransigent and cynical return of the French bearing the assumption that their civilisation was so superior that they had the right to rule the Vietnamese. The Vietnamese who resisted were not turned into an organised, integrated, courageous, committed organisation of people alone by the enthusiasms of nationalism any more than by the organising power of Communists. They were fused into one body by the heat of foreign fire power. When the fire power rose in heat and intensity in American hands the fusing of the Vietnamese extended and strengthened. The power of the Vietnamese resistance has grown continuously until in 1968 it was far greater than ever before. It is thus much a product of foreign attack and grows with the intensity and extent of that attack. It is in a real sense 'the life of the Vietnamese people' and can be destroyed only if, to that extent, the Vietnamese people are destroyed. Continuation of the attack upon the Vietnamese people can only be made if 'our' assumption of their inferiority and 'our' superiority as human beings is strong enough. Fundamentally the attack is not transformed by power politics, or by 'freedom' or 'democracy'. It is motivated into mass killing by the conviction that 'they' are evil or worthless and that 'we' hold the keys of human destiny.[41] Sometimes it appears that a case can be made out for this. But it cannot be in Vietnam.

The return of the French to the north led them to make the practical decision of separating the south from it. Cochinchina was to be a 'separate republic'. Hence the first factor that began to fuse Vietnamese people to the Vietminh was that 'national independence' became more and more a matter of 'national unity' and 'separatism' soon 'became synonymous with treason'. Hostilities had actually begun in Haiphong two weeks before Ho Chi Minh's modus vivendi had been signed in Paris. French units expelled the Vietnamese from their Customs house and the French commander announced that he would take full control of all imports and exports. A protest by Ho Chi Minh to Paris went unanswered. Minor clashes between the French and Vietnamese grew in size and intensity as the days went by and the French were continually making gains. On November 20, 1946, a French patrol boat seized a Chinese junk in the harbour and Vietminh militia (the Tu Ve) intercepted the patrol boat and took three prisoners. There were other minor clashes in which French prisoners were taken. The taking of prisoners by Asians has always been seen as an insufferable indignity by foreigners in Asia. It acutely challenges the assumption of white superiority which seems so fundamental in the whole operation. The French commander, described as 'an irascible colonel . . . Debes', decided to free the prisoners. After heavy fighting the French failed to do so, although the Vietminh were expelled from their areas. Negotiations were immediately sought by the government in Hanoi, which at these talks was conciliatory, agreeing immediately to release the prisoners.

The French retained their gained territory and demanded the removal of barricades protecting the remaining Vietminh areas. When they were not removed the areas were cleared with bulldozers and armoured cars. Fighting with 'increased fury' resulted. Intervention by the Hanoi government produced another cease fire to a chorus of French accusations that the government was unable to control its army. Ho Chi Minh asked for negotiations on the points at issue, but General Valluy, in Saigon, laid it down that negotiations would be acceptable only if the Vietminh evacuated Haiphong. General Moliere, closer to the scene at Hanoi, declined to convey this ultimatum to Ho Chi Minh, reporting to Saigon that the incident was settled and that the demand would 'aggravate an explosive situation'. Aggravation of an explosive situation was just what the French in Saigon wanted and the opportunity was not to be lost. Valluy had foreseen that Moliere would not take advantage of the crisis and so gave orders directly to Colonel Debes at Haiphong. Valluy was in charge in Vietnam in the absence of the man described by Buttinger as 'the bellicose monk', Admiral d'Argenlieu, the High Commissioner, said to be in Paris 'agitating for permission to attack the Hanoi regime'. The Saigon General was doubtless delighted to receive a message from d'Argenlieu just at the critical moment. The High Commissioner had proposed to his co-churchman, Premier Bidault, that the French use the Haiphong incident to teach the Vietnamese a lesson. Bidault gave his consent. 'Can we go so far as to use cannons?', d'Argenlieu asked. Bidault's laconic reply was: 'Even that'.[42]

On the morning of November 23, 1946, Colonel Debes gave the Vietnamese troops in Haiphong two hours to evacuate the city completely. At the end of that time the French put everything they had into the attack. They used tanks, bulldozers, artillery, aircraft and the guns of the cruiser Suffern. Christian civilisation had come back to Haiphong. The Vietnamese claimed there were 20,000 victims. But the French disputed that claim. They said that 'no more than 6,000 (were) killed, so far as naval bombardment of fleeing civilians was concerned.'[43]

Ho Chi Minh continued to appeal over Hanoi radio for the people to keep calm and not to be provoked. And General Giap asked to see Moliere 'to discuss measures to ease the tension'. But the French made no answer. Giap then gave orders for the removal of his regular troops from Hanoi and all larger cities. The return of Jean Sainteny to Hanoi on December 2 brought an immediate meeting with Ho Chi Minh and there were continued appeals on radio, and in the press, by Ho to public opinion in France against 'action by Frenchmen in Indochina.' 'We want peace', Ho kept repeating, 'Neither France nor Vietnam can afford the luxury of a bloody war', but, 'the Vietnamese would do anything rather than renounce their liberty.'

Remarkably a response came from Paris. On December 10, socialist Leon Blum wrote in his party paper that there was only one way for France to maintain prestige and cultural influence in Indochina— a sincere agreement based on independence for Vietnam. Two days later Blum formed an all-socialist government and on December 17 won a vote of confidence in the Chamber of Deputies. On December 18, Blum's Minister for Overseas Territories, Moutet, left for Saigon to make a 'supreme effort for peace'. Knowing how desperate was the situation, and just at the point when the French socialists were going to act, as he hoped they would, Ho Chi Minh sent a cable to Leon Blum in which he stressed the desire of his government to work legally with the French and in which he conveyed concrete proposals to break up the impasse. Saigon censorship held up the cable and it did not reach Paris until December 26, 1946.

In the meantime hostilities had spread between the aggressive, trigger-happy French and the uncontrollable Vietnamese, with continuous gains by the French because of their superior armour and fire power. No doubt Ho Chi Minh's chances of restraining the resistance had now finally come to an end. At 9.30 p.m. on December 17, that thing happened which the French have claimed ever since was the beginning of the war in Vietnam—General Giap gave the order for a general uprising. In this allegation of aggression against the Vietnamese, justifying their action as self defence, the French, of course, ignored all the fighting in the south which had followed their arrival a year before and they ignored all that which had happened in the north since their arrival nine months before.

The die was cast. The war had begun. But it was not because plain words had not been spoken. On August 18, 1945, Emperor Bao Dai had written: 'I address myself to the people of France, to the country of my youth. You have suffered too much during four deadly years not to understand that the Vietnamese people, who have a history of 20 centuries and an often-glorious past, no longer wish, can no longer support, any foreign domination or foreign administration. You could understand even better if you were able to see what is happening here, if you were able to sense this desire for independence which has been smouldering in the bottom of all hearts and which no human force can any longer hold back. Even if you were to arrive to re-establish a French administration here, it would no longer be obeyed; each village would be a nest of resistance, every former friend an enemy, and your officials and colonists themselves would ask to depart from this unbreathable atmosphere. I beg you to understand that the only way to safeguard French interests and the spiritual influence of France in Indochina is to recognise frankly the independence of Vietnam and to renounce any idea of re-establishing French sovereignty or administration here in whatever form it may be.'

CHAPTER FIVE

THE REVOLUTION WINS

The more one looks at the situation the more amazing it appears that the French could have been so blind and so convinced of their own superiority that they would proceed so aggressively to re-establish their rule in Vietnam. But blind and convinced of their superiority they were. At this time Communism played little part in determining or justifying French conduct. Later on when they were in difficulties with the war in Vietnam and when they needed more and more American assistance, the French began to be convinced that they were really fighting Communism on behalf of the free world, and that if they were not helped 'the dominoes' would fall 'all the way to Cairo'. But in 1945-46, and for a long time afterwards, Communism played little part in French justification of the war. For some, this French blindness and conviction of superiority may appear strange in the absence of accusations about Communism. What we can be certain of is that the sense of 'mission' necessary to carry on the war in Vietnam could never have been maintained had it not been transformed in the later stages into a struggle against Communism.

But in 1946 that transformation had to await many years of defeat. We can be sure that Communism came increasingly to justify war in Vietnam, but we cannot be sure that it became of any greater importance in influencing the Vietnamese to believe that the war was being fought in their interests.

All this was implicit in the situation when the French killed 6,000 or 20,000 people in Haiphong on the morning of November 23, 1946. Every shot fired and every bomb dropped in Vietnam since then has been little more than the logical extension of that action.

The French aim of course was to win the war in Vietnam and that meant militarily to defeat the Vietminh and to re-establish French control over the whole of Indochina. For the French, not only north and south Indochina, but Laos and Cambodia were one country; not only Vietnamese, but Thais, and Khmers, and Laos, and Meos, and Muongs and Malayo-Polynesians were to be included in one country, and, over all the French were entitled to rule. If the French ever looked towards 'separatism', as they often did, it was not to give any of these national or racial groups a means of governing themselves but simply to divide them in the interests of French rule. To achieve victory and control, the French needed a military campaign (that has always come first) but they also needed a 'government' able to persuade many Vietnamese that it was a Vietnamese National Government.

The military campaign was aimed at bringing about sufficient 'set piece' groupings of Vietminh forces to allow the killing or capture of those few Vietnamese who were believed to be responsible for it all. They were the misguided evil ones, responsible for making other Vietnamese do what they would never have done unless they had been cruelly or wickedly manipulated. The French, convinced of their own high spiritual intentions, could not believe that a majority, or even many Vietnamese, would ever willingly fight against all that the French were able to do for them. There must be just a few who were manipulating the others, and if only they, and those they had deceived, could be collected together in a few 'set pieces' then the incident would soon be over. Hence the French strategy from 1946 became 'set piece' battles plus the 'Bao Dai solution'.

As time went by and this strategy repeatedly failed, the French began to assert that it was all because of outside 'sanctuaries' and aid in arms and supplies. The assumption was that the insurgent Vietnamese were not really strengthened by support from the people of Vietnam itself and if they had any real strength at all it must have come from outside. French failure never really called into question the assumption that they were strongly supported in Vietnam, and it was never suggested that the Vietminh did have significant support, but French failure began to be more and more explained because of the outside sanctuaries and aid from China and Russia. One can understand the dismay of the French when they saw the first Russian trucks or the first Chinese artillery. These were the things that counted, not the men who were using them. Sanctuaries, supplies and arms from outside were of great value to the Vietminh from July 1953, and they could not have won the war against the French so quickly, or in the way they did, without this assistance. But this cannot be allowed to hide what is fundamental: the thing that determines success or failure in a war of liberation is the support of the people.

Furthermore, the French forces, too, had outside sanctuaries and supplies. France, America and a dozen places nearer to Vietnam were French sanctuaries, and all their arms, most of their fighting troops, and much of their supplies came from outside Vietnam too. Their outside sanctuaries and men and arms and supplies were far more significant for them than the same things were for the Vietminh. But the French lost. This seems to suggest that if we exclude the effort of outside assistance, much more valuable for the French, the Vietminh must have had much more internal support from the people. The importance of this bit of analysis of French military strategy is that the Americans have treated the problem in exactly the same way. The Americans say that the 'Viet Cong' is Communist and, therefore, it cannot possibly be supported by the people of South Vietnam. But what explains why the Americans and their allies cannot win the war? Since they will not admit the people's support of the Viet Cong, they explain it all by 'aggression from the north', or outside sanctuaries in Laos, North Vietnam or Cambodia.

This explanation requires, first, the assumption that North Vietnam is not part of the same country as South Vietnam, and the assumption that Russian and Chinese arms and supplies before 1964 were far in excess of what American evidence shows them to have been. But granting these highly tendentious and doubtful assumptions, what is the net effect of outside sanctuaries and aid? Just as in the case of the French, the American and allied forces in Vietnam have their outside sanctuaries and aid. The United States is an enormous sanctuary—the most powerful in the world. Then there is Japan, Thailand, the Philippines, Malaysia, Australia and dozens of other countries. They are all sanctuaries for the American war effort in Vietnam. And the supply of American men, arms and materials has been vastly greater than anything the 'Viet Cong' have been able to get from outside to help them. Again, as in the case of the French, if outside aid against the 'Viet Cong' is far greater than outside aid for them, then, if they cannot be beaten, they must have much more support from the people. Indeed, in view of what has happened in Vietnam since 1946 must this factor not be crucial to the war and to its outcome? But this factor is concealed, confused and denied in explanations both of the French defeat and of American failure to win.

Because the French held the Vietminh to be without real following among the people, they believed in the 'set piece' strategy; and therefore, until 1948, their military actions were chiefly efforts to kill or capture Ho Chi Minh and his officers. In this way they thought to destroy the 'cause' of the insurrection. These French offensives were aimed at Vietminh battlegroups and headquarters and, at least on one occasion, came within a few minutes of capturing Ho and Giap. These and similar French offensives up to 1948 failed, although they inflicted many casualties on the Vietminh. It seems to be agreed that the French had lost the initiative by the beginning of 1949 and by then the Bao Dai government had lost all its relevance and no longer had a place in French strategy. The victory of the Chinese Communists in 1949 began to allow the French to explain their difficulties in terms of outside sanctuaries and aid for the Vietminh. The Chinese Communist victory, on the contrary, may well have brought a factor which turned the war, for a time, in favour of the French.

The French offensive having failed, Mao-inspired theory told the Vietminh it should now go over to the offensive. Hence, in 1950 and 1951, the Vietminh carried out several large force attacks on the French in the Red River delta, along the Black and Day rivers. After

some early successes it was clear that these offensives, with their con-
centrations of Vietminh troops and their 'human wave' attacks,
could not be sustained. Bernard Fall[44] records the view that: 'June 18
brought the third battle for the delta (which ended) in a Communist
defeat, and Giap retreated to the mountains to lick his wounds and
ponder his mistakes . . . it probably took all his prestige to keep Giap
in the saddle, or more probably Giap was retained because the erro-
neous decision to launch the offensive had been made collectively by
the whole senior Party hierarchy.'

It certainly appears that this decision was a mistake and that it
resulted from a dogmatic application of Mao's rules for wars of
liberation. Mao's victory in China in 1949 brought the weight of his increased prestige to bear upon the Vietnamese leadership and party.
The result, in this case, was a doctrinaire conclusion that the French
offensive had been defeated and it was now time for the Vietminh to go
over to the offensive in Stage Two. This led to a departure from the
basic rule of revolutionary warfare—that success depends upon action
or support by the people and that as long as the enemy possesses great
mobility and fire power it is essential to disperse the revolutionary
forces, sometimes in defensive actions, but preferably in offensive
ones: support and dispersal are the keys to success and cannot ever be
given up as long as greatly superior fire power is likely to be met.

Giap's 'self-criticism', recorded by Fall,[45] is not so much a statement that war doctrine sometimes misleads as it is a criticism of the
assumptions of the war doctrine that had been used. Most Western
experts assume this war doctrine will always be used, that its use is
a 'secret weapon'—and that it explains the success of the revolutionary
forces. At least in 1951, Giap made, it appears, quite a fundamental
change in war doctrine. He wrote in 1951 that the application of this
strategy of long-term resistance required not what Mao or Truong
Chinh had written but 'a whole system of education, a whole ideological struggle among the people and the Party members.' I do not know
whether this was something that Giap worked out, or whether Truong
Chinh agreed or not, but it is a better expression of what is needed
for successful revolutionary warfare than the simplification that appears
in Mao's three stages and written for Vietnamese use by Truong Chinh.
Again it is vastly different from Che Guevara's theory, which, with
great courage, he paid for with his life—that it is possible for 20 or 30
dedicated revolutionaries to bring about a revolution.

Giap's defeat in what had become 'set piece' battles (it is irrelevant whether the Vietminh took up 'set piece' formation to attack the
French, or whether the French were able to attack them in a 'set piece'),
near the Red and Day rivers led him to adopt a general, dispersed
offensive in the highlands, and against the French supply lines, which
were substantially on the ground because of limited air power. It was

precisely this type of offensive which brought about the French defeat, just as in 1967-68 it gave the offensive to the 'Viet Cong' against the Americans and their supporters. In order to deal with it, the French decided on the strategy illustrated by the decision to capture Hoa Binh. This was another 'set piece', expected to become a 'meat grinder' of Vietminh forces as the Americans in Korea had been able to grind Korean and Chinese troops. Instead, the French were forced to draw men and supplies from many places in order to maintain their forces at Hoa Binh.

Up to this point the war had been very costly for the French. Early in 1951 official figures had been released showing nearly 20,000 Frenchmen killed or missing and there were many other than French in the expeditionary corps who were killed or missing. Since 1947, the French had spent between $1,400 million and $2,200 million on the war.

What turned out to be a prototype Dien Bien Phu at Hoa Binh, was followed by the French Operation Lorraine in 1952, and Lang Son in July 1953, with great strain on French resources. These thrusts and attacks brought the French near to breaking point long before Dien Bien Phu. Fall says:[46] 'When the smoke cleared (at Lang Son) the French had suffered their greatest colonial defeat since Montcalm's death at Quebec. They had lost 6,000 troops, 13 artillery pieces, 125 mortars, 450 trucks and three armoured platoons, 940 machine guns, 1,200 submachine guns and more than 8,000 rifles. This abandoned stock alone sufficed for the equipment of a whole additional Vietminh division.'

And so ended another phase of the war against the Vietminh. At first the French thrusts and attacks in pursuit of Ho Chi Minh and his battlegroups failed, then the Vietminh 'set piece' counter offensive failed. Now the Vietminh's dispersed, general offensive had laid the foundation for eventual French defeat. The French answer was a new Commander in Chief, General Henri Navarre, and greatly increased American aid and backing. The Navarre Plan had been the result of strong American pressure on the French to reject the 'peace feelers' from Hanoi in the latter half of 1953. There were also American promises of vastly increased aid. The persuasive dominoes theory had been set out by French General Ely in Washington and basic American strategy began to be formulated that year. John Foster Dulles explained to the Senate Foreign Relations Committee that the Navarre Plan was designed to 'break the organised body of Communist aggression by the end of the 1955 fighting season'.

The Vietminh reply was to extend and intensify their dispersed general offensive and persist with 'feelers' for peace. Their plan appears to have been to make seven main points of attack in the Red River Delta, two along the Black River, several thrusts into northern

Laos, four in southern Laos, two in Cambodia and one into South Vietnam. Most of these single thrusts were in fact a multiplicity of thrusts and attacks and the French assumed that the Vietminh was out to capture Laos, Cambodia and South Vietnam, and hold what they had captured. This was never the case. Navarre's answer to this multiplicity of attacks was to establish 'air heads'—strong ground bases supplied by air—so that he would have forces near at hand to meet any attack or thrust by the Vietminh. Dien Bien Phu with 16,500 men whose purpose was to 'save Laos' became the most substantial and famous. Remarkably enough, the French, out to catch the Vietminh in 'set pieces', had now taken up a 'set piece' position themselves, and the Vietminh were able to disperse at will. In the midst of this dispersal, the Vietminh leadership decided to call off most of their attacks and thrusts towards Laos, Cambodia and even South Vietnam, and mass to inflict a great defeat on the French. Within a few weeks the French found there were four Vietminh divisions surrounding them at Dien Bien Phu. The first attacks cost the Vietminh heavy losses, but soon defeat for the French became certain.

For some time the French had begun to recognise the possibility of a military collapse of their forces. And a new element appeared on the horizon—the idea that peace in Vietnam might help reduce international tensions now seems to have attracted Britain, the Soviet Union and sections of the French power structure.[47]

At any rate a Foreign Ministers' meeting in Berlin between January 25 and February 18, long before pressure on the French at Dien Bien Phu began to be felt, agreed on a conference at Geneva to deal with Korea. But it was the known intention of most of the Foreign Ministers that the conference should deal also with Vietnam. It met at Geneva on April 26, 1954, but did not begin to discuss Indochina until May 8, one day after the fall of Dien Bien Phu.

With the conference still in session, the French guns fell silent at Dien Bien Phu and the white flag went up on French headquarters. Losses on both sides had been heavy but in addition the French had lost the war. French forces shrank back to a perimeter around Hanoi and within days the Vietminh controlled everything in North Vietnam but a few small enclaves, everything else down to the 13th parallel, many areas in South Vietnam, more than half of Laos and three areas of Cambodia.[48]

The war in Vietnam has, of course, passed through many phases, not the least significant being that of 1945-1954. Before 1945 the war in Vietnam had been a purely colonial one—French armed forces against Vietnamese. Between 1950 and 1954, Generals de Lattre, Salan and Navarre wanted a Vietnamese national army but, of course, under French command. The purpose of this army was to defend and pacify French-won territories. Only if this were done, the Generals argued, would the French army have sufficient manpower to carry on the war, let alone win it. The argument had a sense of urgency, if not desperation about it. Most French officers were opposed to a native army not totally subject to French control, and all that had been accepted up to that time was what had been called the 'yellowing' of French units. The influence of the three Generals, and the circumstances of the times, were enough to bring about a change. A Vietnamese military academy was opened late in 1950 and conscription was introduced the following year. The development of a Vietnamese army added a new element to the colonial war. It began to take on aspects of a civil war—Vietnamese against Vietnamese. With these developments came even increased bitterness and greater departure than ever from the 'rules' of war.

Up to 1950 there had been little participation in Vietnam by any foreign nation other than the French. We have seen how insignificant were Japan and China in earlier years. The Japanese occupation between 1941 and 1945 had some influence but little went according to plan for the Japanese. Certainly the part played by Britain and China in 1945 was important, and there was the Potsdam agreement about Vietnam and its consequences. But the situation began to change in a very different way in 1950.

In mid-1949, the Truman administration in America began to regard Bao Dai, the French puppet emperor, as a Vietnamese patriot worthy of American support and aid. This was in part recognition by America that colonialism in Vietnam was a supreme liability and some way had to be found around French control of affairs. But unhappily for the Americans Bao Dai was the kind of choice they were forced to make. Perhaps this was the first of the fundamental contradictions upon which American policy for Vietnam came to be based. In order to get rid of the French so as to get rid of colonialism, America chose to back the leaders and the government the French had backed. For the first time in American history, in turning their backs on the Roosevelt policy, two American Presidents and their Secretaries of State, Acheson and Dulles, each in full agreement, brought the United States into a fully colonial position. That this was done to oppose Communism made no difference at all. Colonialism had always existed in the final analysis, for 'spiritual' reasons; always to save the natives from a terrible fate, and always to advance virtue and civilisation among the underdeveloped and the heathen.

On February 7, 1950, seven months before the French parliament ratified the agreements granting 'full independence' to Bao Dai, the United States Government extended diplomatic recognition to his government. Ho Chi Minh then requested diplomatic recognition from Peking and Moscow and on February 18 and 31, respectively, they responded. The cold war had entered Vietnam, and on American initiative. America's economic and military assistance program began in earnest in June 1950. But, of course, the government of the United States had much earlier shown that it was on the side of the French and against the Vietminh. The first indication the Vietminh had of the post-war attitude of the American government was the immediate use of American weapons and equipment by the French, to be followed soon by an American agreement to sell to France $160 million worth of vehicles and equipment for use in Indochina. By the end of 1950 aid was being supplied at an annual rate of $150 million which grew to $1,000 million by 1954, a sum amounting to about 80 per cent of the total French cost of the war. The French justified their vast import of military equipment by asserting that an agreement for military assistance was signed in April 1950 between the government in Hanoi and the Chinese. But aid from China and Russia to Hanoi did not appear till 1953. Chinese aid was significant at Dien Bien Phu, particularly in artillery and transport, and Russian trucks were valuable.

American aid to France was vital in Vietnam long before 1954, whereas Hanoi was not at all dependent on Russian or Chinese help. Fall records a high South Vietnamese official speaking in New York of 'powerful modern French armies (defeated) by poorly armed Vietnamese fighters who . . . never were helped by Russian or Chinese troops.'[49] Denis Warner states his own conclusion at greater length on this point: 'Weapons mattered less to Giap than tactics and people. His men used sticks, spears, scimitars, bows, and elite, uniformed, battle-tried veterans got the pick of the weapons. The regional troops, full-time and paid for their services but kept within provincial boundaries to support and supplement the regular forces, or to carry out local ambushes and attacks on posts, got what was left over. The village guerrilla units, even at the end, had to make their own. Most weapons came from the French. That was the primary source. While Chinese arms were vital in the build up for Dien Bien Phu, for the rest small-scale arms factories, which were inadequate to meet their needs, and captured equipment, were what the Vietminh had to depend on. Until close to the end the Vietminh had no trucks. A bulldozer, which was used to build the road to Dien Bien Phu, was their only tracked vehicle. The army moved on its own feet, with tiny ponies from the Thai Country in north-western Tonking, bicycles, trishaws, and porters to carry supplies. A division of 10,000 men used up to 40,000 porters.'[50] I have quoted Warner at length because this is an accurate summary of the position of the Vietminh and of the limited nature of the assistance they received from outside. The war effort of the Vietminh was almost completely Vietnamese.

The Vietminh had established ascendency over the French by July 1953 and at that point Chinese and Russian aid was of little importance. Allowing for the largest estimates of Chinese and Russian aid for the Vietminh after that date, it probably did not exceed $150 million by 1955, and much of that was economic aid from China. By that time American aid to France and the Vietnamese since 1950 was well over $1,200 million. The growing involvement of the United States on one side, and it always came first and was far larger, and of the Communist powers on the other, had, from 1950, firmly fixed the war in Vietnam into the international cold war. Vietnam was destined to be the 'battleground for freedom' and she would have no choice in suffering that distinction. This was the beginning of the inevitable transformation of the colonial war in Vietnam, 1858-1950, into a colonial-civil-international-religious war thereafter. This became inevitable, not in 1956, or 1962, but in 1950, when the United States undertook the responsibility of maintaining the war in Vietnam, first for others, but inevitably for herself to fight.

Although the French had given much time to the formation of a Vietnamese 'national' government—the Bao Dai solution—they had never intended that it should have any real power. Every respected nationalist in Vietnam always knew that the attempts to form anti-Vietminh governments were a manoeuvre to avoid making those concessions which the Vietnamese needed and demanded, and which were necessary if there was to be Vietnamese independence at all. Formation of anti-Vietminh governments at all acceptable to the French was not independence and could not be. They were a substitute for it and a manoeuvre to avoid it. But, in fact, there was no other way to meet the challenge of the Vietminh—and even this may not have succeeded—but to grant real independence. There was no other way to fight Communism in Vietnam than to be anti-French. But the Bao Dai camp was led by a group of French 'patriots' or 'hardened collaborators', while those destined to rule South Vietnam under the Americans were their junior officers. Bao Dai understood the nature of independence and he knew that what he was finally given was 'blatant deception'. What he expected to get he could do no more than plaintively ask for (as if true independence could ever be had that way): 'Make me the one who brings to Vietnam true independence', he pleaded, 'and you will see how quickly the people will turn away from the Vietminh.'[51]

Bao Dai governments rose and fell regularly. His series of Premiers began with General Xuan, 'the most notorious of all collaborators'; then Nguyen Phan Long, who had the distinction of looking beyond France to a more powerful master—the United States; then Tran Van Huu, a rich landowner, financial speculator and French citizen; then Nguyen Van Tam who was 'entirely devoted to the French'. Finally, in 1953 Prince Buu Loc became the last Premier, before the French defeat at Dien Bien Phu and American pressure brought about at least the formality of independence (not for those who had won it but for those who had, for years, damned themselves by collaboration, treachery and weakness). Fall draws a fair conclusion:[52] 'Every political concession wrested by the nationalists from the French was first bought by a Vietnamese Communist victory on the battlefields of Tonking, Laos, or the Southern Highlands. There can be no doubt that this historical fact—no matter how well it may be camouflaged behind high-sounding slogans—accounts for the ambivalence of the southern leadership about its role in achieving its now embattled independence.' Francois Mitterand, in the French Chamber of Deputies, put in succinctly: 'We have granted Vietnam "full independence" 18 times since 1949. Isn't it time we did it just once, but for good?'. But, of course, the time was not to come until France had no alternative—and that was created by the victory of the Vietminh.

But the French were even then to continue their long record of duplicity. The French government signed an agreement at Geneva, establishing, until there could be elections in July 1956, an administration in the north, the government of Ho Chi Minh, and their own administration in the south. Yet at the same time they negotiated in Paris an agreement giving complete independence and sovereignty over the whole of Vietnam to the government of Bao Dai. France had so little respect for her signature at Geneva that she signed in Paris at the same time another document that completely contradicted her Geneva commitments.

We can safely say then, that in the war between the French and the Vietminh between 1945 and 1954, the French won nothing by an appeal they made to Vietnamese nationalism and won little respect for themselves or for anyone associated with them. The French were out to win a war by military means, not for Vietnamese independence but for French power in Vietnam. But reliable and influential French leaders were able to see that this aim and method would mean failure. General Leclerc, for instance, said emphatically in 1949: 'France will no longer put down by force a grouping of 24 million inhabitants which is assuming unity and in which there exists a xenophobic and perhaps a national ideal. The major problem from now on is political.' In the same year Leclerc also said: 'Anti-Communism will remain a useless tool as long as the problem of nationalism is not solved.' The problem of nationalism was not solved merely by having some Vietnamese or other in a government or in an army. To solve it, not only were some Vietnamese needed in a government, but that government required real power and, much more important, needed to use that power to bring about real reforms. The test of nationalism was not merely a government that looked national but a government that acted to end exploitation and corruption.

The Leclercs were the exception to the rule. Most of the French leaders remained ridiculously and ignorantly optimistic: victory was always just around the corner. Anti-Communism was relied upon when everything else seemed to have failed. Puppets and collaborators were installed in office, but their offices were empty. As there was no power none of the means to exercise power was needed. It is understandable that this was the result of the work of the French fascists, neo-fascists, Vichyites and tories; but the parties of the Left were little better. We have seen the role of Bidault, d'Argenlieu, Valluy and the others. But in 1948, De Gaulle was with them: 'The true role to observe at this moment in Indochina is not to rush anything. We must know how to take our time. Sooner or later the French solution will have to be accepted.' Perhaps De Gaulle differed from some in that he was able to learn. But by 1955 even the notorious General Salan had come to see the fundamentals: 'We shall win', he said, 'when all vital forces of the nation, from the peasant in the rice field to the bourgeois in the cities, participate in the fight against the Vietminh.'

It has often been written that the most significant failure of all in France to arrive at a better and more workable policy for Indochina was perpetrated by the Socialist Party. The Socialists had an adequate experience and understanding of what causes insurrections in a nation and of the relevance and importance of national independence, economic reform and social justice in preventing them. Socialists opposed the deliberate sabotage of the March 1946 agreement. Blum recognised the right of the Vietnamese to national freedom from France and proclaimed the old colonial system ended. Socialist Party congresses continued to demand negotiations. Despite all this, Socialist Cabinet Ministers acted contrary to all these Party views and decisions. The reason for this behaviour is the same as it is for most Left-wing failure in office. Socialists in office in France believed that the cause of their parties could best be served by getting into power and staying there, even if that obliged them to act contrary to their professed principles and specific programs. 'Power' and office were the things that counted. You could do nothing unless you had power, but it came about that they did nothing about things that counted, when they had power. This, of course, was not power at all. Power for socialists means doing things differently from the way they otherwise would have been done. But the Socialists in office in France treated Vietnam in the same way as did all their political opponents. Power and office were more important than principles and so the Socialists in office gave up their principles about Vietnam, and supported the war. It is to be hoped that they feel that the good they were able to do in other ways made up for their Vietnam policy. But they have a lot to make up for—over two million Vietnamese have died since then and there is still no end in sight.

As the French in Indochina encountered increasing difficulties in the war, more and more attention came to be directed to guns, aircraft and equipment, and less and less concern was shown for a Vietnamese 'national' government and for political, economic and social reform. Escalation has its own self-generating dynamic. This is inevitable, partly because reforms are more difficult to carry out as war spreads and intensifies, and partly because military influence and power grows continuously. The total situation becomes more and more a military one. It was natural, therefore, that as the situation at Dien Bien Phu became desperate in March 1954, the French looked to the United States for increased supplies of aircraft and firepower.

On April 3, 1954, eight senior members of the United States Congress were called together at a secret conference with the Secretary of State, John Foster Dulles.[53] Dulles announced that the President had asked him to call the meeting and said that what was needed was a joint resolution of Congress to permit the President to use air and naval power in Indochina. Dulles is said to have hinted that the mere passage of the resolution would in itself make its use unnecessary. Presumably he expected the Vietminh to call off their attack on Dien Bien Phu, then most successful, at the suggestion of American attack.

Admiral Radford then outlined the plan and there was no mention of the use of nuclear weapons although the aircraft carriers that were to be used, the Boxer and Philippine Sea, were equipped with them. Questions and discussions revealed that if the first strike did not succeed there was to be a followup but Radford was not definite about the use of ground troops and admitted that none of the Joint Chiefs of Staff supported the scheme at all; this, he said, was because they did not understand the situation as he did. Lyndon Johnson wanted to know if Dulles had consulted nations who might be America's allies in the action. Dulles said he had not. Dulles was asked if China and Russia would come in and he replied that he did not think that Moscow wanted a general war and that they could handle China. In the end all eight members of Congress were agreed that Dulles had better 'go shopping for allies'.

This situation had resulted from a dramatic visit to Washington on March 20, 1954, by General Paul Ely, French Chief of Staff, who had told the President that unless the United States gave France assistance immediately Indochina would be lost and the dominoes would, of course, fall all the way to Cairo. This is said to have shocked the American Administration who, 'had been taken in by their own talk of the Navarre Plan to win the war'. But Ely, it appears, got a stronger response than he had expected. He is said to have been 'flabbergasted' by Radford's proposal for American intervention, for which he had not asked. What Ely wanted, apparently, was American aircraft and firepower for French use, not the risk that America would come in and take over. By April 3, the American position was set:

America would intervene provided she had allies in support and provided that France gave Indochina a real grant of independence. But this position had inherent difficulties. The allies were not involved and France was fighting for Indochina, not against Communism. Dulles wanted to fight Communism and was prepared to see France give up Indochina if that was necessary. However, Dulles lost no time. Talks began right away in Washington with diplomatic representatives of Britain, France, Australia, New Zealand, the Philippines, Thailand, Laos, Cambodia and Vietnam (Bao Dai). These were the 'allies'. Dulles ran into 'one rock of opposition', Britain, whose position was finally stated clearly enough by Prime Minister Churchill.[54] He said he would not allow Great Britain to be used 'to assist in misleading Congress into approving a military operation which would in itself be ineffective, and might well bring the world to the verge of a major war.' Australia's leaders, of course, told the Australian parliament little of these events, but at that time they loyally followed Britain, not as now the United States.

British opposition meant that Dulles had to give up his plan for immediate intervention. Instead he put forward the proposal which came into existence because intervention then was not feasible—the plan for the South East Asian Treaty Organisation. With this Churchill and Eden agreed. Dulles began meetings in Washington on April 20 to draft plans for SEATO, apparently hoping that it could replace the Geneva Conference about to begin sitting and which he hoped to stifle. However, events moved rapidly. On April 23, General Navarre reported that only a massive air attack (apparently by the United States) could save Dien Bien Phu. Dulles now took the position that if the allies agreed to an American attack, they need do nothing but support it with words. The President would ask Congress for a resolution authorising the action, and if Congress agreed, which it certainly would, then the strike could be made on April 28. Eden replied that this was a most serious proposition amounting to war and he wanted to know the French position. The French, of course, were desperate, and Bidault said they agreed. Eden, in Geneva, replied that he, personally, would not support the plan and would return to London to consult his government. This he did and returned the day after with a total rejection of the plan. This, coupled with the advice Dulles received from his own military leaders that it was now too late to save Dien Bien Phu, turned him back towards longer-term plans for intervention in Vietnam.

Thus the stage was set for the Geneva Conference. That the Vietminh leadership consented to attend the conference at all has surprised many observers. The French were in a very bad way even before Dien Bien Phu. Their defeat at Dien Bien Phu was inevitable. The French reaction at home against the war was almost general. No

French government could have continued it. Withdrawal must soon have followed. The Vietminh could have expected to win government of the entire country. But they readily agreed to attend the Conference. It is clear that much debate took place. Why did they accept negotiations? There can be little doubt that both Russian and Chinese influences were at work upon Hanoi to attend the conference. This was the orthodox Communist Party line almost everywhere and there was, as yet, no Moscow-Peking split. Furthermore, there would have been the argument in Hanoi that if the fighting went on, American intervention would mean a protraction of the war against a nation far more powerful than the French. But at any rate 'the militant Left', led perhaps by Le Duan lost the argument and negotiations were accepted. It might have been better for Hanoi and for the people of Vietnam as well if they had fought on.

The conference opened on April 26 and began on May 8 to deal with Vietnam. But there were two conflicting forces in the 'allied' approach to the conference. The first was illustrated by President Eisenhower who on the day before the conference opened said that what was being sought in Geneva was a modus vivendi with the Communists. The second was the determination of Dulles, and many others, to retain as much as possible of Vietnamese territory as an anti-Communist area, supported, maintained, supplied and defended by united action by the 'allied' powers. These conflicting forces were securely placed in Vietnamese affairs. They made inevitable the contradictions of Geneva as well as the continuation of war in Vietnam no matter what was decided at Geneva. The Geneva Conference was wrecked before it started. Dulles refused to play an active part in the conference and soon saw that it could make little difference to his long-term plans. But he did not want the war against the Communists to be conducted under the old French colonial banner. Dulles was not enthusiastic about the Radford plan, not because it was military aggression, but because it did not go far enough. What was needed was not a single devastating strike to help the French stay in Vietnam but a complete and comprehensive allied plan which would stop the war from looking like a colonial war. 'Dulles wanted intervention but of a different kind, a far-sighted, comprehensive, long-range operation'.[55]

Dulles could have had no serious regrets about Geneva for it allowed the exclusion of France and the establishment of a suitable anti-Communist base for his new, comprehensive, non-colonial intervention. This was the main practical significance of Geneva—not that it provided for elections, for non-interference by foreign powers and for international supervision.

The ideals and peaceful hopes of Geneva would be brushed away by the march of events. Not only did Dulles have a base for operations

but the Geneva cease-fire and settlement would give time to implement
his plan. Doubtless he would have liked to have all of Vietnam
as a base or a little more of it than that part south of the 17th
parallel. But the French did much better than anyone expected, for it
was thought, by most, that the partition would be at the 13th parallel.
It was this American determination that made the temporary division
of Vietnam into a permanent one. And this is certainly because, as
Buttinger put it, '. . . it was Dulles' view that the non-Communist half
of Vietnam, once it had shed all traces of colonialism, should become
an American-sponsored bastion against any further Communist advance in South East Asia'.[56]

The only point of doubt in Dulles' mind, and in the minds of all
those powerful Americans who supported him, was not whether South
Vietnam should be held as an 'anti-Communist bastion', but how it
should be held. Given this objective it became little more than an
academic question how and where the war would start again. War was
inevitable. The only thing that could have prevented it from being
inevitable was for the Vietnamese to surrender completely their
fight for national independence. Whatever the 'Communists' might
choose to do would be opposed. Escalation of the war was built into
the original decision to maintain South Vietnam as an 'anti-Communist bastion', for that objective remained as strong in 1967 as it was in
1954. In fact it was far stronger, for by then American national reputation, as seen by Americans, was involved.

Dulles of course hoped for something less than war. He had
become convinced by 1954 that if Vietnam was to be won it had to be
won in some other way. At a news conference on July 23, he concluded:
'The important thing for now is not to mourn the past but to seize
the future opportunity to prevent the loss in northern Vietnam from
leading to the extension of Communism throughout South East Asia.
One lesson is that resistance to Communism needs popular support,
and this in turn means that the people should feel that they are
defending their own national institutions.'[57] This emphasis given by
Dulles to popular support was to have some influence on the whole
United States policy in Vietnam in the few years that followed.

Much of the way in which the United States became committed in
Vietnam could be put down alone to John Foster Dulles. But the
policy put forward by Dulles was a consensus of powerful opinion on
both sides of Congress and elsewhere. From what Dulles said and did
we can say American policy in 1954 had the following features:

1. The aim of policy was to retain South Vietnam as an anti-Communist bastion.
2. The French would be totally excluded and so the last taint of
   colonialism would be removed.

3. Intervention in Vietnam would be by all the SEATO allies and not just by the United States.
4. There must be a government in Vietnam of Vietnamese for which there was popular support.
5. The intervention must be limited to financial and military aid to this government. It has been pointed out that the State Department's Policy Planning Staff was influential. One of its members, Louis J. Halle, Jnr.,[58] is quoted: 'A possible variant to the policy of gaining national objectives by eliciting the consent of those who have jurisdiction is to assure jurisdiction for a regime which accords its consent. Such an undertaking may, on rare occasions, be valid and feasible; but all modern history warns that it is likely to be an enticement into quicksands. The only way one can assure jurisdiction, abroad, for a regime that cannot assure jurisdiction for itself is by a species of intervention that, in addition to dissipating the popular consent which the intervening nation might otherwise enjoy, dissipates the consent on which the imposed regime must base itself if it is to establish a tolerable government. When a nation intervenes in a foreign country, it not only tends to turn the people of that country against it, but it also discredits the regime that accepts its support.' The writing was on the wall.
6. The government in Vietnam must bring about political and economic progress. Secretary of Defence Robert McNamara stated this objective: 'We have learned that in Vietnam political and economic progress are the sine qua non of military success.'

Consequently there was built into the American-South Vietnamese alliance, completed by the end of 1955, those forces which would destroy the Geneva agreement and make inevitable ever increasing American intervention. The only thing that could prevent this escalation of war was for the government in North Vietnam and most of the people in South Vietnam, on the one hand, to give up their century-long struggle for national identity and independence, and on the other, for America to give up the objective which meant the destruction of the Geneva agreement and permanent division of Vietnam at the 17th parallel. But equally as much, of course, the American-installed government in Saigon was opposed to the division of Vietnam and planned to unify the country. Tran Van Do, who was Bao Dai's Foreign Minister, declared at Geneva that his government refused to subscribe to any agreement partitioning the country. Before the end of the conference he laid it down: 'Vietnam reserves to itself the entire freedom of action to safeguard the sacred right of the Vietnamese people to territorial unity, independence and freedom'. As early as August 3, 1954, the government led now by Ngo Dinh Diem called on the people of the North 'to rally to the South in order to continue the struggle for independence and liberty'.[59]

And so the stage was set by American policy for the war in Vietnam to start again. There can be little doubt, the Geneva Agreement was destined, even before it came into existence, to have little effect. But this does not mean that it was without significance. Its significance can be seen from relating its contents to the behaviour of the parties to it. This I will do later on.

Geneva was an agreement that can be summed up in several key points:

1. It was a *provisional military* agreement to create a *demarcation line* between two regrouping zones *not a boundary between two countries*. (Article 1.)

2. It was an agreement to have general elections 'which will bring about the unification of Vietnam'. (Article 14a.)

3. Until the general elections, civil administration in each zone was to be in the hands of the party whose forces were to be regrouped there. (Article 14a.)

4. There was to be *free movement between the northern and southern zones,* and the withdrawal of French military forces from the North and Vietminh military forces from the South was to take place within 300 days. (Article 15a.)

5. The introduction *into Vietnam* of any troop reinforcements (Article 16), or arms, munitions and other war material (Article 17) was prohibited.

6. An International Control Commission was set up to supervise the agreement. (Articles 28-47.)

7. Responsibility for the execution of the agreement rested with the parties—the French and the Vietminh—(Article 28) but 'the signatories of the present agreement *and their successors* in their functions shall be responsible for ensuring the observance and enforcement of the terms and provisions thereof'. (Article 27.)

As distinct from the agreement, there was the Final Declaration of the Conference. This document was drawn up as a 'Declaration' so that the parties would not have to sign it because the United States had refused to sign anything that was signed also by China. It provided:

1. That the essential purpose of the agreement relating to Vietnam is to settle military questions with a view to ending hostilities and that the military demarcation line is provisional and should not in any way be interpreted as constituting a political or territorial boundary. (No. 6.)

2. The settlement of 'political problems' was to be on the basis created by the 'general elections' which were to be held in July 1956, under supervision of the International Supervisory Commission. (No. 7.)

3. Individuals were to decide freely in which zone they wished to live. (No. 8.)

4. There was to be no interference in the internal affairs of Cambodia, Laos and Vietnam. (No. 12.)

The representatives of France, Laos, China, Britain and the Soviet Union accepted this Declaration. Cambodia did so with the reservation that she 'did not abandon . . . such legitimate rights and interests . . . Cambodia might have (in) certain regions of South Vietnam'. North Vietnam accepted the Declaration with reservations regarding the Cambodian statement. The Bao Dai government, called the State of Vietnam, did not accept the Declaration at all. The objections of this government were:

1. That there could be no acceptance of 'any agreement that provided any proposal that would lead either directly or indirectly to a permanent or temporary de facto or de jure partition of the national territory'.
2. The French had agreed to evacuate zones vital to the defence and existence of a free Vietnam, but had not done so.

But despite its objections and reservations, the State of Vietnam agreed 'to make and support every effort to re-establish a lasting peace in Vietnam', and 'not to use force to resist the procedures for carrying the cease-fire into effect'.

The United States was not prepared to join in the Declaration. But would:

1. Devote its efforts to the strengthening of peace in accordance with the principles and purposes of the United Nations.
2. Refrain from the threat or use of force to disturb the agreements.
3. In the case of nations now divided against their will, continue to seek to achieve unity through free elections supervised by the United Nations.

CHAPTER SIX

GENEVA GOES . . . WAR COMES BACK

Vietnam, therefore, in and after the Geneva Agreements, remained *one country*, the government of South Vietnam, as it was to become, being more adamant than any other about this point, and the unification of Vietnam was to depend upon the elections *that were provided for in the Agreement*. The Vietminh reluctantly accepted the Agreement, having been persuaded to do so by Chinese and Russian pressure and by an obvious expectation that they could win easily any elections that were held.

So the parties, except the United States and the so-called State of Vietnam, left Geneva with varying degrees of satisfaction, the Vietminh for two years of civil administration of the zone north of the 17th parallel, and the French for two years of civil administration south of it. Or that is what everyone appeared to think. We have noticed, however, that there was a government of the so-called State of Vietnam presided over by Bao Dai, to whom the French had given 'full independence', after they had lost the war to the Vietminh, and even while they were negotiating the Geneva Agreements with the Vietminh, Agreements which created a vastly different situation. In addition, there had been, since 1950, an American Military Aid and Assistance Group in South Vietnam which, apparently, Geneva allowed to be kept up to strength. And American aid to Saigon was to equal about $325 million annually in 1955. The shape of the future lay not in the Geneva Agreement but in these factors.

But the Geneva Agreements of July 1954 marked the end of an era in the long, embattled history of Indochina. Imperialism was to give way to indigenous nationalism and the independent nations of Laos, Cambodia and Vietnam were to emerge. Imperialism meant the presence of a foreign power in Indochina whatever the reason the foreign power thought it had for being there. French imperialism in Indochina had been no different, despite its late discovery that it was to save the country and many others from Communism. The Geneva Agreements meant that Indochina was to be free of a foreign presence in the future. But the appearance of a unified Vietnam, free of foreign control, was to be deferred until 1956. The Vietminh had won independence but the final recognition of it was to be brought into effect in a precise manner laid down in the Agreements. The responsibility of carrying out this agreement, finally to bring into existence full independence, fell upon the French, and the Agreements provided they and their successors were obliged to carry it out. Douglas Pike put it as the Vietminh must have seen it (and very close to the truth) when he wrote: 'Only the Vietminh, the winners, lost (from the Geneva Agreements) or were sold out. Ho Chi Minh somehow was persuaded—apparently by a joint Sino-Soviet effort—to settle for half the country.'[60] But the shape of the future did not lie in these Agreements, won by the Vietminh and forced upon the French by military defeat, but in other factors. The shape of the future lay in the determination of the American government to impose yet another foreign occupation upon Vietnam. How was it to be done?

In July 1954, few observers would have thought the Bao Dai government could survive the winter. The Vietminh was believed to have overwhelming power in Vietnam. But the Vietminh did not begin to give its attention to retaining or developing its strength in the South. It began to withdraw its military forces from the South, and, within the prescribed 300 days, about 100,000 had been withdrawn. Equally as much, the Vietminh began to concentrate on its affairs in the North. No one alleges or suggests that Hanoi did otherwise. No one suggests that Hanoi began to make things difficult for the government in Saigon, or to put any plans into operation to take over the South. The Vietminh had fully controlled quite a few provinces in the South and it withdrew almost completely. Many places were left in the condition, reported by Denis Warner,[61] of Kontum Province, at the northern end of the High Plateau, where the Vietminh left 'only 60 cadres in 1954 to cover an area about the size of the North Island of New Zealand among a mixed population of about 70,000 Montagnards and 25,000 Vietnamese. The cadres were all unarmed, or armed only with knives, and their task was not to fight but to win over the Montagnards.' Hardly the kind of foundation for a military take-over, or even the basis for a long-term objective of that kind. Hardly enough to do even the work necessary to win an election, and yet that seemed to be their purpose.

And the story was probably much the same all over South Vietnam. The Vietminh cadres were not military, but civilian, and the task they undertook was not to fight, but to win the people in a political way. Not only was this the task they undertook but it was the only one they could undertake—nothing more was possible. This was consistent with the decisions of the government in Hanoi, where the National Assembly made it clear that 'the struggle for unity would be long and difficult', and a prerequisite would be the 'consolidation of the already liberated North.' Hanoi wanted to see the South become Communist and unite with the north and wanted to have as much influence as possible over what was done. But this did not mean that Hanoi would seek an armed uprising in the south. In fact, Hanoi did not. This was consistent also with the Moscow line, and, until 1960, not inconsistent with the Chinese one. Moscow was laying it down that 'peaceful co-existence was the only line which was in complete accord with the ultimate aim of Communism'.

Moscow had played a substantial role at Geneva in 1954, consistent with this, but mainly for a far more specific reason. Moscow was as much concerned with Vietnam as with Europe. The Soviet Union wanted to keep France out of further American alliances and saw that, as long as she was dependent on America for support in the war in Vietnam, American influence over her in Europe would be greater— hence it was in the Soviet's interests for the war to stop. Hanoi's support for 'peaceful struggle' in South Vietnam, as we will see, went on till 1960. Moscow's influence was in 1960 still on the side of peace, but Peking's muted criticism of it came into the open in 1960 with assertions that the struggle against imperialism could not be won without fighting. In 1954, Hanoi began its 'line' which remained consistent till 1960. Statements which came over day after day from Hanoi Radio, were like that of the Vietnamese News Agency on September 28, 1954: 'The political struggle demands that our people avoid every provocation and use peaceful methods to win democracy, freedom and bring about general elections to unify the country.' Ho Chi Minh had ordered an electoral effort to be conducted throughout the country, north and south, aimed at 'winning support in all levels of the population with a view to winning the general elections for a United Vietnam.' This was Hanoi's policy and practice in 1954, 1955, 1956 and all through to late 1960 and thousands of broadcasts and Press statements supported this position in those years.

There were men among the leadership in Hanoi who opposed going to Geneva at all, and who opposed agreement at Geneva. There were those who considered the whole arrangement hypocritical humbug and that 'armed struggle' for victory and independence should begin right away. It would be difficult now to prove they were wrong.

It is often reported that the uncompromising 'Peking' line leader, Le Duan, took this stand, and was sent to South Vietnam in 1956 and worked there till 1958. While this may be so there is no evidence that he did anything in the South during that time except carry out Hanoi's policy, which was against 'armed struggle', and for a long-term political campaign. Le Duan doubtless reported against the Hanoi line and found growing support in the South for the position he took. Several of Le Duan's supporters, as well as himself, have later taken some trouble to give publicity to their position, and to their criticisms of the moderate line in Hanoi, in a type of 'I told you so' claim. But while these criticisms went on in Hanoi, probably from late 1956 onwards, the line did not change until 1960. Le Duan lost the argument in Hanoi until the South Vietnamese guerrilla leadership's stand for the 'armed struggle' became so strong that Hanoi could no longer maintain its moderate line.

But there was to be no election in Vietnam and political activity in South Vietnam was to become a crime punishable by death. What was done by the cadres in the South and by the government in Hanoi was in fact what the American State Department reported in 1961 that it had found they had done. In that year a State Department White Paper on the subject was published and it summed up its findings in the following way: 'It was the Communists' calculation that nation-wide elections scheduled in the (Geneva) Accords for 1956 would turn all Vietnam over to them. With total control over the more populous North in their hands, the Communists assumed they would be able to promote enough support in the South for their cause to win any balloting. *The primary focus of the Communists' activity during the post-Geneva period was on political action*—promoting discontent with the government in Saigon and seeking to win supporters for Hanoi. The authorities in South Vietnam refused to fall into this well-laid trap.'[62]

So to avoid this 'well laid trap', the government in Saigon, with the backing of the United States, decided there would be no elections. It is worth noting that the American line in 1961 was not 'aggression from the North'. It was the need to avoid falling into the trap provided by the elections. But much was to precede the decision about the elections. The State of Vietnam, the government in Saigon, had to clear the decks for action. Bao Dai had to go because he had a long record of collaboration which left him totally without appeal to any genuine nationalist. The French had to go, too, if the American expectation—upon which everything appeared to be based—about the removal of the 'last taint of colonialism' was to be realised. The Saigon government had also to get rid of its rivals for power—the Binh Xuen, Cao Dai and Hoa Hao. All this could be done by an overall strength which the Saigon government did not have at the start and which could come only from American backing. Diem was chosen by the Americans to lead the Saigon government. There was no alternative to Diem—although this is not to suggest that he was not very close to American requirements.

America's support for the Saigon government was based on its determination to maintain South Vietnam as an 'anti-Communist bastion'. Phillip Devilliers recorded what was obvious when he wrote: 'As early as September 1954 it became clear that the Americans' desire to hold on to the 17th parallel at all costs would constitute a serious obstacle to the reunification of Vietnam.'[63] It would also provide the reason for American support for Diem—provided he could do the job. Perhaps Hanoi did underestimate the Saigon government, as some writers suggest, but at any rate Hanoi caused it no trouble. In February 1955, the government in Hanoi proposed the restoration of normal relations for posts, roads, telegraphs, air and sea traffic and for trade, particularly in rice. These proposals were repeated many times up to as late as October 1962, but they were always rejected or ignored by Saigon. Similarly, as early as August 1955, Hanoi urged Saigon to take part in the 'consultative conference' about the elections, but this too was rejected because of the 'totalitarian nature of the North' and 'the multiple violations of the (Geneva) Agreement'.

Historian Devilliers found the position to be: 'Repeatedly, in May and June 1956, in July 1957, in March 1958, and in July 1959 and 1960, the DRV (Democratic Republic of Vietnam) returned to the charge, suggesting to Diem that the pre-election consultative conference should be held, and offering to negotiate on the basis of 'free general elections by secret ballot'. Each time it met with scornful silence or stinging replies. Each time Soviet and Chinese support was restricted to kind words, warm gestures of solidarity, and propaganda campaigns.' There was a similar lack of support from the United States and Great Britain, and more surprising, from India, Burma and Indonesia. At each point there was no DRV demand for elections, but only for the 'consultative conference'. Had Diem or the United States been genuine about the elections they would have turned up at the conference, demanded safeguards to ensure free and secret elections, and, if these were not forthcoming, they could have rejected the whole proposal on that ground. But neither Diem nor his American advisers ever gave the slightest consideration to the election requirement of the Geneva Agreements. They rejected it from the start and they did so because they well knew they could not win it. They could not win it if it was secret and free, as none of their own in South Vietnam ever was, nor could they beat North Vietnam at rigging the election even if their intention to rig it had been as great as that of North Vietnam.

The essential question about the election proposed in the Geneva Agreements, is not that it might have provided a genuine test of Vietnamese opinion. It could never have done so. But it did provide a clear admission of who would have won it had it been held, rigged or not rigged, and it clearly indicated who had the most support. It was not Diem and the Americans, any more than it was Bao Dai and the French. It was the Vietminh and the DRV.

Hanoi continued to protest the rejection of its requests and demands for the consultative conference and continued to seek support from the Soviet Union and Great Britain, co-Chairmen of the Geneva Conference, France, China and other nations.[64] None did more than express formal attitudes. Devilliers[65] points out: 'The occasion was a lesson to the D.R.V. (North Vietnam) on the importance which the great powers attach to the problems of their small allies.' Hanoi's efforts to secure the elections were rebuffed by Saigon with growing

American support, and were supported by Communist countries with little more than wordy criticism of the rejection. France acquiesced in the rejection, by her withdrawal from South Vietnam, before the elections were due, and without in any way carrying out her obligations under the Geneva Agreement to ensure that her 'successors would be responsible for . . . the observance and enforcement of the provisions (of the Agreement)', one of which, of course, was for the elections.

Rejection of the elections could have been expected to convince the Vietminh that they had been double-crossed again, at least the 10th time on a matter of importance since 1945. Whatever was to be the longer-term consequences of this, the stage was set for the emergence of Saigon's new Premier. The first to go, to make room for this, was French citizen and air force officer General Nguyen Van Hinh, who commanded the army. This was no easy task.

American support for Diem (as distinct from a government in Saigon capable of winning) had been uncertain and American counsel was divided. Eisenhower's original mandate to Diem of October 1, 1954, was conditional but placed him in a position far superior to that of any rival. It was conditional not upon Diem himself, but upon his 'assurances as to the standards of performance . . . in undertaking needed reforms'. But the performance that was first to count, and was to continue to be paramount, was not political and economic reform but military success. Diem doubtless gave assurances about reforms, and would have had no difficulty in convincing the Americans that the Binh Xuyen and the sects stood in his way and had to be dealt with first. The Binh Xuyen was a Saigon-based band of gangsters who ran the police, brothels, bars and clubs; the Cao Dai a kind of religious sect based mainly on secular writers in America and Europe, and the Hoa Hao a type of militant Buddhism built around one or two individuals and tied to an army to create a kind of local 'war lordism'. These organisations had supported the French, had been financially maintained by the French, but had been prepared to go along with whoever seemed to serve the interests not of their members but of their leaders. They had worked with the Vietminh when it suited them and would later work for a while with the 'Viet Cong'. Of course, to remove these obstructions to power, if not to reform, Diem had to take military action. He could not rely on General Hinh.

Diem acted with resolution and courage in these contests but American money and pressure were always vital. His test of strength against Hinh had been decided by American pressure upon Bao Dai in Paris. The Americans simply pointed out to the French that American aid would be cut unless Hinh was sacked. He was. This demonstration of Diem's power not only brought an end to Hinh, but brought other army leaders into line. It was really the first demonstration of American power and of Saigon's dependence upon it.

Diem's military action against the Binh Xuyen which followed was quick and successful. It would appear sound and necessary to all except those who consider that Ho Chi Minh has been wrong in getting rid of his enemies in a similar way and for the same reasons. It did much to rid Diem of obstruction, to convince the Americans that he was the man to support and to show his rivals that he was dangerous.

But his attack on the Cao Dai and the Hoa Hao took much longer and was much more than a military operation. The hardly accidental withdrawal by the French in February 1955 of their cash subventions to both sects left them very vulnerable to the influence of money. Diem had money. His American advisers favoured compromise but Diem chose to use American money to split and divide the leaders of the sects so that he would not need to compromise. He resisted their collective action and demands for subventions, for territorial recognition and for places in his government and began to deal with their leaders individually. Bernard Fall tells us:[66] 'The total amount of American dollars spent on bribes during March and April 1955 by Diem may well have gone beyond $12 million.'

But the sects still had strong forces of resistance, and solution of the main problem presented by them awaited military action. Most observers were surprised at the speed and extent of Diem's success in defeating them and subjugating most of their territories. Not insignificant remnants were left for some time. It was at this point when Diem had most proved himself that he was most threatened. In a sense it was his success that brought the threat to his position. Bao Dai called him to Paris and most people expected his dismissal. But Diem's successes had removed what was left of Washington's doubts and now Washington did not hesitate. It was Bao Dai who had to go.

The campaign to remove Bao Dai, left Diem personally vulnerable, but he tackled it with great courage and confidence, and did not conclude it until the carefully-managed bogus referendum of October 26, 1955, when he received 98.2 per cent of the votes. Diem claimed a high percentage of success even in 'Communist' areas— an experience which, had his claim been genuine, should have removed his doubts about 'winning' elections in 'Communist' areas. Diem now proclaimed the establishment of the Republic of Vietnam, (not South Vietnam), with himself as President, and members of his family in key positions.

Another of Diem's achievements, and perhaps his most significant one, was the reception of about 700,000 Catholic, and perhaps 100,000 other refugees, from North Vietnam. This was the largest constructive task ever undertaken by Diem and, on the standards of the time and place, it was remarkably successful. Warner records that 'one of Diem's first positive acts had been to ask for American assistance in moving the refugees from the North. His appeals to Washington and to the Catholics of North Vietnam were equally successful. Suddenly a deluge of refugees descended on Saigon. Following the advice of their priests, hundreds of thousands of northern Catholics abandoned everything, their homes, their oxen, and their fields and with no more than they could carry crowded aboard American and French ships at the port of Haiphong.'[67] Among these refugees the most important group were those who had fought with the French and who believed they had no future under the Vietminh.

Although there was something contrived and political about this exodus, there can be no doubt that the refugees were sure they had much to fear in North Vietnam and events proved them right. But the exodus did have significance for other reasons which those who correctly emphasise the above do not even consider. This flood of refugees into South Vietnam was a far more powerful 'interference' from North Vietnam in favour of Diem than anything that ever came from there against him. It provided not only a release from the persecutions and hardships the refugees expected in the North, but it provided the basis of Diem's power in the South. Not only did it provide hundreds of thousands of people upon whom Diem could rely, when he had few, but it added greatly to the strength of those forces that were moving America more and more into Vietnam. It strengthened Catholic support for Diem all over the world. The long war in Vietnam had been colonial, civil, ideological and international. It now became religious and this meant it was going to be more difficult to enforce in Vietnam the Geneva Conventions on war.

Let us now look at the question of Diem's power. Kahin and Lewis[68] say that the refugee group provided 'the most reliable civilian support' of the Diem regime, and formed 'the popular backbone of recent military regimes (in South Vietnam) and (served) as the death weapon against more moderate regimes'. According to Halberstam[69] 'at all vital centers of the (Diem) government power was held by Catholics'. Warner tells us[70] '. . . the Diem regime was Catholic at the vital points of the apparatus'. And Bernard Fall sums it up,[71] 'The arrival of that tightly knit community in a South Vietnam that is largely Taoist, spiritualist, and Buddhist created new political tensions there—the more so as the government of President Ngo Dinh Diem immediately used the Northern Catholics as its major base of political power'. It should hardly be necessary to point out emphatically these obvious facts and developments. It would not be necessary to do so at all if these facts were not so persistently denied in all tame and conventional versions of what happened in Vietnam.

When one ponders the 'separateness' of North and South Vietnam and the assistance of North Vietnamese to the 'Viet Cong', one cannot lose sight of the significance of this 'invasion' of perhaps 800,000 anti-Communists. They came for reasons which for them were well and truly justified, but they did provide 'a major base of political power' for a government in South Vietnam which needed it very much, and which might not have been able to find or maintain that base in any other way.

By the end of 1956, Diem was secure in Saigon and began to enter perhaps his best year, certainly his year of greatest opportunity. His was to prove the only government in Saigon genuine enough in its nationalism to stand a chance of an independent existence. But up to the end of 1956 the Diem government had been very vulnerable and sorely tested. Diem had survived because of his courage, his confidence, his 'lack of colonial taint', his vigorous action against the Binh Xuyen and the sects and, crucially, because of American backing. But throughout this period of struggle not only did Hanoi, the Vietminh, or 'Communists' in South Vietnam not cause the Diem government any trouble, but there were no claims that they did. If these groups were really intent upon aggression or the 'armed struggle', as distinct from 'peaceful political action', they certainly missed many great opportunities in 1955 and 1956: Diem was able to establish himself without any armed opposition from these quarters. It is difficult to find any Diem government claims of casualties or 'terror' before 1958. Between 1957 and 1959 this government reported to the International Control Commission the murder by Viet Cong cadres of 10 servicemen, 28 civil guards, 65 village officials and 51 civilians,[72] a total of 154. The government claimed that 138 were killed[73] in 1959. Hence, it appears that only 16 persons were killed up to and including 1958 . . . hardly evidence to the end of 1958, of any campaign of terror, subversion or guerrilla war, or that Communists had caused any dislocation of government services or ability to carry out reforms. Reforms during these critical years were not prevented by any opposition to the Diem government but by the Diem government's own opposition to them.

In his detailed study, *Viet Cong*, Douglas Pike shows that in the early years the work of the National Liberation Front in South Vietnam was education, indocrination and organisation. The existence and nature of the N.L.F. were given prominence and grievances were identified and fanned into hostility to the Diem government. The whole exercise was essentially political. Organisations were created for farmers, women, workers, youth, students and the professions. Government servants were driven out, after being identified with grievances or injustices, the government was shown as the enemy, and the N.L.F. as the protector of the people. Emphasis was given all the time to the slogan 'we struggle peacefully' and 'the government uses violence'. Pike shows that even through 1960-61 there was little attention to violence, peaceful struggle remaining the theme of all work and propaganda by the N.L.F. But the facts were that in 1961 and 1962 the Diem Government, and fast-growing American assistance, proved too strong for 'peaceful', political struggle to handle. The first Congress of the National Liberation Front in South Vietnam in February-March 1962, according to Pike, was the first recognition of this fact and of the need for violence. Armed struggle began to be emphasised from late 1962 and early 1963. Pike points out the natural consequence of all this: the N.L.F. remained popular through to 1963, but the more it had to use violence and impose greater burdens, risks and losses upon the people the less popular it became. Political struggle to correct legitimate grievances against an unpopular government must be successful. But when the people face violence and have to risk their lives against superior odds, the cause must indeed be strong if it is to hold them. This change was precipitated by the use of massive United States fire power. Pike is of the opinion that the balance from political to armed struggle by the N.L.F. did not shift until September 1963— and then as a result of decisions at a 'military conference inside the Cambodian border opposite Darlac plateau.' The new N.L.F. strategy was the immediate response to the introduction of large numbers of American helicopters, bombs and quick-firing guns.

The conventional American-Australian-South Vietnamese explanation for the war in Vietnam is that it began because the Communist government in Hanoi, supported and incited by the Communist governments in Peking and Moscow, deliberately left behind in South Vietnam Communist Vietminh cadres, troops and arms, and that as soon as the Diem government was seen to be making progress, Hanoi gave orders for these cadres and troops to begin war on the government and its officers and the people of South Vietnam, and then began to send in men, supplies and arms so that it became an attack on the people of South Vietnam from 'outside their country'. This explanation is almost completely false. Action from which the war began was taken by both sides—by the Diem government and by the rebels in South Vietnam. Repressive action by the government and neglect of needed reforms were the vital factors in causing an insurrection and in causing it to grow. In many cases repressive action by the government came first, in some it did not, but in most cases it was necessary to transform a passive resistance in the villages into a situation where people were prepared to fight. Between 1955 and 1960, the government in Hanoi certainly sought to direct and control the movement in South Vietnam, urging it not to use force, but instead to use 'peaceful political methods'. Grievances were to be identified and built upon so that the support of the people could be won first, to win the election expected in July 1956, and then politically to unify the whole of Vietnam under one government. In 1960, the argument advanced by Communists and others *in South Vietnam* was that there was no hope of a political solution to their problems and that the Diem government had to be forcefully overthrown. This, in 1959, was reluctantly accepted by Hanoi. The Soviet Union still supported the 'peaceful' line but Peking asserted that no struggle against Imperialism could be won peacefully. The National Front for Liberation was formed in South Vietnam in March 1960. It was recognised and supported by Hanoi in September 1960. Increased assistance from the North in men, supplies and arms, trickling in before 1960, began to increase in 1961, but did not amount to any more than 10 or 15 per cent of the total even by the end of 1964. This is a summary of what happened in these critical years and the truth destroys the basis for American and Australian intervention in South Vietnam and for the attack on North Vietnam. America and her agents are the aggressors in the war in Vietnam and their aggression is not justified by their claims. Let us look at a summary of the facts upon which this interpretation is based.

Diem began his campaign against the Communists in South Vietnam in June 1955 as soon as it was safe for him to turn away from the Binh Xuen and the sects. This was natural and to be expected. Having disposed of Bao Dai, and the opposing generals, and having secured his rear by the campaigns against the Binh Xuen and the sects, and having won unqualified American support, Diem could not be expected to sit motionless and to wait until he was attacked by the Communists. His was a dedicated anti-Communist government supported by America for the very purpose of clearing Communists from South Vietnam and making it into an anti-Communist bastion. It can be reasonably asserted that the purpose went further: to win all of Vietnam and more as an anti-Communist bastion.

But this was not to be done just by a military campaign. Study of the French war in Indochina and of modern guerrilla war[74] had convinced the Americans that to win a 'revolutionary war' the support of the people had to be won. There was no doubt in American minds, up to 1962, that they had a 'revolutionary war' on their hands in Vietnam.

Many of the Americans who supported Diem in the beginning, like Mansfield, Douglas, Kennedy, Ladejinsky and Buttinger were democrats, if not socialists, who understood what it is that brings about political and economic change, and who found this explanation of 'revolutionary war' consistent with what they knew about history, and the need for popular support compatible both with their experience and with their philosophy. Indeed one of the factors favourable to Diem, for a year or two, was the aura of progress created around him by support of Americans of this type. But Diem was not the same kind of man and his position in society was very different from that of his democratic American supporters. He was not philosophically a reformer and his interests were such that they would be damaged by reforms. He was not likely to adopt reforms to stay in power in Vietnam. Instead he naturally adopted a continuation of the methods which had proved so successful against the Binh Xuen and the sects. But of course, they had no revolutionary basis or backing at all.

And so Diem began his Anti-Communist Denunciation Campaign in June 1955. A year later this campaign was judged to have been so successful that it was reported by the government that 94,000 former Communist cadres had been won over and an additional 5,613 had surrendered.[75] It is not possible to estimate the number killed or sent to concentration camps, but in 1956, the South Vietnamese Secretary of State for Information claimed that between 15,000 and 20,000 Communists and active sympathisers had been detained in political re-education centres since 1954. At the end of 1960, the total claimed was 48,250 for those detained between 1954 and 1960. Phillip Devilliers uses a figure of 50,000 for those gaoled at the end of 1956. The well-known spokesman for the Communist-aggression argument, P. J. Honey, reported that '. . . the consensus of opinion expressed by these people (detainees in camps) is that . . . the majority of detainees are neither Communist nor pro-Communist'. Of the period as early as 1958, writers like William Henderson, anxious to find ways of winning support for America in Vietnam, were able to conclude: 'South Vietnam is today a quasi-police state characterised by arbitrary arrests and imprisonment, strict censorship of the Press and the absence of an effective opposition. All the techniques of political and psychological warfare, as well as pacification campaigns involving extensive military operations, have been brought to bear against the underground.'

As early as 1956 the Saigon government gave itself legal freedom not only to eliminate the 'underground' but any form of opposition. American 'Life' magazine of May 13, 1957[76] summed it up: 'Behind a facade of photographs, flags and slogans, there is a grim structure of decrees, political prisons, concentration camps, milder re-education centers, secret police.'

But in 1957, R. G. Casey, then Minister for External Affairs, in telling the House of Representatives of the position in South Vietnam, began a long series of similar statements by Australian Ministers, based on a complete failure to understand what was happening in Vietnam. He said: 'Now internal security in South Vietnam is better than in most countries of South East Asia, and President Diem's government has won widespread popular support.' Not only did this kind of statement show a complete failure to see the undemocratic nature of the Diem regime but it contradicted the later claim that the Communists were, at the time, a threat to the security of the regime.

Presidential Ordinance No. 6, issued by Diem in January 1956, provides that 'individuals considered dangerous to national defence

and common security may be confined by executive order in a concentration camp.' 'Only known or suspected Communists who have
threatened or violated public security since July 1954 are supposed to
be arrested and re-educated under these decrees,' 'Life' magazine stated,
'But many non-Communists have also been detained. The whole
machinery of security has been used to discourage active opposition of
any kind from any source.' These practices were continued and intensified in 1957 and 1958. But extended powers were obtained and
applied in 1959. Law 10 of 1959 legalised 'long established practices
of suppression' and special military courts were given wide powers over
offences which carried the death penalty. These offences amounted
to no more than speaking or writing of economic, financial or political
grievances which were 'contrary to the truth'—the 'truth' of course,
was what the Diem government and its officials said it was. A five-
week campaign in An Xuen alone is reported by Kahin and Lewis[77]
to have resulted in the surrender of 8,125 Communist agents and
the denunciation of 9,806 'other agents' and 29,978 sympathisers'.

Not only did the Diem government extend its operations over as
much of South Vietnam as it was able to reach, and that was by no
means all, but it extended them well beyond 'former Vietminh cadres
and Communists'. Devilliers says: 'This repression was in theory
aimed at the Communists. In fact it affected all those, and they were
many—democrats, socialists, liberals, adherents of the sects—who were
bold enough to express their disagreement with the line of policy
adopted by the ruling oligarchy'. These views of Diem's conduct were
by 1959 the views of almost every observer who had any standing in
Vietnam. After 1963 they became the views of everyone—even many of
those who had been supporters of the government. Denis Warner
thought that it was 'a tragedy for South Vietnam and for South East
Asia . . . that the qualities which helped Diem to survive in 1954-55
were also the qualities that brought about his downfall'. What had the
Diem government done? Warner answers: 'Like medieval inquisitors,
their witch-hunting for sources of demoralisation was indiscriminate,
haphazard, ineffective and brutal.'[78] It must be remembered that an
anti-Communist campaign is generally concerned with 'sources of demoralisation' not merely political views or activities. Late in 1958, the
National Democratic Movement of South Vietnam made an appeal to
the French and American people: 'We enjoy neither justice nor freedom of the Press, nor free speech, nor freedom to travel and meet
together. A revolt is simmering.'

A revolt certainly was simmering. Apart from social and political
repression in search of 'sources of demoralisation', which was producing
a revolt on its own, what was happening with the economic reform
considered so essential by President Eisenhower? The story is now complete and is documented in many sources. I select some statements by

Denis Warner as an accurate summary of the sources in certain key items: 'In its annual report for the 1960 financial year, the United States Operations Mission in Saigon briefly reviewed the problem that had confronted South Vietnam after 1954. Then it added: "To assist South Vietnam to cope with these many problems, the United States launched a many faceted programme which, since 1954, has totalled £1,302 million".' Then the Report went on to detail what it was claimed had been done in transport, health, education, agricultural production, land reform and development, in which 'United States aid had . . . played a major role'. Then Warner goes on: 'The only inference the uninformed reader could draw from such stuff was that this great volume of United States aid . . . had flowed into productive channels. Nothing could have been further from the truth. A meagre 1.4 per cent of United States aid, or $15 million, went to agriculture between 1955 and 1960. The much-vaunted rural help programme did not exist. Land reform was a flop. Industry was insignificant.'[79] Professor Frank C. Child of Michigan State University, after two years of investigation in South Vietnam, wrote in 1961: 'Today economic development is inhibited not by lack of resources but by lack of effort and inept administration. The rich and the government hoard their resources rather than invest them in economic growth. American aid is administered in a fashion which guarantees the economic and political position of the rich mercantile class, which is vigorously opposed to economic progress.'[80]

Faced with what is now the overwhelming evidence of Diem's repressive action and his refusal to carry out reforms one can share the conclusion of Kahin and Lewis[81] '. . . it is remarkable that a guerrilla type insurrection did not break out earlier.' The reason for this is not only the difficulties and obstructions that such an insurrection always faces, some of which we will notice later, but the fact that Hanoi applied the brakes until 1960 and only then gave reluctant and limited support which still took a long time to have any effect.

Is it not reasonable to expect a revolt in these circumstances? Should people do nothing about their grievances? Should they forever accept injustice and corruption around them? What if they do object? Diem saw to it (when he could reach them), that they were denounced, arrested, re-educated, gaoled or killed. What can we expect those who are left to do then? It was by its home policy that the Diem government destroyed the opportunities it had to establish a stable, non-Communist government in South Vietnam, and produced dissent for which it denied any political or peaceful outlet. This is how and why that force which became the national guerrilla movement in Vietnam originated, not by aggression from the north or from any Communist conspiracy, but in South Vietnam—and not because of, but despite, attempts from North Vietnam to control and direct it against violence and aggression and into political channels. Devilliers correctly concludes that '. . . even among the Communists, the initiative did not originate in Hanoi, but from the grass roots, where the people were driven by Diem to take up arms in self-defence'.[82]

This process and outcome, too, is logical and understandable. The American leaders, as we have seen, made up their minds that South Vietnam, and perhaps more, should be retained as an anti-Communist bastion. To achieve this result they saw, correctly, that the support of the people had to be won. It was their war. It could not be fought for them. If their support was to be won, then first, the 'last taint of colonialism' had to be removed, hence France and Bao Dai had to go. They went. And as a result of American decisions. Yet more was needed. The new government had to carry out needed political and economic reforms. But reforms were not carried out. Diem set up a police state as far as he could reach in South Vietnam, and did not make reforms. And America did not stand behind her own basic assumptions. She went on supporting a government which contradicted them. Hence the struggle had to become more and more military and the war had to become more and more Americanised. But all this originated and remains in the grass roots of life in Vietnam.

Why then did America give up her essentially correct historical and sociological understanding of the 'guerrilla war' in Vietnam and adopt one contrary to the facts and without objective, contemporary content, let alone historical and sociological meaning? Why did America place herself in the position that her administration would have to cover up, conceal and distort? Why did she create a 'credibility gap' between her President and the people? The answer to this lies in the very nature of modern anti-Communism, as it was applied in South Vietnam, and as it tends to be applied in America and Australia. Anti-Communism is not a political or a military method, it is a search for 'sources of demoralisation'. It is a witch hunt. In the final analysis it has no weapon but the force of arms. It was the factor behind the basic change in American attitudes and methods in Vietnam in or about 1961-62. As we have seen, leading American opinion had correctly identified the war in Vietnam as a colonial war in which there was a national revolution. Even John Foster Dulles saw that it was necessary to get rid of 'the last taint of colonialism' and to win the support of the people. Many Americans genuinely thought that Diem was capable of doing this—and he was capable of getting closer to it than any alternative personality in South Vietnam. But he failed. How was that failure to be faced?

The two years 1961-62 were critical years. They began with a visit to South Vietnam by Senator Lyndon B. Johnson. His view was that America must stay in Vietnam and put all her weight behind Ngo Dinh Diem. Johnson must have come away with some substantial

hope that Diem could stay in power but it is obvious that the main
factors influencing Johnson had little to do with Vietnam or the
prospects of any government in Vietnam to win the support of the
people. To Johnson it was a power struggle against Communism that
America must win. The only question was how to win. Hence the
requirement was for experts to be sent to Vietnam to find out. The
experts were Professor Eugene Staley, Professor W. W. Rostow and
General Maxwell Taylor. The two professors and the general took
with them to Vietnam the simple American assumption which they so
well and fully represented—that any problem could be solved if it was
a technical problem, if it was a problem of resources. Staley and Rostow
were technical men—their contribution to geography and economics
was really to make people irrelevant. Staley wrote about the importance of resources, and people were merely one of them. Rostow
convinced himself that he had finally answered Marx and made him no
longer relevant. He had done so by taking history out of economics
and reducing it to tables, curves and categories which in some impersonal sense produced dynamic points of action. Taylor was a general
who, perhaps even less than the other two, ignored the historical and
social factors they all really knew were involved. The question they
faced was how to find ways of using resources to win the war without
changing the social and political structure of South Vietnam in any
way. It was how to win a revolutionary contest without in any way
being revolutionary.

Staley was even more restricted in his job than the other two.
Asked, in effect, how to remove the people from the reach of the so-
called Viet Cong, he recommended the establishment of 'strategic
hamlets', as part of the general strategy which was fundamentally
military. His recommendations became a significant part of American
policy for two years until their failure was fully demonstrated. But
Taylor and Rostow were restricted enough in their scope. I do not
think that Schlesinger exaggerated when he wrote that their terms of
reference 'expressed a conscious decision by the Secretary of State to
turn the Vietnam problem over to the Secretary of Defence'.[83] But
Dean Rusk, Secretary of State, had emphasised in May 1961 that it was
no longer possible to oppose Vietminh threats by purely military
means. The Taylor-Rostow report went well beyond military recommendations. While they all exaggerated the significance of intervention
from the North (by the end of 1961, even by South Vietnamese government reckoning, 'infiltration' from the North was no more than 6,200
and arms were only an insignificant proportion of those used) it is not
true to say, as some do, that the Taylor-Rostow report saw the problem
as primarily a military one. Perhaps the most significant thing about
their report was its stress on the urgent need for reform, while re-

jection of the report highlighted Diem's successful opposition to all reform.

There is no sign that former Professor Rostow gave any emphasis to what might have been the most relevant proposition in his own special academic achievement—*The Stages of Economic Growth: a Non-Communist Manifesto* published in 1959. In it Rostow had emphasised the point that economic 'take-off' in an agrarian society depends upon the shifting of spending power to those who will spend on roads, railways, schools and factories rather than on country houses, servants, personal ornaments and temples. Rostow had emphasised that a 'new elite' was essential—one that would have different priorities and concepts of what was ethically good. Even in his *Stages of Economic Growth* there is little sign that Rostow thought that such a shift might involve social and political disturbances, or that those who held spending power in the agrarian society might resist the change. His main purpose in his academic work was to wish this proposition out of existence so that he could find Communism to be unnecessary and improbable. To think that a simple transfer of spending power from the landlords and officials of an agrarian society would do the trick, was naive enough; but to think that it could happen without resistance was to ignore the essence of the problem in Vietnam. To what extent was Diem and his ruling clique able to modernise South Vietnam? There is little sign that Rostow, Taylor or Staley gave any serious, let alone critical, thought to this at all.

It was perhaps at this point that Washington made its crucial retreat from the need for reforms and thereby committed itself to a dominantly military campaign, although, no doubt, it thought it was really being political. It was not so much that the Taylor-Rostow report recommended such a campaign, it was that South Vietnamese rejection of reform was then most acutely registered and Washington completely accepted that rejection and, therefore, had no alternative but to wage a military campaign. Once America became committed in Vietnam to win the fight against Communism, whether Diem would bring about reforms or whether, in fact, reforms were even relevant, was no longer of any importance. Once it became a matter of national or personal prestige, and it had become so under President Kennedy as much as under any other, or a religious matter, then Diem, or reforms, or the nature of the war, had no bearing on the situation. America then had to stay in Vietnam and do whatever was necessary to win. If America's reputation hinged on winning, or if the reputation of an American President depended upon his not losing, or if the Communists were seen as 'godless goons' who would make us all 'serfs and slaves' and to whom, unless we defeated them, we would be 'betraying the sacred trust of our forefathers' and 'risk bartering our liberties for lunacies',[84] once that stage was reached, then reform in Vietnam no longer mattered. The war then had to be carried on until it was won, and as reforms and the support of the people no longer mattered, then it would become a war fought with fire power alone and it would be an American war. All this seems to have been made inevitable by the decisions of 1961.

At the same time, and as a consequence of these decisions, the prevailing American explanation of the war changed from an historical and sociological one to that of 'aggression from the north', and if this was the case, and if land hunger, injustice and corruption in South Vietnam had little to do with it, then reforms and winning the support of the people, could take very much of a back seat. American action could become more and more military and the war could 'escalate' without limit. If the war was not really a result of poverty, injustice and corruption, for which remedies had been denied by Diem, but instead the result of irresistible aggression starting in Moscow or Peking and likely to overcome the world, then, even if Vietnam and her people were destroyed, this would be justified. But this 'aggression' and 'devil' interpretation, this 'globalism', is unsound and inadequate. It was for this reason that the 'credibility gap', and continuous military escalation, as a result of the new interpretation, became inevitable.

This, of course, does not mean that Communists and revolutionaries played no part. But Communists and revolutionaries can do only what circumstances allow. Political action is hard enough to get anyone to undertake. Apathy is not only a feature of affluent societies. It is just as much, if not more, a feature of poor and badly exploited societies. Political action is hard enough for anyone to induce others to take, but action at risk of life, limb or property is harder to encourage. Any kind of social action is uncommon, action at personal risk is rare indeed. How did it come about that tens of thousands of people who live in South Vietnam are now prepared to risk their lives against overwhelming odds? What gave the so-called Viet Cong that courage and persistence that has driven the leaders of the world's greatest scientific and industrial nation to distraction? This could not have happened in 1900 or 1930 or 1940 or 1945 or 1954. At all these earlier stages of the Vietnamese resistance to foreign interference it is doubtful if today's power to resist could have been generated. How has it come about?

To understand this it is necessary to understand the background of resistance in Vietnam which we have briefly outlined in earlier parts of this story. Everything that happened since April 1847 contributed something to the capacity of the Vietnamese to resist 120 years later.

CHAPTER SEVEN

THE REVOLUTIONARY WAR

In no other country is there a history of resistance comparable in its effect on the people to that in Vietnam. But if we are to understand the strength of the 'Viet Cong' today we have to look very closely. We have to understand what happened in the villages, because this was where it all started. Let us look inside a small village—a microcosm of the greater part of South Vietnam and see what did happen.[85]

We have seen that Vietminh troops were withdrawn to North Vietnam, that the government there concentrated on its own affairs, pressed Saigon on the question of elections and on trade and other relations, and announced and adopted a policy of political action aimed at winning the 1956 elections. Even when the elections were not held, as we have seen, this policy continued till 1960 and changed mainly as a result of Southern pressure. First of all, what was the position of Vietminh troops and cadres? The troops, we are told, had been 'too busy fighting (up to 1954) to marry' and, 'all over the South before the Vietminh evacuation late in 1954, hundreds, even thousands, of weddings took place. At the worst it seemed that separation would be for two years.'[86] But separation was to be for much more than two years. It is beyond doubt, then, that some of these cadres and troops would come back to South Vietnam for their own private reasons. In Quang Ngai, one of the poorest provinces, 'more than 500 weddings took place' and '20,000 families there had close relatives in the North'. Was it not obvious that many of these Southerners 'who left parents, brides and children and went north with the Vietminh in 1954' would later return when elections were refused and separation grew beyond two years? Is it not surprising that the number claimed to have returned by 'infiltration' from the North is not more than the 1,800 'confirmed' and 2,700 'estimated' in the famous American White Paper, 'Aggression from the North', up to the end of 1960? Can such 'infiltrations' be properly claimed as 'aggression' by one country upon another?

It is believed that about 3,000 to 5,000 civilian 'cadres' were left behind in 1954. Warner tells us there were 60 in Kontum, 100 in Pleiku and 40 in Dalac. Who counted them? How many were Communists? Who decided they were 'cadres'? We do not know. Was it Diem officials who were busy carrying out the 'medieval inquisition' that Warner himself thinks it was? But assuming that all were 'cadres' that were claimed and assuming that they got orders direct from Hanoi—what did they do? Surprisingly enough, Warner reports what we would, from our own examination, expect—'. . . their original orders were to work among the people in preparation for the 1956 elections'. And Warner's findings confirm what we would expect— 'Apart from those on liaison duties, few Communist cadres made their way south before 1957. Ho was preoccupied with internal problems'.[87]

But there seems to have been something sinister about these cadres. Some of them took jobs. That is to say, they 'infiltrated' into Diem's anti-literacy classes or opened classes of their own where the government did not. They even took jobs as drivers and conductors on buses so that they could travel about and keep in touch with the people. What did they do in a village? They began to look for legitimate grievances. They must have known that you can't get very far on grievances that are not legitimate. 'What legitimate grievances', asks Warner, 'could the Communists find to exploit? The answer was land.' In most places, except for the refugees from the north, there had been no land reform at all. In some, the Vietminh had given land to the peasants and Diem officials had restored it to the landlords and ruled that back rent, since the confiscation, had to be paid. But even when grievances were the most legitimate it was difficult to get the peasants to act. 'The task was not easy', writes Warner. 'At first Diem's mobile troops were active in the area, and especially in two neighbouring villages which were on dry land. During the first years of peace, when the Lao Dong Party made several attempts to become active, Diem's men three times broke up the organisation. Three party members were killed, two secretaries arrested and more than 100 cadres and others taken into custody. Finally one cadre remained and he commanded no local support.'[88] It certainly does not look as if the Communists began the war here or that Diem was slow to act. In any case it looked then, and that was sometime in 1957, as if it was all over in 'XB' village, which is referred to in Warner's 'The Last Confucian'.

But we are told that in this 'typical village', 'higher level' assistance came finally in 1959, not from North Vietnam, but from other areas in South Vietnam and Cambodia. These helpers 'gathered scattered party members and instructed them in re-establishing destroyed Party bases'. One of their reports, presumably captured by Saigon government forces and examined by experts, pointed out: 'Things were so difficult then that the members were forced to hide in the fields and marshes during the day, and only at night could they slip back into the villages to do propaganda work among the farmers'. But what about this period of perhaps two years—1957 to 1959? What was North Vietnam doing all that time while the 'Party bases' were being destroyed and the members were hiding in the fields and marshes?

What indeed was Diem doing? What about the reforms that were needed? What about winning the hearts and minds of the people during those two years? Was it these scattered party members hiding in the fields and marshes who prevented the Diem government from acting? What indeed about all the others? What about the nationalists, the democrats, the socialists and the Catholics who might have competed with the 'scattered Party members' for leadership of the village? What about the legitimate grievances of the village—who was attending to them? The year 1959 came and nothing had been done.

Was it surprising then that the 'Party members' were so successful with their propaganda? We are told it was propaganda they used (they must not have known that power really grows out of the barrel of a gun). The 'Party' had in 1961, 26 members, 30 members were in the Lao Dong Youth, 274 in the Farmers' Association, 150 in the Youth Group and 119 in the Liberation Women's Group. 'Two thousand people, or two thirds of the villagers', the captured report said, 'take part in Party-led activities'. Perhaps the report exaggerated but Warner was impressed. 'From one outlawed man', he wrote, 'to the active control of 2,000 seemingly willing recruits in the space of two years!'[89]

But the Diem forces remained strong in and around the village. How was their power and influence to be dealt with? Denis Warner is ready with another of those misleading suggestions that he generally slips in at crucial points. It was 'terror'. Leaving the story of XB village, he stops to tell us at this point that in 1959 and 1960 there was a 'vast increase in indiscriminate terror', and quotes *two* cases from *other* parts of Vietnam. Then he returns to the story of XB village and we find that 'terror' does not have much relation to it.

We can have no doubt, the Viet Cong killed many people viciously, cruelly and unnecessarily and Warner gives a vivid description of one of them—Father Theo Bonnet in Kontum in 1961. But the Viet Cong would have won very little support by killing Father Bonnet. This was not the basis of their support and strength, and it was support and strength they needed in XB village at this point of the development. Warner recognises that the Father Bonnet type of killing was inconsistent with village needs and he points out—'Summary Viet Cong justice for a village chief guilty of corruption or brutality did not offend the peasants.' If there was to be killing in XB village at a point where Warner introduces 'terror' as an explanation it would be this latter type. But in XB village at that stage it does not even appear that killing was relevant at all. The report goes on to say that the 'Party' had proceeded with its propaganda and had been successful in demonstrating the link between the village notables and security agents and Mister H, the cruel landlord . . . who would return to the village and collect back rent. It was a 'good method' the report said, 'after a while, even certain notables refused to work for the enemy and some took the side of the people'.

What happened then? The report tells us that the 'U.S.-Diem clique' tried to win back the people by distributing drugs in the village. The offer was flatly rejected. 'Civic aid' does not count for much when land and back rents are involved. Yet no significant change had taken place in the village. The report puts it: 'At this stage XB village had merely turned from being for and with the government to being for itself'. But, of course, this was not enough. If the village was to hold on to what it had or to contribute anything to the 'liberation of South Vietnam' it had to become more than 'for itself'. Awareness of the land question and identification of the link between the landlords and the government and village officials is knowledge for the villagers but knowledge alone achieves no reform. Action is needed for that.

Reform can sometimes be achieved by the action of voting, but not in South Vietnam. Even the village chiefs were no longer elected. In 1956, Diem abolished the elected village councils, replacing them with officials appointed by his provincial governors upon approval by the Minister for the Interior. They were all, no doubt, checked against the ever growing list of names compiled by Nhu's secret police. Village elections could not be held because many 'Communists' would be elected. And the result—'At one stroke the autonomy which South Vietnam's 2,560 villages had enjoyed even under the French rule was swept away, and a centralised administration usually out of touch with their problems' was substituted.[90] Furthermore, political activity, meetings, speeches and distributing pamphlets were outlawed as criminal offences.

Hence XB village had to fight if it was to get anywhere. It had to fight if it was to prevent the imposition of the old rents by Diem officials and soldiers. Denis Warner agrees: 'It had to fight, and the more it could be made to fight, and the more the government forces would be encouraged to fight it, the more rapidly would the people become fully identified with the Communist goals which do not merely seek to exclude the government from rural areas but to overthrow it.' But how could the village come to the point of being willing to fight? Few people want to fight. Few people want to risk their lives if they can possibly avoid it. Much more was needed in XB village to make it fight. Hence, the report said the 'Party' had to extend its work. Public health, sanitation, education, and even the marketing of produce had to become its concern. The government failed to start a school in XB village so the 'Party' did. By the end of 1960 such progress had been made that 'the public establishment of the National Liberation Front in the village became the occasion of a quasi-religious festival'. It wouldn't be long now before Diem's troops attacked the village and made it fight. Warner too sees it this way: 'The establishment of the

National Liberation Front was in a sense the crossing of the watershed for XB village.'

The 'Party' had to work now 'to get the people to make rudimentary weapons' (apparently there were none available from Hanoi, Peking or Moscow and none had been found in caches left by the Vietminh) and to 'join in turning XB village into a combat village'. But still 'Party' officials met with resistance, and it was the cadres and self-defence troops who had to lay metal and bamboo spikes and make 'naily boards' to stop the troops who would come. The people 'thought this was illegal and would result in terror and reprisals by the soldiers'. But the soldiers were coming sooner or later anyway. 'In the light of this', says Warner, 'Party members had to lay the boards themselves, while endeavouring to educate the people.' But 'once during a terror sweep one of the soldiers was injured by a naily board (a hideous booby trap made from needle-pointed and barbed nails set in wooden blocks) and the soldiers withdrew.' This was taken to be a victory 'which encouraged the villagers.' However, the village was still not strong. Everything was defensive and confidence was low. There was a tendency to give way on defensive action and even on 'legitimate grievances'. The village thought it had gained a good deal. The report said: 'Once the people are satisfied about land the movement degenerates'. The people could not be persuaded to act and to fight unless they had good reason. It was not a matter of a Communist conspiracy, manipulation or a miracle of organisation. Whatever else was present, strongly-felt grievances and interests were essential. Even when these factors were present and recognised, people did not go beyond a defensive position. Few wanted to be identified as targets for reprisals by government troops. This was what 'terror' meant to XB village.

What is it that changes this passive, defensive situation? What was it that took the 'Viet Cong' to an offensive that brought the Saigon government to the point of defeat four years later and robbed the American forces of the initiative all over South Vietnam seven years later? Warner agrees that this defensive situation 'is true everywhere'. Yet it changes. How? Warner provides the answer '. . . the ARVINS (Saigon government forces) follow the French examples. They assume guilt by association in the areas [like XB village] beyond their control. Tragically few seem to appreciate that this sort of war is lost, not won, by killing people.'[91] Of course, it was not long before the 'ARVINS' swept into XB village, killed many, burnt much and captured some, just as they swept into hundreds of other villages. Just as the French had done before and the Americans and Australians were to do later. The fate of XB village disappears into the smoke of bombs, shells and fire but Warner concludes his story of the village with a reference to what happened in the area. 'The following month after the army had retired, leaving behind it thousands of unhappy peasants, Buddhist bonzes petitioned the province chief in Tra Vinh against shelling of hamlets and pagodas and to demand the release of their imprisoned fellows. Some months later their leader Superior Bonze Son Vong, appeared on the lists of the central committee of the National Liberation Front.'[92] And, of course, it would not be so difficult to get the people in XB village to make and lay naily boards now.

While all this was going on in XB village, in Tra Vinh and in perhaps a thousand other places, what was Hanoi doing? We have noted that from August 1955 through to July 1960, Hanoi was mainly concerned to agitate for the elections it felt sure it could win. In January 1957, Hanoi announced that 'the struggle would be long and difficult' and that a 'prerequisite would be the "consolidation" of the already liberated North'. But by June 1957 there were radio stations in South Vietnam which claimed they spoke for armed insurgents and they were saying things very much in conflict with Hanoi. In 1958 a new radio station in South Vietnam began using the theme song of the former Vietminh resistance radio, identified itself as the Voice of the *South Vietnamese* Liberation Front [emphasis mine] and raised consistently the theme of 'struggle against oppression by the dictatorial American Diemists'. Almost immediately Hanoi denounced these broadcasts as provocations by Saigon and American agents and called on the people of South Vietnam not to follow them.[93] Kahin and Lewis conclude: 'Every one of the numerous recorded Hanoi broadcasts dealing with the Front attacked it violently.' From June 1958, according to these writers, the Front was accused of 'using their broadcasts to distort Marxist-Leninist theories. They . . . have falsified the policies of the Vietnam Lao Dong (Communist) party and D.R.V.N. (Hanoi) government.' Hanoi attacked such Front statements as 'the working class considers the bourgeois and petty bourgeois class as enemies'. Hanoi, of course, argued that a much wider front was needed than this would allow. Hanoi also attacked the 'South Vietnamese Liberation Front' for not supporting its demand for a consultative conference on elections prescribed by Geneva, for showing no interest in the election, and for lack of support of other claims put forward against Saigon by Hanoi. But the South Vietnamese Liberation Front, by this time, was convinced it could get nothing from Saigon by asking for it. The government in Saigon, it believed, had to be overthrown. Hanoi had not yet come to accept that. We can be sure that insurgents (perhaps the people) in South Vietnam were more and more likely to accept the extreme view put forward by the Liberation Front, but we can be even more sure that Hanoi did not. Kahin and Lewis point out the reason for this: 'The tenor of Hanoi's statements revealed sharp anxiety that its overall strategy for reunification was being jeopardised by the militant tactics and socially radical policies advocated by the

Liberation Front radio.'⁹⁴ Just as in the case of the confrontation with the French in 1945 and 1946, Hanoi sought to postpone war as long as possible, and use political methods to consolidate and build up strength. Hanoi was still intent upon the same program in 1960.

Vietnam was certainly one country and Hanoi was not giving up plans for its reunification. Hanoi was as firmly committed to that as was Diem. But neither could have imagined that re-unification would come soon. Hanoi said it would be a 'long struggle'. In this struggle Hanoi would have wanted to control the insurgents in the South, to determine their policy and to decide how and when it would be applied. But North Vietnam had to come first. The North had to be built up as the basis of the revolution for the whole of Vietnam, and perhaps Cambodia and Laos, as well, and this could be set back by premature action. Furthermore, if the ground was adequately prepared by winning over as many people as possible the final acts of the revolution would be less difficult and the chances of greater American intervention would be reduced. Fewer people would be killed and less cost involved. So many people argue senselessly that Communists in Vietnam want exactly the opposite results. The evidence does not support this argument. Not only could the North and the South be endangered by a too radical and militant policy but such a policy could destroy any prospects of success at all. If a revolution is to be won support must be won. People need much more to persuade them to support a revolutionary party than they need to make them vote for any other kind of party. It is not easier for a revolutionary party to win support, it is more difficult. It cannot perform the far greater task of bringing about revolutionary changes unless it does win support. Certainly not all 'revolutionary parties' win support but no party can succeed with a revolution unless it does win general support.

Diem was proving much stronger and more durable than anyone expected and American aid was coming in faster and, in a military sense, it was being quickly and effectively used—compared with anything that could have been expected. It was not that Diem was able to convert the whole of South Vietnam into a police state, far from it. There were large areas of South Vietnam where his writ never ran. But Diem proved a much more powerful and independent factor than anyone expected and than the Americans really hoped for. We have seen in the case of XB village that it needed a 'terror sweep' by the ARVINS to convert the village from passive resistors to a 'combat village'. Not only was this needed in XB village but we can be sure that it was needed all over South Vietnam. Diem struck more and more as his effectiveness grew and as American support gave him the tools for the job, and in striking he changed the passive insurgency into an armed uprising—not general but significant. Armed uprisings cannot be produced by signals from Hanoi, Moscow or Peking. They need long and deep preparation. They need deeply-felt grievances and they need rejection of reform by the authorities. Then they need that reaction by the authorities which transforms the rebel defiance into attack. Then, as in every other war, the strongest side wins. Leadership and organisation are all necessary but these are secondary factors in the sense that they can be produced by capable men who understand the situation. A revolutionary movement will not fight because of leadership and organisation alone. A revolutionary movement will only fight when it has to. It is fused into a fighting body by the attacks of its enemy. The theory of guerrilla war, assuming that the 'enemy' will have greater fire power and mobility, is little more than a reflection of what could have been worked out in XB village. As the counter attack, caused by some revolutionary action, escalates, support for the revolution grows. It seems that, generally, the revolutionary side will avoid combat as long as it can, but provided that it does not give up its revolutionary intent, combat must come. It may be that once a 'revolutionary' war reaches a certain point it cannot be won by the 'counter revolution' no matter how powerful it is. Killing and destruction in a revolutionary situation win no friends. The killing and destruction must take place among the people because the 'revolution', if it is genuine, is in the people. Even those who are left in the ruins will not be fond of those who caused the ruins. This we will look at later.

But in any case we can be certain that the process in South Vietnam by 1957 was moving faster than Hanoi knew or expected or wanted. By 1961 it was apparent that the stage of 'armed struggle' had fairly generally been reached. But up to that point it was a southern insurrection, the product of southern experience. Insistence on 'armed struggle' became dominant in South Vietnam in what has been called the 'landmark' statement of March 1960. This was the 'Declaration of the Resistance Veterans'. It was a detailed and considered statement 'justifying . . . departure from Hanoi's policy of peaceful struggle in South Vietnam as the inevitable result of Diem's oppression.' 'If the people take up arms', the Declaration said, 'it is only to defend themselves.' Certainly the people would not have been attacked by Diem, and would, therefore, have had no need to defend themselves if they had done nothing about land, corruption and brutality. There would have been no need for self-defence if the people had remained satisfied with their lot. At this stage of the war revolt had been based on more than nationalism. But nationalism was linked to the economic and social needs of the people. The Declaration appealed to 'all classes, all social strata, all milieu' to struggle against 'repression by the South Vietnamese authorities and to expel all forms of American interference'. The picture was completed with the call to replace the Diem regime with a broad coalition and liberate South Vietnam from sub-

mission to America. By this time not only the impatience of the movement but its strength must have become apparent to Hanoi. Jean
Lacouture has written that emissaries from the North, sent to test
public opinion in the South after the Declaration in 1960, were badly
received, called cowards and asked 'What are you waiting for to help
us? If you don't do anything, you Communists, we will rise up against
you too.'[95] But it was not until six months after this experience, after
the 'southerners had taken matters into their own hands, that Hanoi
made a public endorsement of their stand'.[96]

The Third Congress of the Vietnamese Lao Dong Party met in
Hanoi in September 1960. It sanctioned the formation of the National
Liberation Front in South Vietnam and approved a program for the
violent overthrow of the government of Ngo Dinh Diem. Even then
the Congress stated the two 'strategic tasks' of the Vietnamese revolution and it placed first 'to carry out the socialist revolution in the
North'. 'Closely related' was the task 'to liberate the South from the
rule of the American imperialists and their henchmen (and) achieve
national reunification and complete independence and freedom
throughout the country.' How different had been Hanoi's goals in all
previous years: 'To consolidate the North and actively take it step by
step towards socialism'. For the South the goal was 'to compel the
other side to carry out correctly the Geneva Agreements, to re-establish
normal North-South relations and to hold consultations on general
elections to reunify the country'. Southerners were offered a 'heartfelt
salute' for their sufferings.[97] But perhaps as significant as this change
in attitude, in revealing the relations of North and South, was that at
the Third Party Congress a decision was made to *cut* defence expendi-
ture in the interests of development of North Vietnam. None other
than the Minister for Defence, Vo Nguyen Giap, put the resolution
to the Congress. 'Today', he said, 'the economic construction in the
North has become the central task of the Party. Therefore, it is necessary to cut down the defence budget, adequately reduce our army
contingent so as to concentrate manpower and material in economic
construction.'[98]

In December 1961, what was called the first congress of Communist representatives in South Vietnam was held and it decided to form,
in South Vietnam, a Community Party—the Vietnam People's Revolutionary Party—and on January 1, 1962, this Party came into existence.
This Party was not established, as some assert, on directions from
Hanoi. It was, like the National Liberation Front, established in
South Vietnam and recognised by Hanoi. Before its establishment,
Communists in South Vietnam would, if they were members of a party,
be members of the Lao Dong Party. Now they could be Communists
and members of a southern party. This is hardly likely to have been
organised by Hanoi to give it more control over southern Communists.

It would have rather the opposite effect. And so, by 1961, the first
phase of the post-Geneva war in Vietnam was over. All available evidence supports the conclusions drawn up about this phase by the
American historians Kahin and Lewis and I choose to sum up this
phase in their words:

'In sum, the insurrection is Southern-rooted; it arose at Southern initiative in response to Southern demands. The Liberation Front gave
political articulation and leadership to the widespread reaction
against the harshness and heavy handedness of Diem's government. It
gained drive under the stimulus of Southern Vietminh veterans who
felt betrayed by the Geneva Conference and abandoned by Hanoi.
After the withdrawal of their troops to the North these Southern
Vietminh were left with no effective means of enforcing the political
terms of the Armistice—either the conducting of the elections or
protection against reprisal. They were denied the promised opportunity to reassert their political ascendency through elections and
then savagely persecuted for their past political affiliations. Not
surprisingly, they lost patience with the Communist North and
finally took matters into their own hands. Hanoi, despite its reluc-
tance, was then obliged to sanction the Southerners' actions or risk
forfeiting all chance of influence over the course of events in South
Vietnam.'[99]

This is an accurate statement of what happened on all these vital
points. It is contrary to all American and Australian government explanations of the causes and nature of the war in Vietnam. Abundant
evidence is now available to test the truth of the matters involved.
The official American and Australian line is false. Never before
have we been involved in a great national commitment based so much
on false assumptions and assertions. Naturally the visible 'credibility
gap' grows every day. Naturally the campaign in Vietnam fails to
achieve its objectives.

This assessment of the position should be related to what the
International Control Commission said about breaches of the Geneva
Agreement. The Commission made 12 reports up to 1962—the period
under review here. What did these reports say? The Geneva Agreements of 1954 were intended to end control of Indochina by foreign
countries—in other words to bring an end to 'colonialism', to grant
independence to Indochina. Indigenous nationalism, whatever it was,
and it was assumed by all that the Vietminh was dominant, obtained
the right to determine the future of Vietnam. Laos and Cambodia were
recognised as independent nations whose future was in the hands of
their own people. But the appearance of a unified Vietnam was to
await only a military settlement and was to come into existence as the
result of supervised elections in July 1956. This latter provision was
as fundamental to the Agreement itself as it was in the Declaration.

Commonly, it is alleged that the Geneva Agreements were broken only by North Vietnam and the 'Viet Cong'. But the Geneva Agreements were broken by the French who withdrew and made no effort to pass on to their 'successors' their responsibilities to ensure that the elections were held as the Agreement provided. The Agreements were broken by the government of the 'State of Vietnam' (South Vietnam), whose breach of the Agreements was made possible only by American backing.[100] These breaches of the Agreements are set out in detail in the early reports of the International Control Commission.

As early as 1955, the Commission pointed out what it was to stress several times later in identical language: 'It is obvious . . . that there is room for improvement in the implementation by both parties of the Articles of the Agreements dealing with democratic freedoms . . .' The Commission recognised the difficulties arising out of 'eight years of strife' which both sides faced, but said that both sides 'have been sadly lacking in a sense of purpose and urgency in dealing with these matters'. The Reports gave many details which justified these conclusions and leave the conviction that the conclusions are meant to apply equally to both sides. In 1956, the Commission made another statement that was repeated in identical language in later reports. This was its conclusion in para. 84 of the 1956 report about assistance and co-operation given to the Commission's investigating teams. The conclusion is as follows: 'Neither party has fulfilled in their entirety these obligations. As has been revealed in the preceding paragraphs, the degree of co-operation given to the Commission by the two parties has not been the same. While the Commission has experienced difficulties in North Vietnam, the major part of its difficulties has arisen in South Vietnam.' Although the Commission's criticisms of South Vietnam grew in detail in later years, we find in the 1958 report a paragraph (38) repeated at least twice in later reports, which read: 'It will be seen from these chapters that while in North Vietnam the Commission generally continued to receive the necessary co-operation, it did not receive the necessary co-operation in keeping a team at . . .' (and then follows reference to one place in each of the reports). Criticism of North Vietnam was not general but usually referred to a particular place. All the reports to 1962 detail the complaints of breaches of the Agreements made by both sides. But far more complaints were made by the North against the South, than by the South against the North, and fewer of the South's complaints were found by the Commission to be established.

And then, of course, came the Special Report of 1962 in which the Commission drew up its conclusions about both sides. These conclusions are as follows:

'Having examined the complaints and the supporting material sent by the South Vietnamese Mission, the (Legal) Committee has come to the conclusion that in specific instances there is evidence to show that armed and unarmed personnel, arms, munitions and other supplies have been sent from the Zone in the North to the Zone in the South with the object of supporting, organising and carrying out hostile activities, including armed attacks, directed against the Armed Forces and Administration of the Zone in the South.'

The same report also states:

'Taking all the facts into consideration and basing itself on its own observations made in the United States of America and the Republic of Vietnam, the Commission concludes that the Republic of Vietnam has violated Articles 16 and 17 of the Geneva Agreements in receiving the increased military aid from the United States of America in the absence of any established credit in its favour.'

'The Commission is also of the view that, though there may not be any formal military alliance between the Governments of the United States of America and the Republic of Vietnam, the establishment of a U.S. Military Assistance Command in South Vietnam, as well as the introduction of a large number of U.S. military personnel beyond the stated strength of the MAAG (Military Assistance Advisory Group) amount to a factual military alliance, which is prohibited under Article 19 of the Geneva Agreements.'

The first extract shows that the commission merely 'noted' findings of its Legal Committee, but in the second extract the Commission states its own conclusion. The first extract refers to 'specific instances'. It is hardly likely that they are different from, or are additional to, those listed in detail in later reports from which the total of weapons from the North which were captured in the South has been arrived at. The conclusions of the International Control Commission in the first extract are as strong and not one ounce stronger than the detailed evidence in the reports. In addition, it might be noted that the first extract says clearly that it is based upon 'material sent by the South Vietnamese Mission', whereas in the second extract the commission says that it is 'basing itself on its own observations'. For what it is worth, the Polish Delegation stated in the 1962 Report that the 'Indian and Canadian Delegations have presented a picture of the situation in South Vietnam which . . . does not correspond with the real state of affairs.'

But something that is of greater weight is the Indian comment on the Canadian report. It is:

'In order to clarify the factual position, the Indian Delegation draws attention to quotations in the Canadian Statement of so-called "conclusions" of the Legal Committee. The reference to the

Special Report of 1962, from which the extracts above come, made in the third sentence of para 3 of the Canadian Statement concerned only specific cases. The other quotations which immediately follow in the same paragraph purported to be "conclusions" of the Legal Committee have neither been presented to, nor have the sanction of, the Commission or any of its Committees.' No reference to this important statement was made in the U.S. White Paper, nor, as far as can be ascertained, in any other official American or Australian Government statements on 'aggression from the North'.

At this stage we can sum up the work and findings of the International Control Commission about breaches of the Geneva Agreements. Both sides broke the Agreements. But the first and most substantial breaches of it were by the Government of South Vietnam and the Government of the United States. The volume and power of American intervention in South Vietnam, most of which was a breach of the Agreements, precedes and is far in excess of the intervention of North Vietnam, China, the Soviet Union and all other Communist countries. Indeed the reports of the Commission, although they do not state it that way, are consistent with the interpretations that the Communist side did not turn away from political to military methods until they were forced to do so by the rising tide of American arms, materials and men. The Communists wanted to win a revolution but they wanted to win it politically and peacefully if they could.

CHAPTER EIGHT

THE UNWINNABLE WAR

It seems that in 1962 the Diem government's military victories based on American air power gave rise to another batch of optimistic predictions about winning the war, and, more significantly, helped to persuade Washington to accept Diem's rejection of reforms and his military obsessions. The result was not only a bad year militarily in the 1962-63 dry season for Diem, but a social and political policy which provoked widespread opposition. It was not the 'Viet Cong' who were really responsible for the over-throw of Diem when it came; it was the general resistance in the cities led by the Buddhists. Diem's rule was a tyranny, and for many it was a tyranny worse than the worst picture of the Communist one, for the simple reason that people in South Vietnam were living under Diem's tyranny. For most at the time, and for almost everybody since, the conclusion of Denis Warner appears to sum it up: 'There was no alternative now [in 1963] but a coup d'etat.'

But there could be no move without American support. Having raised Diem to the status of President, maintained him in office, paid his bills and supplied him with the means of power, the Americans faced a Diem grown strong enough to enforce a policy that many Americans knew would fail. It had failed and now he had to go. '. . . the United States floodlit the way for the enemies of the regime. Coldly, calmly Lodge set the scene.'[101] Yet almost to the day of the coup, American officials remained optimistic. In September, the American Pacific Commander announced: 'We can win this war in three years.' In October 1963, McNamara and Taylor made a fact-finding tour of South Vietnam and reported that the military program was sound in principle and so successful that 1,000 advisers could be withdrawn by the end of the year, and the major part of the American task would be completed by the end of 1965. At the same time President Kennedy re-stated the long accepted objective (and the continuing recipe for failure) when he announced: 'We want the war to be won. What helps to win the war we support. What interferes with the war effort we oppose.'

Many pressmen in Saigon reported that McNamara and Taylor had been 'given the usual treatment' and had come up with the 'usual mistakes'. A few days later a 'Viet Cong' unit dealt government forces what was described as 'one of the bloodiest blows of the year', and in September the 'Viet Cong' were able, for the first time, to capture a provincial capital—Cai Nuoe and Dam Doc were both taken and held for a short time. Fourteen days later Mr. Averell Harriman welcomed those who had overthrown Diem, hailing them as a government having 'every appearance of offering the kind of leadership the South Vietnamese people want—religious freedom, greater personal liberty and vigorous prosecution of the war against Communism.' In Saigon, it was reported that Mr. Cabot Lodge looked like 'an old riverboat gambler who had won it all.'

Two things should be emphasised. First, Diem had failed. It may be argued that had the military campaign against the Buddhists been ruthlessly carried out, as it was later by Cao Ky (and as Madame Nhu at the time wanted), their resistance would have been swept aside and Diem, like Ky, would have established supremacy. No one can be certain whether this is true or not, but what is certain is that the position in 1963 was not the same as it was when Cao Ky was able to stifle Buddhist opposition. The second thing was that the overthrow of Diem proved that all real power lay with America. It made obvious the fact that there could be no more Vietnamese independence under America than under France. If power exercised in Vietnam by another country was imperialism then Vietnam was as much subject to imperialism in 1963 as it ever was. It is important to note that the fundamental reason why America disposed of Diem was opposition to him by the 'people'. It was the Buddhists, students—'the people'—of Saigon and Hue who made it impossible for America to continue support for the 'medieval inquisitors'. Certainly the situation then was different from that later on when Cao Ky was able to do what Madame Nhu would have done in 1963. In 1963 there was a great deal of military opposition to Diem because he had hamstrung and discredited many of the generals. Those who led the coup, Minh, Don and Dinh, were, far more than was Diem, the tools of America, and they were no more the voice of the people.

Finally, the Americans were not prepared in 1963 to go as far to maintain a regime against popular resistance as they were to be in 1965 and 1966. The reality of Vietnamese independence was still important enough in 1963 to make unacceptable any military action to sweep aside the Buddhists, the students, 'the people'. Little of the reality of this remained in 1965 and 1966.

It is interesting to note that the coup junta talked constantly about 'the people'. Minh is reported to have said: 'My stand is that we must first win the support of the people before we can win against the Communists.' Diem was in fact overthrown because he had not won the support of the people. But Minh and his fellow officers were no better situated to win the support of the people. He was a general. They were all generals. Every move had to be a military move. The rising tide of Buddhist-led and inspired popular action made it impossible for

America to continue support for Diem; but was this popular factor to have any longer term significance? If popular action was to have any weight in South Vietnam, some very essential changes had to take place. Some did. The first change resulted from the war itself. The more widespread, intense and damaging the war became, the greater became the number of people who wanted to stop it. Hence popular action became associated with 'neutralism' if it wanted the war to stop, and with 'Communism' if it wanted to come to terms with the 'Viet Cong'. Certainly this was what happened in Saigon and Hue, and most of what is South Vietnam is in the 2,500 villages. But the fate of governments in Saigon was not determined in the villages.

So, in 1963, Saigon relaxed in obvious relief and pleasure when it heard that the Diem regime was overthrown. Its bustle and urbanity, its color and variety were even more apparent than usual and revealed a people ready for change. They wanted to determine their own affairs. But how could any of them look at the new military junta without the scepticism that decades had implanted? Could the idea of democracy be anything but incredible? It is not surprising that most people were preoccupied only with ending the war.

Still, freedom appeared to have come. The gags were removed from the Press, students elected their representatives, trade unions began to speak up and make higher bids for wages. Within a few days the political prisoners stepped on to the Saigon wharf, where so many prisoners had stood before, after their release from the notorious Poulo Condore. Dr Pham Quan Dan, carried away in triumph after nearly two years of a seven-year sentence, told the crowd that there must be real elections within six months. A few days later Pham Khac Suu, released from an eight-year sentence, announced that the regime must be democratised. Lacouture reports that the 'liberation of the prisoners of the Diem regime gave me a chance to verify that torture and ill-treatment had been practised in the prisons and camps. . . Hundreds of students of both sexes had been subject to ill-treatment. At the detention camp in Le Van Quich 40 prisoners at a time were thrown into a cell in the hot sun. Others had their nails torn out; still others were blinded; one student died of a crushed liver.'[102] There was certainly plenty of room for democracy and there must have been a great demand for it.

But the Minh regime was not ready for democracy. The war had first to be won. If there was to be democracy there would have to be popular action. There would have to be politics. There would be criticism of corruption and demands for reforms. There would be talk about the war. How would Minh and his junta react to this? Almost immediately they began to close newspapers again and censor others. It was not long before any critic began again to be called a 'neutralist' or a 'Communist'. There were officially-organised demonstrations against the French and against 'neutralists'. There was a strong argument, convincing for all the military people, that all this talk and politics was harmful and must be stopped. There could be little democracy in the middle of a war, but always there was the basic idea that popular support was the *sine qua non* of successful military action. How was this contradiction to be solved? What had happened was both a threat and an opportunity; both a chance to learn from the past as well as a fear of the present. It was now recognised, as Robert McNamara put it, that the Viet Cong had 'large indigenous support' and 'a band of loyalty'. At least large indigenous support had to be won by Saigon if it was to defeat them. But how could Saigon win this support if there was to be no politics?

The fall of Diem came as a shock to most of those who had given their support in full measure to his government. But not many spoke as did a Belgian priest to Lacouture: 'Who is responsible for that catastrophic situation, the total failure of the Diem regime, the confusion in which our Christianity now finds itself?' The question was rarely asked and when it was asked the answer invariably placed the blame elsewhere. The conclusion was that the overthrow of Diem left the majority of people in an unchanged position. It rearranged things inside the 'command structure' and concerned only a small number of people. The fact that alongside this 'command structure' was another one, the American Command, with money and resources without which there could be no command at all, removed even further from the Vietnamese people any power to make decisions. But the people existed and they had their needs—and the most intense need was an end to the war.

The Minh army junta were not power mad, nor a 'Vietnamese variety of fascists'. They were the sons and brothers of landowners, officials and merchants wealthy enough to have been educated in France, and 'imperialist' enough to have grown accustomed to the corruption that is part of imperialism. It is not surprising that they thought mainly in the language of armoured vehicles, helicopters and strategic villages. It is not surprising that they never thought about land rents, usurious interest rates, state-owned factories, or elected village officials. These thoughts to them meant Communism, and to oppose Communism was the purpose of it all. Perhaps the junta was more likely than Diem to be able to think of talking to Hanoi and they were not so single minded about the war itself. Too many mistakes had been made for them to think there was a simple answer to everything, and so '. . . the men of November 1 (the day of the coup against Diem) quickly provoked the disappointment of the Americans',[103] who soon began to look for alternative leaders more confident that the war could be won.

In the early days following the coup official figures placed the

Viet Cong at 90,000; showed they were capturing $2\frac{1}{2}$ weapons for every one lost; that they were still predominantly armed in this way, and that of 432 strategic hamlets in Long An and Dinh Luong only 20 per cent were militarily viable. In Camau the Viet Cong ruled the country-side. American officials reported: 'We're ever-extended. All we can do is defend ourselves.' General Duong Van Minh told them: 'I am a soldier, but I tell you that this war will not be won by arms.' In December the Viet Cong over-ran Hiep Hoa, 20 miles from Saigon, and officials told newsmen: 'This used to be cowboys and Indians stuff. Now one of our battalions may meet one of theirs toe to toe like World War II.'

It looked as if Generals Khanh and Duong Van Duc were the most eligible to meet this desperate situation. Before long General Harkins, the American commander, was alerted to a plot. General Nguyen Van Vy, former chief of staff removed by Diem, had returned from Paris and was said to be a 'neutralist'. Generals Don, Kim and Vy were said to be ready to negotiate with the National Liberation Front. On January 30 these three generals and Generals Dinh and Xuan, the core of the Minh junta, were arrested and the day after, General Khanh was able to convince Mr. Cabot Lodge that he had forestalled a move by these 'neutralists', supported by France. Within a few hours, Khanh was accepted as President of the Revolutionary Council which contained a Nguyen Van Thieu but as yet no Cao Ky. This was a group totally opposed to anything like 'neutralism' and ready to carry on the war with confidence. This is what they meant by the word 'Revolution' which they used with relish and vigour. But this very fact meant that they were further away from the people and from politics and reform than were Minh and his colleagues. If popular support was the *sine qua non* of military success, as Mr. McNamara said it was, this had not been a move in the right direction. But it was the second coup that had been brought about by fears of 'neutralism'.

President Johnson, early in 1964, promised Duong Van Minh 'the fullest measure of support . . . in achieving victory'. And in July he told reporters: 'We do not believe in conferences called to ratify terror; our policy is unchanged.' The New York Times concluded that this was a reversal of the Kennedy policy.[104] According to this newspaper, President Johnson's letter renounced unequivocally 'any prospect for a neutralist solution for South Vietnam . . . at a time when neutralist sentiment has been gaining currency in some political and intellectual circles (in South Vietnam).' A few days later, Robert McNamara made it even clearer that America had no room for neutralism or negotiations when he said three days before the Khanh coup: 'The survival of an independent government in South Vietnam is so important to the security of South east Asia and to the free world that I can conceive of no alternative other than to take all necessary measures within our capability to prevent a Communist victory.' In the face of the serious military situation of late 1963 and early 1964 and of the persistent calls for negotiations, American officials began to argue openly that unless the war was carried to the North, the South Vietnamese government would fall and fighting would never end in South Vietnam because a majority of villages either supported or did not oppose the 'Viet Cong'. Some dramatic escalation did not seem far away.

Not only did military victory remain the aim of the American Administration—there was greater emphasis upon political factors under Kennedy—but so too did the 'need' and intention to attack North Vietnam. General Maxwell Taylor had written in his report of November 3, 1961: 'It is clear to me that the time may come in our relations to South-East Asia when we must declare our intention to attack the source of guerrilla aggression in North Vietnam and impose on the Hanoi government a price for participating in the current war which is commensurate with the damage being inflicted on its neighbours in the south.' At this time, and for three years to come, it must be noted that American Administration spokesmen, generals and officials admitted that the 'Viet Cong' was predominantly made up of men who had never been out of South Vietnam and who were almost wholly Southern born, and that their weapons were either captured in South Vietnam from the Saigon regime and American forces or home-made. But the objective of attacking North Vietnam, firmly planted in American militaristic intention, required only the appropriate conditioning of the American people and the appropriate occasion. America now had a President whose political abilities for this task were outstanding. Johnson was to prove capable of serving his military hawks to their obvious satisfaction.

General Harkins reported at the end of his term that the strategic hamlets 'were cutting the Viet Cong lifeline,' but McNamara appointed a joint team to investigate the whole project. In the Delta alone it was found that the Viet Cong had captured 3,500 fortified hamlets of the 7,000, and 11,000 weapons. There was terror in Saigon and Newsweek reported local and Pentagon officials in saying: 'Often the heavily-equipped government troops are powerless to stop guerrillas—who are sometimes armed with little more than home-made rifles and hand-made grenades. . . The Viet Cong have little, but they are ingenious, possessed by clenched-teeth determination. We have too much and we are complacent.' These circumstances gave emphasis to the demands to extend the war—everywhere ran the argument that America faced another Korea and that the obsession against committing American troops to the mainland of Asia must be given up. Rostow proposed his plan No. 6 . . . to blockade Haiphong, for

P.T. boat raids on North Vietnam installations, then strategic bombing raids either under the U.S. or South Vietnamese flag. But McNamara publicly remained committed to the aim of victory without escalation. Although the details of the operation are not yet clear, we can be certain that the United States decided late 1963 and early 1964, to oppose neutralism and negotiations and to enforce a policy calculated to win the war, even though both the Saigon junta and public opinion were favourable to negotiations and to a neutral South Vietnam.[105]

Yet the trend towards more war did not go unresisted. Pressures on South Vietnam continued and the Khanh junta never got firmly into the saddle. Militarily, 1964 was a bad year and the Viet Cong made substantial gains. Corruption was even more rife and there was not even talk of reforms. The problems the junta had in remaining in office meant that even the war was almost forgotten. These difficulties in the South, and demands for attacks on the North, were naturally associated with ever growing claims about the significance of North Vietnam in the war. These claims grew in volume and influence all through 1964. As early as March 6, 1963, perhaps to rebut them, General Paul Harkins, U.S. Commander in South Vietnam had stated: 'The guerrillas obviously are not being reinforced or supplied systematically from North Vietnam, China or any place. They apparently depend for weapons primarily on whatever they can capture. Many of their weapons are home-made.' But claims of aggression from the North went on and became more acceptable as American difficulties in the South grew.

The Senate Foreign Relations Committee concerned itself closely with the matter. On May 21, 1964, Senator Wayne Morse told what had happened before that Committee in a statement which remains uncontradicted:

'I have cross-examined witnesses for some time on South Vietnam from the Pentagon and State Department. When I put the question to them: "What military personnel have you found in South Vietnam from Red China, Cambodia or elsewhere?", the answer is always "Practically none". So when I press the witnesses further with the question, "Am I to understand the Viet Cong are South Vietnamese almost entirely?", the answer is "Yes". The same is true of their weapons. The Viet Cong have armed themselves from Government stocks, not by foreign imports from Communist countries. The so-called supply lines from North Vietnam that so many politicians want to bomb are little more than a myth.'

The supply lines from the North existed, and they were used probably from 1961, but it was not until early 1964 that supplies of much significance came along the thin and scattered tracks. But argument went on in 1964 to convert the interpretation of the war, ac-

cepted by all American authorities up to 1962 as a civil war between
the Diem-led government and Communist-led insurgents in South Vietnam, to one of an attack upon the people of South Vietnam by the
armed forces of North Vietnam. But during 1964 the American administration still stood strongly in the path of this pressure. American
magazine Newsweek, during 1964, reported these events and on July
27, 1964, stated: 'In answer to General Nguyen Khanh's charges of
"overt invasion" from the North put forward to justify his campaign
to send ground troops to the North, U.S. Secretary of State Robert S.
McNamara strongly refuted these claims and "stated flatly" that he
knew of "no North Vietnamese military units in South Vietnam".'

Matters in Saigon and South Vietnam went from bad to worse
after June 1964. Khanh's 'radical plan to attack Viet Cong strong-
holds' and establish a 'welfare state' for citizens was not even effective
propaganda. ARVN casualties reached 1,000 a week. Dr. Pham Huy
Co, after a four-month tour, reported morale low and that the Vietnamese soldier was often hated by the peasantry. Pentagon officials
answered that armies were always unpopular. Khanh was warned that
the American people were not yet ready for an attack on North
Vietnam and that there was to be a Presidential election soon. But in
June the United States admitted bombing areas in Laos and the tempo
of the war was stepped up in the centre and north. Khanh admitted
that since the overthrow of Diem an additional five million people had
come under Communist administration. America added $125 million
to the support program and the Roman Catholic Church's Caravelle
Hotel announced a $10 million extension program. But nothing
appeared likely to halt the deterioration of the war in South Vietnam
and an attack on North Vietnam loomed more probable every day.

There is still uncertainty about the origin of the pressures and
claims that there was aggression or invasion from North Vietnam.
It had been claimed for years that North Vietnam had been responsible
for giving the orders for the insurrection to begin, and for inciting and
encouraging it, as well as controlling its tactics and strategy. But it was
only after the fall of Diem that the physical invasion or aggression
argument took the centre of the stage. It was the South Vietnamese
military leaders like Khanh, Khiem and Ky who were most voluble in
advancing the theory. It may have been that they had American Army,
State Department or C.I.A. support for the argument from the beginning, but the American Administration was able to withstand the
pressures until about August 1964. In keeping with a familiar pattern,
McNamara's strongest resistance to the argument for escalation preceded by only a few days the Administration's submission to it. This
submission occurred with the Tonkin Bay incident which gave the
President full powers to conduct the war just how and where he liked.

On August 3, De Gaulle called for a Geneva-type conference and

Washington's rejection was quick and predictable. On August 4, 1964, just eight days after the statement above quoted from McNamara, the American destroyers Maddox, one of the most powerful, and Turner Joy, reported that they had been attacked 65 miles off the coast of North Vietnam by torpedoes fired by North Vietnamese vessels. From as early as July 10, it had been reported that South Vietnamese vessels (American-built with South Vietnamese crews) had been attacking North Vietnamese fishing boats and bases and American destroyers had acted as a protective cover and to 'spy' or collect 'intelligence', well within the '12-mile limit' claimed by North Vietnam and rejected by America. The incident of August 4 followed one on August 2 in which North Vietnam admitted an exchange of fire with the Maddox, and the Maddox claimed to have been narrowly missed by torpedoes from two PT boats and to have sunk at least one boat. The Americans claimed the destroyers on August 4 were not in territorial waters, the North Vietnamese claimed they were; the Americans claimed they had been fired at and the North Vietnamese claimed there had been no attack. At 8.36 p.m. the Maddox in mountainous seas had signalled an attack from unidentified vessels. At 9.30 p.m. the Maddox reported the craft were 50 and 100-ton Soviet-built torpedo boats and at 9.52 p.m. the Maddox and Turner Joy were under 'continuous torpedo attack'. Jets from the carriers Constellation and Ticonderoga came to the aid of the destroyers and it was claimed that two torpedo boats were sunk. Within a few hours of the incident American jets on orders from Washington went in to attack North Korean PT boat bases at Quang Khe, Phue Loi, Vinh, Hon Gay and Loc Chau. It was claimed that 25 patrol boats of the 30 sighted had been damaged or destroyed, seven anti-aircraft installations silenced, and 90 per cent of the oil-storage facilities at Vinh destroyed. American losses were stated to be a Skyhawk and a Skyraider but North Vietnam claimed to have shot down 15 planes.

The President's decision to attack seemed in America to be a political master-stroke. Harris polls showed 42 per cent support for the President but soon after August 4 the President was found to be supported by 72 per cent of those interviewed. America's action was supported by every Western ally but France, while it was reported that Russian and Chinese reactions were 'a few pale strictures'. President Johnson, in Washington, was said to have 'exuded calmness and confidence' and 'lauded the unity, calmness and strength of purpose of the American people'. Two days later the Senate and the House of Representatives passed with a mere five dissenters a resolution authorising the President to 'take all necessary measures to repel any armed attack against the armed forces of the United States and to prevent further aggression'. The facts are not as yet finally clear but the most recent event was a U.S. Senate Foreign Relations Committee enquiry in 1968 which threw doubt on the official version, and a statement by the captain of the Maddox that the radar signs taken to be evidence of torpedoes were probably caused by the vibrations of the destroyer's own propeller. But whatever was the truth of the incident it was taken to give the President full and complete personal power over the course of the war and to begin attacks on North Vietnam. It was a vital step in the escalation of the war. It was the result of affairs in Saigon and not of anything that may have happened in Tonkin Bay.

The significant thing about the Tonkin Bay incident was not its nature, but how it was used by President Johnson to get something he had wanted for some months. Tom Wicker, New York Times Washington correspondent, wrote of it: 'Usually the timing is precisely his own—as when he presented his Vietnam resolution to Congress the day after the Gulf of Tonkin crisis. He had been carrying it around in his pocket for weeks waiting for the moment'. What would be its result? On September 28 Newsweek felt compelled to ask: 'How is it that the greatest military power in the world, virtually unchallenged by its one international peer, is unable to win or even seize the initiative in a limited war to which it has committed not only its prestige but its own soldiers.'

Yet the 'initiative' of attack on North Vietnam on August 4, which had won for the President 30 per cent in the public opinion polls and almost unanimous backing by Congress, had not saved the government in Saigon, and, according to Newsweek had provided only a 'brief period of euphoria', and 'all of Washington's manoeuvres have proved bewilderingly futile'. The President was left with the 'Vietnam Dilemma' and because of it, indeed because of Khanh's over-reaction to the attack on North Vietnam, the third coup in Saigon was under way.

General Khanh's reaction to the President's dramatic step was to announce a new constitution drawn up by himself and two friends 'which concentrated in his hands all civil and military power'. Buddhist-led students and 'the people' soon began to move and on August 27, assembled outside Khanh's house and demanded his appearance. Khanh was harangued for some time, hoisted on to a tank, and found himself echoing the words of the crowd: 'Down with military power. Down with dictatorships. Down with the Army.' For several days after this Khanh retreated from the wrath of his colleagues and talked of resigning, his survival was said to be 'a day-to-day question now', but the American Administration stood behind him and the slogan 'It's Khanh or chaos' seemed to have official authority. But Khanh not only had denounced military authority, he had promised a civilian government. The move towards escalation of the war by attack on North Vietnam to save the government in Saigon had suffered a temporary setback. This would mean that the escalators would increase their efforts. The failure of escalation would not mean less escalation or a re-assessment, it would mean more. The dynamics of the third coup lay in the conflicts among 'the people'—those outside who demonstrated or followed; in the conflicts for office among the generals; and in the need for escalation of the war because of the over-all weakness of the Saigon government and its armed forces. Only greater American involvement could now save the government from 'neutralist' overthrow and its forces from defeat. It was at this point that the war in Vietnam was at its most sensitive and desperate point —it could so easily have gone on to a vast escalation or reached a settlement at the conference table.

Lacouture reports that just before the coup of September 13, there were rumours of a 'Catholic coup', and rumours of moves by Generals Duong, Duc, Phat and Nguyen Cao Ky. It was perhaps at this time that South Vietnam most lacked a dominating figure among the contenders for office. On September 13, troop movements began, but no one was sure of their strength or which columns were for whom. Perhaps the most vivid clue to understanding can be seen in Cao Ky's airmen flying above the tanks carefully counting and weighing their strength. The result was a compromise between Ky, who emerged as a figure of power for the first time, and Duc, Khanh and the Deputy American Ambassador, Alexis Johnson—General Maxwell Taylor was in Washington reporting on the distressingly bad state of the war. Kahin and Lewis[106] say that Taylor advised that the Viet Cong insurgency could not be ended unless the war was made so costly to the Communists, and particularly to North Vietnam, that rather than risk further heavy losses they would discontinue the struggle. Congress had now given the President power to make the war costly for North Vietnam.

September saw an oft-repeated conclusion that went something like this: by his handling of the Tonkin Bay incident the President in one stroke had regained the initiative and disposed of Vietnam as an election issue, but paradoxically all it did was allow Khanh to destroy himself, and to create even greater difficulties for the government in Saigon. There can hardly be any doubt that the confusion in Saigon during these months would have provided the 'Viet Cong' with a chance to create havoc. But they did not. Their restraint suggests that the war was balanced on a knife's edge at this time and 'Viet Cong' attacks would have helped to push it further away from the negotiations and neutralism which in August 1964 still remained their aim and a possibility.

But, of course, the September coup solved very little. Khanh had been temporarily saved by American intervention and because there were too many rivals for office. But he was now completely dependent upon the American Ambassador and continually pressed and embarrassed by the Buddhists and students with whom he had some real affinity. Equally as much he was opposed by the Catholic component of 'the people'. Government in South Vietnam was still a matter of the American will applied in tank and aircraft manoeuvres. At this point a further proposal for negotiations was made. U Thant asked Washington and Hanoi secretly to send emissaries to Rangoon. Hanoi accepted the proposal but McNamara rejected it on the grounds that the government in Saigon would not survive the opening of negotiations.[107] It was then that Ky made this point clear. He would use his planes, and the tanks would have to follow, against any 'pro-Communist or neutralist elements', whether they sought to act by elections or by coup. This was the dominant attitude in 1964 which was not only fully acceptable to the American administration but was the only one that could allow the survival of the Saigon government and of American policy.

Roger Hilsman, soon to resign as Assistant Secretary of State for Eastern Affairs, pointed out in September 1964 that there were few grounds for optimism in Vietnam and that the chief error was in putting major responsibility on the military for what was essentially a political problem. The Administration, he concluded, was not going to be able to make South Vietnam into an anti-Communist bastion [which had always been its aim] but the best it could hope for was an independent state. This was the spirit behind the next coup of September 20 which disposed of the National High Council. The Council, had preserved some of the older generals, who stood in the way of promotions and who still carried a little of the popular revulsion against the war which had found its way to the top through the Minh coup. These moves further weakened Khanh and now his only strength lay with 'the people' or with the Buddhist-student section of them. Khanh emerged from Dulat, having thrown off his 'mental ailment', with an anti-American line, and joined in the campaign for a civilian government. These developments created problems in Washington. James Reston wrote that President Johnson, actually conducting his election campaign on a platform of restraint in Vietnam, against the escalating Goldwater, was anxious to resist those 'most powerful voices around the Administration' who saw that survival in South Vietnam depended upon backing the Ky line and argued that things were so urgent that a decision could not wait until after the election. It is impossible not to be impressed by the skilful wording of Johnson's attacks on Goldwater and the advocates of escalation. Attacking proposals for escalation now, Johnson always left his options open so obviously that he implied that what was wrong about Goldwater was that he was premature.

October brought to South Vietnam a civilian government with Phan Khuc Suu as Head of State. He had returned from Paolo Con-

dore a year before calling for democracy. Tran Van Huong was Premier. General Taylor had denounced the military coup of October 20
and warned that Washington would reconsider its close alliance with
Saigon unless the 'fabric of legal government was restored.' Suu and
Huong were the answer to this warning and they were advised to resist
the demands of the generals even to the point of resigning. The value
of Suu and Huong, and the sole reason for their appointment, was that
they could give a show of legality, and of opposition to the generals
who wanted to attack North Vietnam and escalate the war. While this
ideally suited President Johnson's election campaign, it met none of
the needs of the situation in Saigon. Khanh met the appointment of
the civilian government in October by 'forbidding' any restoration
of civilian authority, which he had been calling for a little earlier; and
he publicly attacked General Taylor for intervening in Vietnamese
affairs by appointing such an authority. But Buddhists and the students
came in behind Khanh and 'Out Taylor' banners appeared in the
streets. Khanh was performing a 'political balancing act on the high
wire'. Cao Ky's event of the month was to divorce his French wife and
marry a Vietnamese air hostess, and South Vietnamese casualties
reached the highest monthly total since the war began.

In November Hanoi alleged bombing and shelling of North Vietnam and the end of the rainy season brought increased extent and
intensity of 'Viet Cong' attacks. On November 1, the 'Viet Cong' scored
what was called 'the most stunning military victory in 10 years of civil
war'—a 'Viet Cong' mortar team set up six 81 mm American-made
mortars and with 80 shells in 30 minutes destroyed six B57 bombers,
three Skyraiders, and a helicopter. After causing $10 million damage
the 'Viet Cong', pursued seven hours later, were not even seen by their
pursuers. November 30 brought the biggest American action of the
war. Operation Brushfire used 115 helicopters and 7,000 troops against
the 'Viet Cong' in Boi Loi woods 40 miles north-west of Saigon. Four
days later $2 million had been spent and officials claimed 93 Viet Cong
dead and 68 captured. In December, Maxwell Taylor left again for
Washington to make 'his grimmest report yet'. Even before he landed
he made it plain he would call for 'a drastic remedy . . . escalation . . .
bombing raids on supply lines in Laos and North Vietnam.' South
Vietnam was described as a 'land of despair', with 'crucial fighting'
and political clashes going on in the streets of Saigon. Premier Huong
declared: 'We are on the brink of national disaster.' Taylor's arrival
in Washington brought a 'full dress review' of Vietnamese policy and
McNamara advised: 'It would be impossible for Max (Taylor) to talk
to these people (the Press) without leaving the impression that the
situation is going to hell.' The war for America was going from bad
to worse.

December 1964 was a black month. Talks with Sihanouk broke

down. 'Viet Cong' battalions were involved in 'stand up fights' and captured $250,000 worth of equipment. Saigon was in upheaval and there was a feud in the armed forces command. The 'Young Turks' demanded the dismissal of nine senior generals accused of 'neutralist' tendencies. Resistance in the field to the 'Viet Cong' depended absolutely on American aid and fire power, which might save the day, but what else? The factors in the situation that were bound to extend the war and destroy the chances of negotiations were clear before the end of 1964. While South Vietnamese politics were obscure, the forces within them were the declining pro-French moderates led by Doung Van (Big) Minh, the first coup leader; the 'neutralist' Buddhist section whose military leader was really General Nguyen Chanh Thi; and, finally the rigid anti-Communist Catholic wing led by General Nguyen Van Thieu. The public strength of Thieu's section was the well-organised Catholic community most of whom had come from North Vietnam. But whatever else the government in Saigon might be, it was weak and fully dependent on America. Yet American politics at the end of 1964, because of the Presidential election, did not allow this continuing crisis to be brought to an end. It was not until after the elections in America that it was possible for the American Administration to bring in American power behind the officers who took the hard anti-Communist line and to carry the war into North Vietnam.

On January 3, 1965, with the Saigon government on the verge of collapse, thousands of people demonstrated in Saigon. Strikes took place in Saigon, Hue and Danang. Newspapers called for negotiations and for neutralism. The Saigon government admitted on January 8, that 'the authority of the government is trampled underfoot—martial law is not being respected—the forces of law and order have lost control.' These events demanded action. On January 20, General Thieu and Marshal Ky were given portfolios in the Huong government and the swing to the Right began. Naturally the Buddhist-led protest against this move was widespread and increased the intensity of the street demonstrations. Seven days later, Khanh, who could see the writing on the wall, staged a successful coup against Huong. Buddhist leader Thic Tri Quang was perhaps then at the height of his power, and there were demands not only for neutralism but for American withdrawal from Vietnam.[108]

Here emerged a crisis more significant than any in 1963 or 1964. This one went to the root of power in South Vietnam. It threatened the continuation of the war in a way no other had. Unless action was taken conflict and chaos in Saigon would grow.[109] What was remarkable was that the 'Viet Cong' seemed again to have taken so little advantage of the situation. The only adequate explanation seems to be that 'Viet Cong' pressure would have hindered the moves towards negotiations and neutralism, strengthened the hard-liners and pushed

the war into North Vietnam. This the 'Viet Cong' did not want nor did
North Vietnam. But 'Viet Cong' action was the factor that was used
as the pretext to set in motion all these forces which in fact the 'Viet
Cong' did not want. One final move came before the storm. On
January 9, the London Economist had reported that the situation in
South Vietnam had deteriorated so much that to put it right 'it will
almost certainly be necessary to mount air strikes against North
Vietnamese targets.' On January 27, General Taylor went to Vientiane
and Bangkok and American air activity in Laos intensified and Hanoi
accused the Americans of using bases in Laos and Thailand to bomb
North Vietnamese villages. It was apparent that what America needed
now was a new government in Saigon and a dramatic development of
the war which would prove that she would not withdraw or slacken
her efforts to win.

Then early in February came a fresh event that disturbed the
trend of things. Soviet Premier Kosygin announced that he would visit
Hanoi. The New York Times saw the significance of this event in this
way: 'Now again the Asian Communists, this time in South Vietnam,
seem ready to bid for power through a negotiated settlement. The
Soviet Union, apparently fearing that a continuation of the war in
South Vietnam may lead to United States bombing of North Vietnam
and its own involvement, is reappearing in the role of a diplomatic
agent.' Kosygin had gone to Hanoi to press for negotiations. But the
Saigon government could not stand a weakening of American power
and support. Something had to be done. Then came the Pleiku incident. It was a Saturday afternoon in Washington. A 'Viet Cong' unit
made an attack on the American base at Pleiku and within 12 hours
of the beginning of the attack American planes had begun to bomb
North Vietnam.

American historian H. J. Morgenthau saw the events of April 1965
in a way which the evidence has since confirmed: 'The United States,
stymied in South Vietnam and on the verge of defeat, decided to carry
the war to North Vietnam not so much in order to retrieve the fortunes of war as to lay the groundwork for 'negotiation from strength'.
In order to justify that new policy, it was necessary to prove that North
Vietnam is the real enemy. It is the White Paper's purpose (that of
February 17, 1965) to present that proof. Let it be said right away that
the White Paper is a dismal failure. The discrepancy between its
assertions and the factual evidence adduced to support them borders
on the grotesque. It does nothing to disprove, and tends even to confirm, what until the end of February had been official American doctrine: that the main body of the Viet Cong is composed of South
Vietnamese and that 80 to 90 per cent of their weapons are of
American origin.'

The American interpretation of 'aggression from the North' solved no problems but appeared to put things in a much more acceptable light. It enabled the Administration, and in particular its advisers, to find enormous relief in being able to put aside the intractable problems of the South. Not only would it justify the illusion that the war could be won by bombing attacks on the North but it obviated the embarrassment of being seen to intervene in a civil war. This view allowed the President to imply that the enemy was just like Nazi Germany and Japan. Certainly it should have put America in a position in which the war would have been much more acceptable both in America and overseas. Things would have been much worse than they were had somebody failed to get the bright idea, or to refurbish the old idea, of Communist aggression from 'outside the country'.

It is important to note some implications of the position thus chosen by the American Administration. First, it was false. Sooner or later, the falsity was bound to emerge because America is a free society in which the truth emerges more quickly and relentlessly than anywhere else in the world. Sooner or later, an 'agonising re-appraisal' was inevitable. Second, the Administration could have chosen simply to say 'we are going to bomb North Vietnam to force them to submit.' While this in fact was what was being done, it could not be admitted because the American people would not accept such an action and, when it finally became obvious through the 'credibility gap', they rejected it. Then again, the belief that North Vietnam could be bombed into submission implies an assumption that the North Vietnamese people or government were inferior. This assumption would not as likely have been made about a white, non-Communist nation. The fact that it was made about North Vietnam tells us more about the Johnson Administration than it tells about Vietnam.

Not only was the position taken about North Vietnam false in general, but the position taken about the attack on Pleiku was false in particular. Immediately at the United Nations, American Ambassador Adlai Stevenson said: 'Key items of equipment, such as the mortars employed in the attacks of February 7, have come from North Vietnam.' Reporter Malcolm Browne revealed what has since been admitted: 'The attackers (against Pleiku) numbered no more than 50 men and their weapons were wire cutters to get through the perimeter fence, American grenades, and a large number of TNT blocks wrapped into bamboo pole bombs . . . the explosives used in the mortars appeared to have been extracted from captured American shells.' And the mortars used had not come from North Vietnam at all (but as reported by Charles Mohr in the New York Times the very next day), they were 81 mm. American-made mortars. Mohr also pointed out that the attack had been made not by North Vietnamese but by a company or less of 'Viet Cong' who had escaped without being seen or detected by the guards or military personnel. Drew Pearson, in the Washington

Post on February 28, pointed out that 'Hanoi could not have planned to have all South Vietnamese personnel and all Americans asleep' a crucial factor in the success of the attack. Senator Mansfield pointed out that at the time there were no more than 400 to 500 North Vietnamese troops in South Vietnam. And it was apparent even from the Administration's own figures in the White Paper that infiltration from North Vietnam had not increased.

As soon as the bombing started Kosygin brought an end to his visit to Hanoi and returned to Moscow by way of Peking. On February 16, after his return to Moscow, Russia submitted to Peking and Hanoi a new proposal for an international conference on Indochina. President De Gaulle called for the reconvening of the Geneva Conference, the French government stated that Hanoi had urged France to intensify efforts for a negotiated settlement and De Gaulle said the Chinese would be prepared to attend such a conference. The immediate American reply was that France had been given no mandate to act as mediator and that the United States was not interested in a return to the conference table at this time.[110]

But on February 24, the Soviet Union called for the reconvening of the Geneva Conference. On the same day, the United Nations Secretary-General, U Thant, said he had been conducting discussions for a long time aimed at starting negotiations about Vietnam and he now proposed a workable conference. France, the Soviet Union and North Vietnam immediately announced their support for U Thant's plan.[111] President Johnson 'insisted the U.S. would not negotiate now.'[112] The U.S. reply was simple: 'There are no authorised negotiations under way with U Thant.' Secretary of State Dean Rusk added to this by explaining that no one was authorised to speak for the United States and that no one would be allowed to negotiate until North Vietnam had agreed to respect the independence and national security of South Vietnam. Another of the hawks-in-chief, William Bundy, made it clear that the American aim was an 'independent and secure South Vietnam' and stated that North Vietnam 'would not go for that at the present time.'[113] It was again clear that America was in the war to keep South Vietnam as an anti-Communist area and believed that this could not be achieved by negotiations. It was at this point that U Thant chose to make his famous statement: 'I am sure the great American people, if only they knew the true facts and the background to developments in South Vietnam, would agree with me that further bloodshed is unnecessary. As you know, in times of war and of hostilities, the first casualty is truth.'

The subject of negotiations is so important that it is desirable to collect together in one place those many incidents which make up the remarkable story. While Franklin Roosevelt was President of the United States the Vietnamese national independence leaders were treated with respect and the possibility of negotiations and diplomatic relations with them was genuine and meaningful. The change that began with the Truman Administration and intensified under Eisenhower, Kennedy and Johnson, made sincere and meaningful relations with these leaders impossible. We have seen the almost desperate efforts made by Ho Chi Minh to avoid war against the French and to gain independence, gradually enough, by negotiations. We have seen, too, how, although under some pressure, Ho Chi Minh and a majority of Vietminh leadership accepted negotiations at Geneva in 1954, the Agreements that emerged and until 1960, with little more than protest, the destruction of the Agreements that made war again inevitable. The record up to this point shows that the Communists and most other nationalist leaders in Vietnam were dedicated to winning national independence, and to accepting Communist leadership of it. But they did not prefer violent methods. They were characterised by tenacity and persistence, but equally they were characterised by moderation in the degree of force they chose to use. On almost every occasion they were willing to accept far less than they wanted, but always what they did accept was consistent with the march (seen as a long and hard one) towards complete national independence. It was possible, of course, after 1960, that they might change. It was possible that the 'hard-liners' like Le Duan might have convinced the rest that moderation was cowardly and mistaken; that nothing could be won by consent; that no agreements would be kept and that talking was all a waste of time. The 'hard-liners' must have had a strong case that convinced many, and weakened the position of Ho Chi Minh. This leader, as dedicated as any to the cause for independence, by his whole life gave convincing proof that the struggle for national liberation is long and difficult, and allows gains only in small instalments.

About September 1963 there was a French proposal for discussions among the parties to arrive at a neutral and independent Vietnam. On November 8, a week after the overthrow of Diem, Hanoi radio broadcast an appeal for negotiations between interested groups to arrive at a cease fire and a solution to 'the great problems of the country'.[114] Kahin and Lewis record at the same time the NLF sent a manifesto to General Duong Van Minh calling for negotiations and a settlement among all the 'forces, parties, tendencies and strata of the South Vietnamese people'.[115] At a Press conference in Washington on November 2, Dean Rusk summarily rejected any suggestion of negotiations.[116] His rejection, of course, was for obvious reasons. The American position was so weak they possessed no basis upon which to negotiate. In November 1963, the Manchester Guardian quoted some 'unimpeachable source' that Hanoi was 'willing to discuss the establishment of a coalition government in Saigon'.[117] And on February 24, 1965, U Thant said: 'In my view, there was a good possibility in 1963 of arriving at a satisfactory solution.' In September 1964, U Thant continued, or took up again, initiatives he had begun in 1963. On his approach North Vietnam agreed through the Soviet Union to a meeting. Apparently with the agreement and encouragement of Adlai Stevenson, U Thant arranged with Burma for a meeting to take place in Rangoon. Ne Win, Burmese Head of State, replied affirmatively on January 8, 1965. But within a few days Washington rejected the whole plan. Adlai Stevenson gave the rejection to U Thant and it stated two reasons—that the United States could not enter into discussions with Hanoi without the presence of the Saigon government, and such talks would risk ruining the morale of that government. The bombing of North Vietnam began less than two weeks later.

It was at this point that U Thant made his well known statement about being sure 'that the great American people, if only they knew the true facts and the background . . . would agree with me that further bloodshed is unnecessary.' In December 1964, Ho Chi Minh notified the French Government of his desire to discuss 'an accommodation with the United States'. Early in February 1965, before the bombing of North Vietnam began, and before the visit of Premier Kosygin, President De Gaulle, at the 'urging of North Vietnam, requested a reconvening of the Geneva Conference to discuss the future of South-East Asia.'[118] North Vietnam had already claimed that its territory had been bombed and attacked by the United States, bombing of Laos had been intensified, and North Vietnam knew that a great extension of the bombing was close at hand. This it obviously did not want. The American official reply to the French initiatives came from several spokesmen, including Dean Rusk, who said the French had no authority to act as mediator and his government was not interested in any return to the conference table at that time.

On April 1, 1965, William Warbey, a British Labour MP, had talks in Hanoi with Ho Chi Minh and reported that the only Hanoi precondition for talks was an unconditional cessation of the bombing and of all other warlike acts against North Vietnam. Warbey asserted that none of the other 'conditions' mentioned by Hanoi were conditions for the *commencement* of talks but were Hanoi's *objectives* to be achieved in the talks.[119] Early in April, both in South Vietnam and Washington statements were made and leaflets were dropped from aircraft declaring that the National Liberation Front would never be recognised since 'it is only an instrument created by the Communist North Vietnamese'. On April 7, President Johnson spoke at Johns Hopkins University to make his dramatic 'unconditional negotiations' proposal. According to Evans and Novak the reference to 'unconditional negotiations' was a 'last-minute' concession to the Peace bloc that 'amazed those who had seen an earlier version'.[120] It must have amazed Australian Prime Minister Sir Robert Menzies, too, for he,

the night before, asserted he had an identical position with President
Johnson in saying if he 'were the last Prime Minister to reject negotiations' he would remain so. He was. In May 1965, French Foreign
Minister Couve de Murville told Pressmen in Paris that 'North Vietnam had signified a willingness to talk without conditions' but '(he)
had found Washington unreceptive to the news'. When asked about
this Dean Rusk said 'neither side had nominated attorneys'.[121]

In April, with bombing of North Vietnam under way, and marines beginning to take part in combat in South Vietnam, and after
Johnson's 'unconditional negotiations' speech, there is no doubt that
the position of both Hanoi and the NLF hardened. Premier Pham
Van Dong stated that the four points—withdrawal of American forces,
recognition of the sovereignty and territorial integrity of Vietnam, re-
unification and neutralisation of Vietnam, settlement of the affairs of
South Vietnam in accordance with the program of the National
Liberation Front—were the basis on which Hanoi would agree to a
Geneva-type conference. In mid-May, hard-pressed by critics at home
and abroad, the United States halted the bombing of North Vietnam
and announced the suspension could be extended if there were 'significant reductions' in Communist attacks on South Vietnam. A permanent end to the bombing could come if there was a permanent end
to these attacks. There was now no mention of negotiations, 'unconditional' or any other kind. The day before the bombings were
resumed, after five days' cessation, North Vietnam contacted the
French government and asked it to inform Washington that North
Vietnam was prepared to negotiate on the basis of its four points
without demanding the prior complete withdrawal of American forces
from South Vietnam.[122]

It was in August 1965, that Dean Rusk said he was waiting for
some 'key signal' from Hanoi but that his 'antennae' had not yet
picked it up. He admitted that it was true 'that last autumn Ambassador Stevenson was informed by Secretary-General U Thant that he
had been informed indirectly that Hanoi would be willing to have
contact with the United States and that the Secretary-General had
suggested Rangoon as a suitable site'. The State Department also confirmed that the North Vietnamese had approached the French on May
20, 1965, about peace negotiations.[123] At this point Rusk went on to
make it clear exactly what was the Administration position about the
war and about negotiations. He said the United States had at its dis-
posal a great deal of other information which it interpreted as meaning
North Vietnam was not prepared to call off its 'aggression against
South Vietnam'. He was asked did this mean that the United States
did in fact impose a condition for the cessation of bombing—that
North Vietnam should call off its 'aggression against South Vietnam'—
and if so how could the President speak as he had done on April 7,

about 'unconditional negotiations'? Rusk was then specific. He said: 'There has never been any lack of opportunity to bring this matter to peace—to the conference table—if the other side is prepared to stop trying to impose their will by force on South Vietnam.'[124] Later Rusk made it clear that when he said North Vietnam must call off 'its aggression against South Vietnam' he meant that this included the 'Viet Cong' as well. The 'Viet Cong', in his view, and in that of the Administration, was only the tool and creation of Hanoi and it had to surrender or withdraw. Was there then anything to negotiate about? Did it not mean that America would go on bombing until North Vietnam and the 'Viet Cong' were prepared to give up their objective and stop fighting? Did it not mean that the American bombing would go on until this happened? This was the reality and logic of the American negotiating position and it was perfectly understandable. That was what America had gone into Vietnam for, and it was to be expected that she would be prepared to stop for nothing less than that. And Rusk had now made it clear. It was only in those circumstances that it could correctly be said that Hanoi and the NLF had refused to negotiate.

It was negotiations of this kind about which President Johnson spoke at a Press conference on July 13, 1965, and it was negotiations of this kind about which he continued to speak. The Report of the American Friends Service Committee wrote of his July 13 statement: 'One cannot but be amazed, in view of these seven documented missed opportunities (all listed above) for exploring the sincerity of North Vietnamese offers for negotiations, that President Johnson declared at his Press conference on July 13, "I must say that candor compels me to tell you that there has been not the slightest indication that the other side is interested in negotiation or in unconditional discussion, although the United States has made some dozen separate attempts to bring that about".'[125] What President Johnson was saying was that Hanoi and the NLF was not interested in giving up completely all influence and say in affairs in South Vietnam and handing it over to an anti-Communist government dependent on the United States. Hanoi was being asked to stop all connections with the South, and the 'Viet Cong' was being asked to stop fighting, accept the Saigon government or leave the country. The President's position was: 'This is what we want to negotiate about, and Hanoi and the NLF continues to reject our offers.' He was perfectly correct.

At the end of 1965 U Thant privately communicated to the United States the result of his search for peace in Vietnam. On March 9, 1966, he made his recommendations public. He said that he had reason to believe that peace negotiations could be initiated on the basis of three points and in no other way. The points were: (1) cessation of the bombing of North Vietnam; (2) substantial reduction by all parties of all military activities in South Vietnam; (3) the participation of the National Liberation Front (Viet Cong) in any settlement.

Again the Secretary-General found that Washington was not interested.[126] U Thant went on to stress through 1967 and 1968 that there could be no negotiations till the bombing stopped; that the NLF, although now receiving substantial help from Hanoi, was in no way a stooge and had an independent policy; and that the leaders of Vietnam were independent and obsessed with the principle of non-alignment. Furthermore, he asserted, he did not subscribe to the view that 'if South Vietnam falls, then Country X, then Country Y, then Country Z will follow'. 'In my view,' he said, 'the destiny of every country is shaped by its own peculiar circumstances, its national background, its own political philosophy. What is true of Country X is not necessarily true of Country Y or Country Z.' It seemed, even early in 1966, that U Thant's three points would inevitably have to be recognised by the United States, but a refusal to recognise them remained the basic American *condition* for negotiations held consistently through 1965, 1966, 1967 and 1968. Equally, Hanoi and the NLF refused to accept these conditions.

The year 1966 went on apparently with each side making a closer examination of the other's 'points'. For North Vietnam there were four, for the United States 10,[127] and the National Liberation Front's 10-point program issued in December 1960 had often been summed up in four.[128] In evidence before the Senate Foreign Relations Committee on February 18, 1966, Rusk said the United States could accept three of Hanoi's four points, the exception being what he called the 'hard core of the Communist position'—that the internal affairs of South Vietnam should be settled in accordance with the program of the NLF. What did that mean? According to Rusk it meant the prior recognition of the NLF as the 'sole spokesman for the people of South Vietnam'.[129] It is difficult to understand how Rusk arrived at this interpretation or how he was able to maintain it. Always a basic point in the program of the NLF was to 'establish a coalition government'.

The NLF program went like this: 'The present rule is a disguised colonial rule. The South Vietnam ruling clique is a servile administration carrying out U.S. imperialist policy. Such a regime and administration must be overthrown and be replaced by a broad, national and democratic coalition government composed of representatives of every sector of the population, various nationalities, political parties, religious communities, and patriotic personalities.' This was issued in December, 1960, as the first of 10 points; on July 20, 1962 as the third of four points; and on November 17, 1963 as the sixth of six points.

Of the power and ability of the NLF there can be no doubt. It is perhaps the most powerful and effective *political* organisation in the world. Nor can it be denied that its Communist leadership is powerful and effective. The NLF would dominate any coalition government into which it entered. The possibilities and prospects of this will be examined later, but all that should be said here are the two points: (1) the NLF is an expression of the profound social revolution that has been taking place for some years in Vietnam, that it expresses the grass roots needs of the people growing out of poverty and suppression, and the need for national identity. The NLF and 'Viet Cong' are only a minority but their fervour exerts a powerful influence over the majority mainly because it expresses what they feel. (2) The conditions out of which this revolution, and in turn the NLF and 'Viet Cong' grew, were the conditions imposed upon Vietnam by colonial occupation. First, there was the 'presence of foreigners', and second there was foreign support for a Vietnamese ruling class whose interests, and very existence, depended upon blocking those changes which would have removed the forces that produced the revolution in the first place.

At first North Vietnam had stressed as their point 3 the *program* of the NLF. Rusk had chosen to interpret that to mean the NLF as an organisation. A year later, Ho Chi Minh demanded precisely what Rusk had alleged—the United States must recognise the NLF as the sole genuine representative of the people of South Vietnam and engage in negotiations with it.[130] Not only was this a hardening of North Vietnam's position but it reflected the increased power, significance and independence of the NLF as an organisation. On November 11, 1965, two Italian visitors to Hanoi, one the former Mayor of Florence, met Ho Chi Minh. On November 20, Italian Foreign Minister Fanfani, informed President Johnson[131] that Hanoi would join in talks if there was a ceasefire and an acceptance of the Geneva Agreements as a basis for negotiations, which North Vietnam regarded as embodied in their 'four points'. On December 4, Rusk sent Fanfani a letter disagreeing with Hanoi's contention that their 'four points' were an authentic interpretation of Geneva and asking him to get further clarification. On December 13, Fanfani informed Rusk that five days earlier he had sent such a communication on its way to Hanoi. On December 15, before any reply was received, American aircraft for the first time bombed a major industrial target, a thermal power plant, 14 miles from Hanoi. Hanoi never replied to the Fanfani query and this was the end of this particular adventure in negotiations.

But on December 4, 1966, a similar exchange began. On that date Polish Foreign Minister Adam Rapacki[132] sent word to Washington that Hanoi was prepared to have unconditional talks at ambassadorial level in Warsaw, and Washington was asked to send a special representative. A later communication gave more particulars and said that

Hanoi was prepared to engage in 'secret exploratory discussions' with the United States, did not mention the cessation of bombing as a condition for this meeting, and put up 10 points for discussion. One of these was that North Vietnam would not make any public acknowledgment of its forces in South Vietnam. Washington replied asking that this point be 'clarified' to mean that the North Vietnamese forces should be withdrawn from the South. Before this difference could be taken any further, and on December 13 and 14, the bombing was again stepped up this time by attack on the railway yards within Hanoi itself, and by President Johnson's giving permission for the first time, for bombing within the city limits.[133] These attacks caused widespread damage to civilian areas. Again there was no further reply from Hanoi.

President Johnson began his 1967 propaganda campaign by listing on February 2 the many approaches that had been made to Hanoi and claimed that Hanoi had 'not taken any step yet' that could lead to negotiations. This led to the Washington Post's[134] publication of the story of the Polish Foreign Minister's endeavours which are referred to above. British Prime Minister Harold Wilson told the House of Commons on February 7 that he was fully informed about the 'Polish discussions' which had failed because of a 'very considerable two-way misunderstanding'. Later Wilfred Burchett stated that these talks had been 'foiled' by the bombings of December 13-14. No effort was made to re-establish the discussions in Warsaw. Early in 1967, President Johnson had also said that he was prepared to suspend the bombing of North Vietnam, and when asked what steps the other side would have to take, Johnson said, 'Just almost any step'. A reply soon came from North Vietnam's Foreign Minister, Nguyen Duy Trinh, who informed Wilfred Burchett on January 28, that only the bombing of North Vietnam stood in the way of talks. In a well-known and widely-publicised interview, Burchett reported Trinh as saying, 'It is only after the unconditional cessation of bombing and all other acts of war against the Democratic Republic of Vietnam that there could be talks between the Democratic Republic of Vietnam and the United States. . . . If the bombings cease completely, good and favourable conditions will be created for the talks. President Johnson said he was only waiting a sign. Well, he's had the sign.'[135] But despite a great deal of pressure at home and abroad (and it was at this point that Senator Robert Kennedy returned from Paris with a feeling about 'peace talks' and had a heated meeting with the President), the position of the Johnson Administration did not change.

By now the North Vietnamese position was clear and unambiguous—talks could start if the bombing stopped. President Johnson recognised this and 'noted' that the position had been confirmed by 'serious and responsible parties'. But President Johnson rejected the proposal and gave as the reasons that a halt in the bombing would tell the world that discussions were going on and would impair the necessary secrecy of such talks. A second reason was that North Vietnam would use the halt to 'improve its military position'. And so the American position was stated: 'I am prepared to order the cessation of bombing against your country and the stopping of further augmentation of U.S. forces in South Vietnam as soon as I am assured that infiltration into South Vietnam by land and by sea has stopped'. The bombing truce that was under way was to end on February 10, but that was the day President Johnson's letter reached Hanoi, and the truce was extended by two days. There were intense diplomatic activities but to no avail. On February 13, President Johnson announced resumption of 'full scale hostilities' including intensified bombing of North Vietnam. He attributed blame to Hanoi for the decision, saying that the truce had been used for 'major resupply efforts of their troops in South Vietnam.' I. F. Stone[136] was exceedingly critical of the Pentagon claims of supply efforts from North Vietnam. He pointed out that the original tonnage claimed of 35,000 had been reduced to 23,000. The trucks that had been sighted were seen only from the air, and there was no way of knowing whether they carried military supplies or not, or whether they were all bound for South Vietnam or not. As these reports were crucial to the decision for the resumption of bombing, Stone considered that something much more definite should have been obtained before such strong conclusions could be drawn. He called the whole exercise sloppy and unconvincing. At the same time, American Air Force officials made their normal announcements —on February 8, the first day of the truce and the day the President's letter was handed to Moscow, 2,762 tons of equipment was carried by cargo planes to American troops. The total for February 8-10 was over 7,000 tons and more than 17,000 troops were carried by the Air Force alone. The probability is that a vast amount more would have been landed at this time by ship in South Vietnamese ports in a 'major resupply effort' for American troops. And so the negotiation manoeuvres ended until another season. Next time the result would be different but until then many more bombs had to fall.

Meanwhile, on the political front in South Vietnam, Khanh's coup against Huong resulted, on February 15, 1965, in another civilian government. Phan Huy Quat, one of the 18 petitioners arrested in 1961 by the Diem government, was now Premier, but none of Maxwell Taylor's closest collaborators was even in the cabinet. Quat's cabinet was perhaps the most representative that Saigon has ever had. But it was not an 'American cabinet'. Hence another coup was on the cards.

It came within three days of Quat's appointment and it was directed against Khanh. This coup was described as a 'Catholic coup' and seems to have originated with Colonel Thao and General Khiem in Washington. It was thought by the New York Times to be 'abortive', was according to that paper 'hatched in Washington', but it meant the end of Khanh, who became a roving ambassador, and it moved the balance of power in the junta to Thieu, Ky and Khiem, who all said they were delighted with the result. Thieu became Chairman of the Armed Forces Council in place of Khanh, and Ky became its spokesman and announced that the Council now controlled South Vietnamese politics and would get rid of anyone who talked about negotiations or neutralism. Quat seemed now a prisoner of the junta and announced that South Vietnam was acting in self defence against an attack from the North and that there would be no peace until the Communists had been taught their lesson, and were ready to stop their unprovoked aggression. On March 2, 1965, American bombers attacked North Vietnam in the first raid that was not claimed to be a retaliatory one.

But the raids on North Vietnam and the hard-line of Thieu and Ky in the Saigon Government did not bring an end to agitation and demonstration for negotiations and neutralism. There were reports, for example, from 'informed sources' that the Quat government was interested in finding a peaceful solution. In April the deputy premier, Tran Van Tuyen, gave an interview to Le Monde[137] in which he said: 'This war must be stopped. In such a context, the Left-wing South Vietnamese forces could find a place.' As a result of these moves and these ideas, the Quat government was attacked by the Catholic elements and demands were made for a government that would never compromise. It was soon after this that the Quat government is said to have asked Australia to send troops to Vietnam. But the government outlasted these circumstances and this request by only a few days. On June 11, yet another coup, not surprisingly, brought down the Quat government and installed the military junta dominated by the explosive combination of General Thieu and Air Vice-Marshal Cao Ky.

The take-over of office in Saigon by Thieu and Ky through which American power could be fully exercised in Vietnam was the most critical turning point in the war. It meant that the internal logic of the continuing crisis since 1960 had now fully worked out. Since 1960 in South Vietnam, the strength and influence of those who wanted negotiations and neutralism to bring an end to the war, had grown both among 'the people' and within the small groups that formed the succession of governments. Opposed to them had been a large number of generals, officials and war profiteers, supported among 'the people' largely by the Catholic communities who were refugees from North Vietnam. It had been the fundamental aim of American policy to maintain a government in Saigon through which South Vietnam could be maintained as an anti-Communist area. To achieve this aim the

American Administration was compelled to oppose negotiations and
neutralism and to support the groups in South Vietnam who were
most vigorous and uncompromising in their opposition to negotiations
and neutralism and to oppose those who wanted to bring an end to
the war. For this purpose it was necessary, at crucial points, to escalate
the war so that any chance of acceptance of negotiations by Hanoi
or the N.L.F. would be removed and the hand of the 'hard-liners' in
Saigon would be strengthened. But, because of political conditions in
America the Administration could not admit a policy of this kind,
hence there were delays and appeals for negotiations, all of which were
framed so that they would not be acceptable. This, then, was the
record until the war against North Vietnam was well under way and
until there could be no serious threat to the hard-line military junta in
Saigon. One final significant point emerges from all this—American
intervention and policy always went against those influences which
emerged from 'the people' in South Vietnam, and went always in
favour of the most aggressive of the generals. This is because 'the
people' wanted the war to end while most of the generals wanted it to
continue. If the American Administration was to secure its fundamental aim the war had to continue until all Communist influence
in South Vietnam had been destroyed or had surrendered and South
Vietnam was a secure anti-Communist area.

Of course, the United States Administration would have liked to
win its objective without a 'wider war'. It would have liked to win its
objective without putting American troops into combat at all. It would
have liked to win its objective without a war at all. But it was primarily concerned to win its objective, and if war was necessary then
war had to be undertaken even if the war had to widen. There were
two reasons for the extension of the war in North Vietnam. The first
and most important was that it was necessary to commit some dramatic
act that would convince everyone, particularly allies in South Vietnam,
that America would not withdraw and leave them to their fate.
Nothing could achieve this more effectively than attack on North
Vietnam. Indeed this was so often and so vividly demanded by the
hard-line generals in Saigon, that it was the vital test of American
commitment. America passed the test—she was tough enough to last
the course. The second reason for the attack on North Vietnam was
that aid from and through North Vietnam to the forces being fought
by America in South Vietnam was becoming more and more significant.
Prior to February 1965 most American interpretations of the war in
South Vietnam had been that it was a 'revolutionary war' in which
the guerrillas had to have, to a crucial extent, the support of the
people if they were to win. It was always said that Communists played
a dominant role in any action and that North Vietnam sought to
control, direct and aid the action taken. But through most of the

period the enemy war effort was recognised by Americans as mainly
an indigenous one that depended upon popular support in South
Vietnam. Indeed so much was this so that the winning of popular
support against it was laid down by Dulles, as a primary factor, and
by McNamara as the *sine qua non* of military success. But in February
1965 the whole emphasis changed. The new interpretation was laid
down in the American State Department White Paper, 'Aggression
from the North', issued on February 17, 1965. What was being said now
about the war was clearly put in the opening statement that the White
Paper was 'The record of North Vietnam's Campaign to Conquer
South Vietnam.'

The war was now no longer seen as a civil war. It was 'flagrant aggression' by North Vietnam against all the people of South Vietnam.
Indeed President Johnson chose to say on the opening page that the
attack on the people of South Vietnam was from 'outside their
country'. The purpose of the White Paper, and the American Administration's new interpretation of the war, was to show that what
America was fighting in South Vietnam was just another case of
aggression by one country against another, like that of Nazi Germany
or Japan, which had nothing to do with the national aspirations or
desire for reform by the people in South Vietnam themselves. Whether
this interpretation was valid or not could be tested only by evidence
of the movement of men and materials from North Vietnam into South
Vietnam. That 'aggression from the north' was a *new* interpretation is
attested by the position taken in the 1961 State Department White
Paper, 'A Threat to the Peace; North Vietnam's Effort to Conquer
South Vietnam.' Here is an extract from it: 'The weapons of the Viet
Cong are largely French, or U.S.-made, or hand-made on primitive
forges in the jungles. The Communists have avoided any large-scale
introduction of Soviet-bloc arms into South Vietnam for that would
be too clear evidence of their direct involvement,' and Secretary of
State Dean Rusk admitted as late as August 3, 1965, before the House
Foreign Affairs Committee[138] 'that the official estimate of guerrilla
strength in 1959 was only 3,000 and they were South Vietnamese.' Rusk
and Under-Secretary George Ball did not appear to think, even in 1961,
there was much strength in the Viet Cong in this 'determined and
ruthless campaign of propaganda, infiltration, and subversion by the
Communist regime in North Vietnam to destroy the Republic of
Vietnam.'

The division of Vietnam was already accepted as a permanent fact.
But who now in 1961 were the 'Viet Cong?' The White Paper put it:
'Undoubtedly there are some volunteers. But the record shows that
many young Vietnamese are dragooned into service with the Viet
Cong. Some are kidnapped; others are threatened; still others join to
prevent their families from being harried.' Under-Secretary George

Ball put it: 'The guerrillas whom the Vietnamese army (of 350,000) is fighting are under distinct handicaps. In many cases they are poorly trained and equipped and not motivated by deep convictions. Rather they are merely unsophisticated villagers or peasants who have only rudimentary training in weapon handling and tactics. Their equipment may be makeshift, often just what they can capture or fabricate themselves.'

It is worth while here to summarise the findings of Douglas Pike, who, in 1966 published in his book 'Viet Cong'[139] the result of his specialised work as a foreign service officer with the U.S. Information Agency in Vietnam since October 1960. Pike had access to captured documents and no one could claim to have a fuller access to, or knowledge of the captured evidence of the organisation and activity of the 'Viet Cong.' Pike chose to sum up the phases of 'Viet Cong' organisation in three periods: First, 'Social Movement Propaganda Phases', to February-March 1962. Then the 'Political Struggle Movement', from early 1962 to late 1963. Finally, 'Legitimisation-Militarisation Phase', from 1964. Pike states conclusions like the following: 'It was true that the leadership in the 1960-61 period did not put much priority on the violence program, nor was there much direct appeal to any segment to employ terror techniques' (p. 155). 'It is important to understand the essentially political rather than military nature of the NLF's activities in the first period in order to appreciate the marked changes that followed in succeeding years' (p. 156). 'Virtually no mention was made of violence; the language was in terms of the "peaceful struggle movement" ' (p. 156). 'The end of the social movement propaganda phase was marked by the meeting of the NLF First Congress [in South Vietnam, of course] in February-March 1962' (p. 157). 'By mid 1964 . . . most of the effort during the period was such as to suggest that the NLF was in search of a negotiated settlement, a coalition government with NLF primacy. At any rate the balance from the political to armed struggle tipped late in the summer of 1963. In fact the exact moment can probably be fixed. It was the first week in September 1963, when the two DRV generals convened the 'military conference', apparently held just inside the Cambodian border opposite the Darlac plateau' (p. 162).

The publication of Pike's book should have brought an end to controversy among those who accept the official American version. Pike's work shows that the 'Viet Cong' and NLF did *not* initiate the military, or armed force, part of the war in Vietnam. They wanted to win power in South Vietnam, but they used political methods almost completely till the end of 1961, and the scales did not tip towards armed struggle till September 1963. Hence the war was initiated by Diem and the United States. The NLF and Hanoi wanted to win above all else, but wanted to win without war. War was forced upon them by Diem and America who could not hold their own in the 'political struggle' conducted by the NLF primarily, and by Hanoi.

War made it much harder for the NLF. The people do not want to carry the burdens of war and the NLF became less and less popular as they were compelled to impose upon the people the cost of the war in taxes, death, wounds, damage to their homes and villages and the physical burden of carrying equipment and supplies. War was far less of a burden to America's Vietnamese because Americans paid for it, America supplied everything that was needed and carried it all in ships, aircraft and land transport. For many of America's Vietnamese war was a career and for hundreds of thousands of others America's war provided a 'sanctuary' in the cities in which they could live on the war. Pike's figures confirm this characterisation.

They are as follows:

	Military incidents	Military attacks	Kidnappings	Assassinations
1957-60	no figures	no figures	2,000	1,700
1961	500	no figures	no figures	1,300
1962	19,000	13,000	9,000	1,700
1963	19,500	15,000	7,200	2,000
1964	25,500	15,500	1,500	500
1965	26,500	15,500	1,700	300

Of course 'incidents' and 'military attacks' are by no means all incidents or military attacks initiated alone by the 'Viet Cong', although this is the basis of the classification. The importance of these figures is that they show how few there were before 1962.

Pike takes a typically American viewpoint of the rise of the NLF. Few American or Australian writers have shown any understanding of the historical, national and sociological nature of any movement for change and how excruciatingly difficult it is to *organise* anything or to move any one to do anything which is not a purely self-centred action. Pike thinks the essence of the 'Chinese revolution' was strategy, that of the Vietminh spirit, and that of the NLF organisation. Everything the NLF did, he says, 'was an act of communication. . . I take a communicational view of social change.' This is largely superficial.

It is of vast importance to show the nature and significance of 'communication' in any social movement as Pike does for the NLF. There can be no social movement or real political party without it. But you can organise or communicate until you are blue in the face and unless there is something to organise or communicate about you may as well take up fishing. Someone said there is nothing so powerful as an idea whose time has come. Unless there is an idea whose time has come there will be no change of any kind. The idea whose time had come in Vietnam was the idea of getting rid of foreigners, of bringing

about economic change and the realisation that these were both criti-
cally tied together. The NLF could have had every skill and device of
organisation and communication man has ever thought of, and without
these ideas they would have moved people no more than would a
Billy Graham crusade. The Vietnamese people might have sung and
prayed or their Vietnamese equivalents as a result of communication
and organisation, but they would never have died for mere organisation and communication. What happened in Vietnam was more than
organisation, communication and a military campaign. No one ever
doubted that the Second World War in Europe and Russia had been
the result of a military expedition by Hitler's Germany. German
tanks and aircraft swept across frontiers in their thousands. No one
ever suggested that the attack on Pearl Harbour was a civil war, or
that the fall of Singapore had been brought about by native guerrillas,
or that the battle of the Kokoda Trail was a revolutionary insurrection.
Do they expect us to believe that the war in Vietnam was in any way
similar? Stupidity, prejudice and lack of interest are common but
not that common. The age of double-think came earlier than 1984
but the facts of the war in Vietnam have delivered it a serious blow.
It is not yet dead and it will be resurrected in order to insinuate that
whatever happens in Thailand must have been imported completely
from China. Let us review how this double-think was managed in the
case of Vietnam.

   The 'White Paper' of 1965 set out to prove that the war in South
Vietnam was a 'campaign' by North Vietnam 'to conquer South
Vietnam'. This 'campaign' was 'inspired, directed, supplied, and controlled' from 'outside' the country by 'North Vietnam'. Such was the
task undertaken by the White Paper. Much of the evidence presented
in the White Paper was collected by the officials of the government in
Saigon who always had a strong motive to exaggerate. Much of it had
been presented to the International Control Commission as the years
went by and the Commission reported on it. It will be useful and per-
tinent therefore to look also at what the Commission found.

   The evidence, broadly, divides into two kinds—evidence of the
movement of men, 'infiltration', into South Vietnam and the capture
in South Vietnam of arms and ammunition that had come from Communist countries. Let us look first at 'infiltrations'. The White Paper
claims that infiltrations began in 1959 and between then and the end
of 1964, there were 19,550 'confirmed' and 17,550 'estimated' infiltrations. The International Control Commission states that there were
2,000 more. In both cases almost all of the men who infiltrated to the
end of 1964 are admitted to be South Vietnamese who had left South
Vietnam, as required by the Geneva Agreement. They had close relatives, including wives, in the South and, when it was apparent that
there was to be no unification of Vietnam by election in 1956, they

returned to their homes. For the greater part of the 'infiltrations' it is just as reasonable to conclude that they came South to rejoin their families as it is to conclude that they came South to fight. This is even more the case when we realise, as we have seen earlier, that up to 1961 it was not the policy of North Vietnam to encourage an insurrection in South Vietnam, but to oppose it and encourage political action instead. But if one assumes that all those who 'infiltrated' did fight, what proportion would they have made up of those who were officially claimed to be Viet Cong regular and irregular forces? Below is a table which shows the result:[140]

Year	Viet Cong: regular and irregular forces	Largest Confirmed and Estimated Infiltrations	Percentage of Infiltrators to Viet Cong forces, assuming (a) no casualties and (b) 50 per cent casualties per year	
			(a)	(b)
Prior to 1961		4,500		
1961	45,000	6,200	24	—
1962	70,000	12,800	33	23
1963	95,000	7,900	33	17
1964	115,000	12,400	38	18
1965	220,000	7,900	15	8

The White Paper itself points out that those in charge up to 1964 sought to fill 'their quotas' with those born in the South and that the casualty rate was high—it is usually assumed about 50 per cent a year Furthermore, the White Paper points out that most of the 'infiltrations' claimed as above were Southerners who had gone North before 1954 and 'those who were in fighting trim 10 years ago are no longer up to the rigours of guerrilla war'. Taking all these factors into account there can be little doubt that the largest numbers of 'infiltrations' ever claimed were never worth more than one-fifth of the total Viet Cong forces, and these were mostly of far less value as fighters in the guerrilla war.

It is, of course, claimed that the men who came from North Vietnam were especially important because they were trained in guerrilla warfare, were most capable in political indoctrination, and they came with authority. Doubtless this was true of some, but detailed reports show that initiation of action and organisation was mostly the work of men who had lived all their lives in South Vietnam. Douglas Pike in his *Viet Cong* shows the NLF organisation was more highly developed than was that of the Vietminh. The probability is that experience in the South was much more important in winning battles and influence than was reputation and authority in the North.[141]

Turning now to the supply of arms and ammunition. The White Paper gives an amazingly small total of arms—far less than one would expect. Between May 12, 1962, when it was claimed that the first weapon from a Communist country was captured in South Vietnam, and December 31, 1964, it is claimed that 184 weapons from Communist countries were captured in South Vietnam. In 1962 the total was 23, in 1963 it was 161. The International Control Commission, purporting to give details of all the weapons captured during the period to the end of 1964, provides the following list: 580 Russian Massin Nagant rifles, 150 Czech machine guns, 14 Chinese 75mm. and 57mm. recoilless rifles, 30 Chinese 7.92mm. and 7.65mm. rifles, 49 Chinese machine guns, four Chinese bomb launchers, five East German rifles, three unspecified 7.92mm. machine guns—a total of 835 weapons. If we add to this total those arms mentioned in the American White Paper which may not be included in the Commission's list, the total of all weapons from Communist countries captured in South Vietnam up to the end of 1964 is 911. Now, during the same period it is officially claimed that 15,100 weapons in all were captured from the 'Viet Cong'. Hence of this total, only 911, or 6 per cent, were from Communist countries. Where did the rest come from? During the same period it is officially admitted that at least 27,400 American weapons were lost to the 'Viet Cong'. It is probably a fair assumption to say that the proportion of weapons from Communist countries captured from the 'Viet Cong' would be similar to the proportion of weapons from Communist countries actually carried and used by them. If we make this assumption we can say that the value to the 'Viet Cong' of weapons from Communist countries, up to the end of 1964, was less than one tenth of the weapons they had captured from Saigon government and American forces. The value of ammunition and supplies would be much the same. Indeed up to the end of 1964 the Viet Cong war effort in South Vietnam was almost certainly 90 per cent South Vietnamese.

The hollowness of the official American claim in the White Paper is shown by the dramatic emphasis given to one shipment of arms, ammunition and supplies captured on the coast of South Vietnam on February 16, 1965, nine days after the bombing of North Vietnam had started, and included in the White Paper as part of the evidence justifying the bombing of North Vietnam. This shipment contained '100 tons of small arms mostly Chinese' and included 1,500 grenades, 1,000 submachine guns, over 2,500 rifles, one million rounds of ammunition, other explosives and medical and other supplies. This was many times more than had been captured in South Vietnam during the whole of the war up to that point—and in one barge. The New York Times chose to write of the capture: 'Apparently the major new evidence of a need for escalating the war, with all the hazard that entails, is a 100-ton cargo ship loaded with Communist small arms and ammunition. A ship that size is not much above the oriental junk class. The standard Liberty or Victory ship of the Second World War had a capacity of 7,150 to 7,650 tons.' The New York Times went on to point out that, small as this was, very few like it would ever have got through for 'about 12,000 vessels are searched every month by the South Vietnamese coastal patrol force, but arrests are rare and no significant amounts of incriminating goods or weapons have been found.'[142] We can be little surprised that the distinguished American historian and diplomat Hans Morgenthau summed it up: 'It [the White Paper] is a dismal failure.' But Presidents, Secretaries of State, Prime Ministers and public figures all over that part of the world dependent upon America still go on repeating the assertions as though the case had never even been questioned.

It was not, therefore, actual 'aggression from the North' that caused the escalation of the war in South Vietnam and the attack on North Vietnam. Aggression from the North was merely used to justify them. Escalation of the war was caused by the continued deterioration of the strength and influence of the government of South Vietnam and its forces in 1964. One argument alone prevailed—the war had to be won and it would be won if the Communists were hit hard enough. But the war in 1964 became the top question in the public opinion polls in the United States; officials and the Press were increasingly questioning Administration policy; Senators Morse, Gruening, Church, Gore, Richard Russell, Fulbright, Mansfield and others spearheaded the Senate opposition. Some answer had to be given. For over a year escalation had worked well as an answer. The Administration reaction to Tonking Bay had put the President way out in front. With Huong and Suu holding only the trappings of power against a 22-man military junta in Saigon, who depended upon escalation, then escalation was an obvious answer.

One of Britain's most authoritative writers on Vietnam, P. J. Honey, diagnosed the situation in a way that nicely met its needs. 'The war in Vietnam is not lost' he wrote, 'things have not been going too well. What can we do to turn the tide?' That was the question, what was the answer? '. . . in terms of the short haul', decided the expert from Britain, 'the U.S. would have to face up to the prospect of a "selective" carrying of the war to the north, Perennially short of food, overcrowded, and industrially backward, North Vietnam is economically the most vulnerable state in the world. . . A few carefully planned bombing raids would be capable of inflicting economic chaos on the entire country.' Not only, it seems, was Honey an expert on the condition of North Vietnam but he was a strategist as well. He went on to advise the United States: '(You) might then warn North Vietnam that, unless a halt were called to her intervention in the south, selective bombing might continue on a graduated scale until Hanoi concluded it was against its interests to continue the war. Then, and then only, would it be possible to negotiate a peace settlement with any prospect of lasting results.' This must have been the kind of advice the American Administration wanted and finally acted upon when it chose to use the 'Viet Cong' attack on Pleiku to launch the bombing of North Vietnam on February 9, 1965. But General Henri Navarre gave to America advice a little different from that of Honey. He recommended a strategic bombing attack on North Vietnam, but he warned that this would not be enough. 'Without U.S. combat troops en masse (in North Vietnam) you will suffer a defeat similar in degree to the French 10 years ago.'

To some it remained unclear where Maxwell Taylor stood.[143] U.S. Brigadier General Marshall is sure that 'despite recent stories' he understood that Taylor did not 'in his recent report' recommend 'an extension of military operations within South Vietnam or the bombing of North Vietnam.' 'This is what Johnson wants', said Marshall, 'and Taylor is delivering the goods.' What was the reason? Marshall put clearly what everyone knew: 'The Vietnamese are demoralised . . . haunted by fear the U.S. will pull out . . . something has to bring them back.' Deciding that 'our schemes are about half as good now as they were 10 years ago', Marshall was not in favour of an attack on North Vietnam. Had Taylor changed his position? Marshall believed that the war had to be won in the South and he thought that 'three or four American regimental combat teams, reinforced by armour, would do it . . . guerrillas have always been beaten by conventional tactics.' But the deterioration in the South was the crucial factor and Bernard Fall warned that it was not caused by Diem's overthrow. 'It had been going to hell since 1959 . . . a stalemate for a decade . . . the U.S. can only hope to win a better place at the bargaining table. The best we can hope for is a non-committed, non-Communist South Vietnam.' However much the military experts may have differed one from another about tactics, one thing seemed certain—everything pointed to an attack on North Vietnam, and mainly because there was no other feasible way that critical deterioration in South Vietnam could be avoided. Two questions only seemed to be argued. Would the attack on North Vietnam stop the deterioration and give President Johnson the political lead at home against his critics? Would the attack cause the Soviet Union or China or both to retaliate? All the experts agreed that the answer to the second question was 'no', while to the first the answer was 'it has worked successfully before.' So the stage was set.

January saw two American fighter bombers shot down over the Plain of Jars in Laos, and in South Vietnam the monthly total of 'Viet

Cong' actions more than doubled. The Saigon generals were not satisfied by the offers Huong was prevailed upon to make to them and Ky would not give up control of the air force for a place in the Cabinet. But on February 8, the 'Viet Cong' 261st Battalion retreated at Up Bac and left 153 dead and three recoilless rifles. It was said to have been the most successful action ever fought against them and the key was seen to be the speed and precision of American bombs and napalm. The tactical balance, it was argued, could shift if this type of warfare was adopted. But politically things got worse. Huong was removed for Harvard-trained economist Nguyen Xuan Oanh, then a six-man civilian and military council was to pick a Head of State and a Premier. Taylor hated Khanh and Khanh hated Taylor and all that could be hoped was that fire and bombs could 'manage the mess'. And so came Pleiku and bombs on North Vietnam. The 'Viet Cong' attack on the American base at Pleiku in central Vietnam was made with U.S. mortars and satchel explosive charges. American casualties were seven dead and 109 wounded—the largest number so far in any single action—but American aircraft losses, six helicopters and six reconnaissance aircraft, were not high. A few hours after this normal attack President Johnson met the National Security Council and the order was given to carry into effect the plans the Pentagon had long since drawn up. Twelve hours after the attack on Pleiku began, the counter-blow was under way. Bombers attacked North Vietnam and the stated purpose was that it was a reprisal for the attack on Pleiku and to discourage further Viet Cong attacks. But there was no evidence that North Vietnamese arms or men had been involved at Pleiku and no evidence that the attack was anything but identical with so many others on American bases, some of which had been stronger and had caused more damage. February 15, 1965, saw Newsweek reporting: 'With startling abruptness, the whole character of the war changed... After months of public vacillation the Johnson Administration in the course of a single night escalated the war.'

But the public reaction was not so favourable as had been hoped. Immediately there was what the Press called 'public and private disquiet'. It was not Tonking Bay all over again. There was a concerted attack in the Senate. In April, 15,000 students picketed the White House and 'teach-ins' began and spread widely on University campuses. The public opinion polls did not show a clear result—Harris, for instance showed 83 per cent in favour of the 'retaliatory strikes', but 75 per cent favoured 'asking for negotiations'. Around the world, much of the reaction was that the President's decision was understood as a strike with a purpose—and the purpose was to cause North Vietnam to agree to negotiations. Much of the acceptance it won was induced by the hope that negotiations would come about as a result of it. If they did not it could be expected that the reaction against the President would be all the greater. Outside America there was pressure for negotiations. Unease in Paris, London, Moscow, Bonn, Rome, New Delhi and at the United Nations turned people towards negotiations. But there was no response from Washington. The attack had been made because of American weakness and it had to go much further before that weakness could be changed into the strength without which negotiations would be inconceivable to the Americans. The passivity of China and the Soviet Union, in the face of the attack upon their 'heroic comrades', made the American task so much easier. But it was not only a bombing attack on North Vietnam that was involved. In March, American marines arrived at Da Nang. It was the first American combat mission on land in Asia since Korea. The marines at Da Nang and the bombs on North Vietnam worked wonders for South Vietnamese government morale.

But warnings persisted about this 'unwinnable war'. Bombs and marines would not be enough. Again, as at all turning points in the war, it was strongly asserted from many official quarters in South Vietnam that the rural areas could not be won without those fundamental reforms which the Saigon government would not and could not accept. Again, as at all turning points in this war, proposals for negotiations came thick and fast. U Thant proposed a meeting of the United States, Britain, France, China, the Soviet Union and the Vietnams. On April 12, came the appeal by 17 non-aligned nations. Washington turned them all down flat, and now, North Vietnam turned them down too, although the New York Times reported that North Vietnamese officials privately said that they would be prepared to negotiate on the basis suggested by the 17 non-aligned nations.

As the raids spread into North Vietnam, what was described as the 'largest, bloodiest battle of the year' took place in the 'cleared out' southern delta area. Government forces lost 21 dead and 85 wounded and American planes and helicopters left 258 'VC' dead on the ground. The significant military fact since December was that almost all of the battles in South Vietnam had been decided by air power. The American raids on North Vietnam were answered by Soviet missiles, which may well have been on the way earlier, and by the middle of May, 1965, McNamara was claiming that the 'great bulk of weapon requirements of the VC are supplied from external sources.' But it seems that the Soviet missiles supplied to North Vietnam were limited in range and power so that American naval vessels and some base areas could not be reached. McNamara claimed that, for the first time, North Vietnam had sent a regular army combat unit into South Vietnam.

The Administration story of the arrival of North Vietnamese regular troops into South Vietnam is yet another example of the inaccuracy, lack of care or straight lying which characterised the story as a whole. During 1964 McNamara and others had said that there were few North Vietnamese troops in South Vietnam and no regular units. Several times, early in 1966, Dean Rusk claimed that 'From November of 1964 until January of 1965 they moved the 325th Division of the North Vietnamese Army down to South Vietnam.' Rusk used this to show that North Vietnamese regular Army intervention was not 'an answer to the American escalation by bombing North Vietnam' but that in fact the North Vietnamese had been responsible for escalation.

Oddly, there was no mention of the 325th Division in the State Department's White Paper of February 17, 1965. It mentioned that one private of the 2nd Battalion of the 9th Regiment said his entire regiment had infiltrated in May 1964; another prisoner said that one Viet Cong battalion got 80 North Vietnamese replacements in February 1964. It seems remarkable that if the entire 325th Division had been infiltrated between November 1964 and January 1965, that this fact would not have been mentioned. Did the American officials not know of the whereabouts of the 325th Division in February 1965?

The Secretary of Defence, Robert McNamara, first mentioned it in April, 1965, when he said that evidence 'accumulated last month' confirmed the presence in the north-west sector of the '2nd Battalion of the 325th Division . . . of the order of 400 to 500 men.' By August the battalion had become a regiment. In that month, General Earle Wheeler, Chairman of the Joint Chiefs of Staff, said there was in South Vietnam 'at least one regiment of about 1,200 to 1,400 men, I think, of the 325th Division.' Late in 1965, Bernard Fall reported: 'As of the time I left a few days ago no Intelligence officer was ready to swear that the 325th as a unit had joined the battle in South Vietnam.' The Mansfield report of January 1966, following a visit to South Vietnam, reported that North Vietnamese soldiers in South Vietnam in December 1965 numbered about 14,000 and no mention was made of the 325th Division. But all the way through 1966, Rusk continued to claim that the whole of the 325th Division was in South Vietnam 'before we started the bombing'. On April 27 and May 17 he was pointed and specific in this latter claim. On June 16, 1966, Senator Mansfield went to some trouble to say: 'When the sharp increase in the American military effort began in early 1965, it was estimated that only about 400 North Vietnamese soldiers were among the enemy forces in the South which totalled about 140,000 at that time.' (See Congressional Record, Senate, June 16, 1966, pp. 12856-58.)

When Mansfield's statement was referred to McNamara, the Secretary of State for Defence made the reply: 'The figures attributed to Senator Mansfield are accurate and reflect the confirmed North Vietnamese force presence in the South at that time.' He also said he was well aware of the 'wide difference' between the Defence Department's 'confirmed figures' and 'other estimates'. But after all this, on August 25, 1966, in a joint television appearance of Rusk and McNamara, Rusk repeated his statement that the North Vietnamese had moved 'one of their divisions' into South Vietnam at the end of 1964 and the beginning of 1965. McNamara made no comment. And in Saigon in June 1966 I myself found it impossible to get any American official to be specific about North Vietnamese regular Army presence in South Vietnam and not one American official was prepared to name a Division or even part of one.

Cao Ky asserted that the bombing raids had not reduced the movement of men and supplies from North Vietnam (in fact, the probability is that they had increased); and he demanded a full scale invasion. A rising chorus of legislators, educators and writers in America attacked LBJ and his policies in Vietnam. America then urged Australia to send combat forces to Vietnam. On April 29 the Menzies Government responded. The first all-American heliborne raid of the war took place. American officials began to be optimistic again, and as US forces in Vietnam reached 45,000, 'VC' casualties, kills and defections, were claimed to be up one-third, and their weapon losses doubled. But still most of the captured weapons were American. The kill ratio was now said to be six to one, and some American officials claimed that the 'pendulum had swung', or that the 'VC will lose'. Now there were universal and confident claims that America 'couldn't lose'. The 'pendulum had swung', but it was not because of the bombing of North Vietnam. In fact there had been an increase of supplies from the North and the bombing had caused that increase. The 'pendulum had swung' because of American bombers and helicopters and communications in South Vietnam.

Despite the improvement in South Vietnam, the end of May found Johnson, according to Newsweek, in 'Chaos . . . osmosis and apprehension'. It was reported that 'all the manifestations of the so-called Korean war syndrome are gone. There is no longer the same fear of fighting a great war in Asia.' Why then the chaos, osmosis and apprehension? First of all, the Administration did not want a bigger ground war in South Vietnam. McNamara answered those who now saw that the American people could be induced to accept a ground war, by saying that he did not believe 'that American troops could be used to substitute for South Vietnamese troops on the ground.' Secondly, as early as the end of May 1965 the Administration had come to realise that the bombing had failed. It would not force the North Vietnamese to surrender or negotiate. It had not reduced the infiltrations and the supplies. It had increased them. What was to be done now?

It seems to have been about this time that the decision for Americans to go into full combat was made. In February, 1967, in a Department of State Bulletin, General Wheeler wrote: 'By the late spring of (1965) . . . the Viet Cong-North Vietnamese Army was threatening to overwhelm the armed forces of South Vietnam. That summer, at the request of the South Vietnamese, the United States made a decision to commit major forces to halt aggression.' But of course, the build-up of American forces for combat had taken place since March 1965. 'Early in 1965' was the time General Westmoreland chose as the point when he made a decision to build up American combat troops rapidly because 'we knew that the enemy hoped to deliver the *coup de grace* by launching a major summer offensive to cut the Republic of Vietnam in two with a drive across the central highlands to the sea.' McNamara always expressed the view that the decision to put American troops fully into combat was made 'in the spring of 1965.'

June 1965 was a bad month for the United States in Vietnam. There was growing evidence that the bombing raids were not breaking the morale of the North Vietnamese despite the increasing severity of their application to civilian targets. The monsoon rains, blinding for aircraft, allowed the 'Viet Cong' to 'emerge from their lairs and smash government positions with devastating effect'. The offensive began near Quang Ngai where it cost the government 500 casualties. This was described as 'one of the biggest victories the Communists had won since the withdrawal of the French'. 'Viet Cong' attacks followed in Darlac, Pleiku, Dongxeai and Phu Bon. These events made clear that Saigon Government forces could not win in the dry without air-power, or in the wet at all. Full-scale entry of American forces into combat was not far off, and the following week brought White House authorization for American troops to go into battle.[144] On the heels of these lost battles, Premier Pham Huy Quat, who was supposed to have invited Australia to send troops to Vietnam, as we have seen, resigned with his Chief of State, Phan Khac Suu, and South Vietnam was firmly in the hands of the generals. The bad military situation brought B-52 bombers from Guam to pour 550 tons of bombs on to a small target near Ben Cat for the loss of two bombers and no known enemy casualties. A search of the target area later revealed not one dead person, 'Viet Cong' or otherwise. The political situation was worse than the military one for there was no simple act like B-52 raids from Guam that could be brought to bear on it. Ky, Thieu, Thi, Khiem and several others were as divided from one another as they were from the enemy and each lived in constant expectation of death far less from the consequences of the enemy than from each other. Ky was selected as Premier because he had absolute control of the 10,000 man air-force—the most effective weapon to determine the balance between the warring generals and their tanks. July brought the resignation of Maxwell Taylor as Ambassador in Saigon and his replacement by Cabot Lodge.[145] It was obvious now that the main Administration drive was to get combat units to Vietnam as fast as they could be made available. One of the many illogical quirks of the war came again—at a time when Vietnamese policy was going military—a general was replaced as ambassador by a politician. The change was followed up by 'New and serious decisions' by President Johnson and his advisers. Plans were under way for a large build up of American forces in Vietnam and for their involvement in combat.[146] The President laid new stress on the 'aggression' against the expeditionary American forces 10,000 miles away in a foreign country, and it was hinted that there might be as many as 200,000 Americans in Vietnam to meet it by October.

McNamara returned from Vietnam at the end of the month with a report that in all departments the war had deteriorated during the past 15 months. Newsweek, more objective than most, was still able to write about Lyndon Baines Johnson under the heading of a 'Portrait of a Master. Lyndon the Magnificent? Lyndon the Good? Lyndon the Just? Improbable . . . Lyndon the Powerful? . . . Yes.' The magazine thought that he held more raw power than any other peacetime President and that he had wielded it 'with remarkable skill'. President Johnson was still the remarkably successful President, accessible, earthy, positive and above all successful. No one would have thought then that a second term for him was not a certainty.

The President's skill was obvious in the way he coupled the dramatic build up of American forces and their deployment in combat with a 'peace offensive'. 'Fifteen efforts have been made to start . . . peace discussions', the President told the world. He gave the impression that his Administration was prepared to agree anywhere, anytime, to peace 'without conditions' to which the sole barrier was the rejection by North Vietnam of all he had done. But as August passed the war became worse. With the 'Viet Cong' now in command of much of the areas outside the cities, plans were examined for American forces to control five big coastal enclaves and to venture out with helicopters and heavy fire-power. The last fortnight in August brought the first big American entry into combat—Operation Starlight near Chu Lai. Marines claimed 560 dead guerrillas, and perhaps 1,000, while their own casualties were stated at 50 killed and 165 wounded.[147] The battle gave ground for 'cautious optimism' about the war and a growing conviction that American 'regulars' could win against the 'Viet Cong'. Perhaps, the ground war could be made acceptable? And September was a month of 'peace'. The President set all his men upon the paths to find an end to the war. But it was not an end that could be *negotiated*. The only end he would accept was an end in which North Vietnam would terminate all contact with South Vietnam and the 'Viet Cong' would give up the fight in South Vietnam. For the President, 'negotiations' were talks about how these objectives could be agreed to and achieved, not about how North Vietnam and the 'Viet Cong' might have some say in what happened in South Vietnam. For those who believed that Communism could never be accepted this was a logical position, but it was a position inconsistent with 'negotiations'. It was consistent only with carrying on the war until it was won militarily. The Johnson position was not yet popular enough in America. But things were going well. The end of September found the Harris poll reporting about half those questioned agreeing with something like 'Now that we're there we should go all the way?' There had been a slight increase during the past three months in those who agreed that the war should be carried to the North, a reduction in those favouring negotiations, and an increase in those who wanted to 'hold the line'. The hawks were still flying well.

The latter part of 1965 saw an improvement in the government in Saigon. Ky, Thieu and Thi came to terms and Ky emerged as a political, civilian figure, photographed often with his new wife and several children. 'In my job,' said Ky 'I have to be a military man, a politician and a movie star.' As the year went on few could deny that he was being successful in all three roles. But military maps still showed that the 'Viet Cong' 'dominated or infiltrated' almost all the country in South Vietnam outside the cities. Bases were being held, GI's were pouring in and Ky was combining his triple roles with rising power and influence. The bombers, fighters and helicopters played a key role as the rain eased and the 'unofficial total of U.S. aircraft shot down' reached 400 for the year since February. The enemy claimed much more. The end of the year saw Army Chief of Staff General Harold K. Johnson claiming that 'the allies' have at least 'stopped losing' the war. The allies were engaged in planning how to win it, and to convince everyone that they wanted to stop *now* for negotiations. Time was needed and the main aim at the end of 1965 was to gain time. But the casualties rose and the pain and tragedy of the war increased.

Before going on with the story of the war into 1966, it is appropriate to examine the state of it at the end of 1965. By then the main lines of American action had been determined and these lines of action had been firmly implanted in the pattern of American nationalism, psychology and prestige. The President began the year with his State of the Union Message. His Message trailed from visions of the Great Society at home to the war in Vietnam. 'Tonight', he said, 'as so many nights before, the American nation is asked to sacrifice the blood of its children and the fruits of its labor for the love of its freedom.' The fight in Vietnam was unquestionably a 'fight for freedom' as had been all the other great experiences of American history. It was pure, just and vital. America sought nothing for herself. 'We fight' he said, 'for the principle of self determination, that the people of South Vietnam should be able to choose their own course.' This was not just a partial involvement, not just a matter of aiding the South Vietnamese in a war that was theirs. This was a great American moral responsibility. It was America's 'manifest destiny'. 'We will stay in Vietnam because a just nation cannot leave to the cruelty of its enemies a people who have staked their lives and independence on America's solemn pledge.'

The President's continuous talk about restraint, limited escala-tion and an ever readiness to stop the attack at the slightest sign of re-sponse from the enemy, could never be reconciled with his fundamen-tal assumptions or those of Dean Rusk and the main weight of Admin-istration advice. This was a war to which America was fully committed for freedom and one America must win as she had always won. In the final analysis, when the position had been put like this to the American people, most of them had fully accepted it. It was only a minority that was opposed. But the minority, the 'other America', was large, growing and influential.

Yet the Administration position did nothing to answer the vital questions about what was happening in Vietnam. To what extent was it a national revolution? How much did the people support it? Why was the Saigon government unable to bring about 'essential reforms'? What was the significance of 'aggression from the North'? What was the validity, if any, of the 'dominoes theory'? Would America sustain, at growing cost of men and money, a land war in Asia? All these ques-tions were avoided or clouded by the Administration's stand. Even its 'peace offensive' was reported to be adding to public confusion.

Basically, of course, the American administration recognised that the Viet Cong was strong and that an end to fighting now, or in the near future, would leave them strong enough to make impossible an anti-Communist South Vietnam, or even a neutralist one. Similarly the Administration recognised that if any negotiations were to be genuine, in that they gave the parties a say in what was to be done, then there could be no anti-Communist base in South Vietnam. Many influential voices in America were raised to show that unless the Administration was willing to recognise the National Liberation Front, then talk about negotiations was at best self-deception, and at worst hypocrisy. This proposition was fully implied in the position taken by Senators Mansfield and Fulbright from March 1966 and perhaps by a Senate majority by the end of the year. Unless the National Liberation Front was given some kind of recognition then the war would not only have to be carried on but would have to escalate—first in South Vietnam, and if it looked like being 'won' there, then into North Vietnam. And a 'win' there would not mean an end to the war but an extension into China.

The extent to which the Johnson Administration was committed to military victory became more and more apparent as 1966 went on. On June 11, 1966, the New York Times editorially wrote: 'This escalation (like those preceding it) is not likely to force Hanoi to sue for peace or negotiations (but suggests), that the United States now believes it must achieve its political aims in Vietnam through military "victory".'

The first significant event in 1966 was the bombing pause. It was supposed to be designed 'to coax Hanoi to the conference table or to put the onus for the resumption of raids on the Communists.' The strong probability, understood by the American Administration, was that Hanoi would not respond and yet there would be political and propaganda losses for them, and gains for the Administration, if they did not. There were signs that Hanoi was prepared to respond but with no alacrity or enthusiasm. But few people in America were happy at the abortiveness of the bombing pause. James Reston warned that '. . . we are just at the beginning of an enormous battle for Asia . . . (that would) go on for the rest of the century.' What he warned against was the belief that, a 'smashing victory' against people, shown by their refusal to negotiate to be guilty, could end it all. He wanted firmness but not escalation. It was then that General Gavan came in with his 'enclaves' plan and General Matthew Ridgway supported him. Gavan wanted the Administration to maintain 'enclaves', fortress areas along the coast, desist from bombing the North, and avoid pouring in more men, which could lead only to an ever widening and deepening war. A 'solution', according to Gavan, had to be sought through the United Nations or at a conference at Geneva.

And so the bombing pause came to an end. The last American bomb had fallen on North Vietnam the night before Christmas 1965 and for five weeks there had been no more. The pause was of great value to the Johnson Administration. It had convinced great numbers of people in America and in all her allied countries that Johnson was a great peace maker and that only Hanoi was to blame for the fact that the raids just had to start again. During the pause men and materials had continued to pour into South Vietnam from the North as much as the roads and the mountains would allow. But neither did the ships and aircraft stop bringing American men and materials into South Vietnam. The pause had its uses but it did not bring negotiations. And so the ritual went on. Councils of war continued in the White House. The President, Rusk and McNamara sat together at the side of the table and the same sort of conclusions were reached on the same sort of diplomatic, military and CIA advice. The President dismissed the plans of Gavan and Ridgway with the telling reply—'It's the first time I've heard it argued that a good defence is the best offence.' It was not defence that the President wanted. It was 'offence'. The President asserted that 'everything humanly possible' had been done to bring Hanoi to the conference table and now he had no alternative but unwillingly and with great sadness to send in the bombers again and carry on the war. Mansfield and Fulbright disagreed as they had done before, but now when the President played his trump card against them as he had done so often before, asking, 'What would you do, Mike?', the answer came back: 'Continue the bombing pause and recognise the Viet Cong as a legitimate party to peace negotiations.' To this, the President and Rusk made ambiguous and tendentious replies, which appeared to mean that the Viet Cong were free to come to the negotiations if they wanted to. But it is hardly likely that the Democratic Majority Leader in the Senate and Chairman of the Senate Foreign Relations Committee would be stressing recognition of the 'Viet Cong' if negotiation could have been achieved without recognition. And so the bombers were sent back to their task, and new plans to counter, with air and fire power, the 'main force' Viet Cong capability were put into operation. There was still no sign that the basic questions of strategy were being examined. How much more bombing would be needed? How much more air and fire power would have to be used to destroy the 'Viet Cong's' ability to interfere with that visionary anti-Communist South Vietnam so much desired by the Administration? What cost in American men and money would be likely to be involved? Would the American people accept what was probably necessary? Would the Press, the educators and the legislators go along with the kind of public relations job the Administration needed if a task of the kind probably involved was to be accepted? For a great and successful politician, Lyndon Baines Johnson was certainly leaving many obviously vital issues unexplored. It may have been obvious to some even then that he was undermining the second term he so much wanted. Republican spokesmen cheerfully took a prominent part in giving the President the kind of support he needed to proceed with his escalation, and manoeuvre himself out of office.

And so they all went to a war conference in Hawaii. The Administration went in great force to improvise a military program; the military rulers of South Vietnam went to be told who was really the boss; and the allied Heads of State, Prime Ministers and Premiers went to see the same thing for themselves. The essence of the Declaration of Honolulu was that America would never surrender the fight in South Vietnam but there must be a great program of social, economic and political reform. The essence of the Thieu-Ky position was that they would never deal with, or recognise the Communists, or the National Liberation Front. To this position the whole Johnson Administration gave its blessing and approval. Never before had so many American Secretaries (Ministers) and advisers been together outside America for any purpose. There were the Secretaries of State, of Defence, of Agriculture and of Health, Education and Welfare. There were the nation's top military 'brass' and experts in agronomy, forestry, fisheries, irrigation, education, health and, of course, there were the men from the State Department with their plans for a free and democratic election in South Vietnam better than any ever before held in a country at war. Westmoreland, apparently, won the President to the view that he had a better, stronger and more convincing case for a military victory (although it would perhaps take five years) than the case presented by McNamara, on whom the President had relied before. Ky, apparently, convinced the President that the failure of all his predecessors to bring about social, economic and political reforms, which, of course, were vital for victory, sprang from the fact that they were lesser men than he. He could 'root out the Viet Cong from the rural areas and root ourselves in.' Everyone went away terribly impressed by Westmoreland and Ky. They were certainly a very impressive pair. The President is said to have lapsed 'into Texas patois'. 'The plans are fine' he said, 'but we want results. We want to see those coonskins nailed to the wall.' Few men in the whole sorry story of the American war in Vietnam could have been more convincing than Westmoreland and Ky. They were unquestionably the men 'to nail coonskins to the wall.'

What was the significance of these conferences in 1966? Decisions made at the conferences reversed the roles of the Americans and South Vietnamese forces in the war. The Americans were now openly admitted to be the force that was to do the fighting and the South Vietnamese were to look after pacification and guarding the cities. Remarkably enough that was what Ky had proposed a year before as evidence of the strength and durability of his fighting men and their acceptability 'as a revolutionary force' to the people of South Vietnam. The South Vietnamese Defence Minister was frank and proud of the change. He said 'The entire Vietnamese Army will switch to a pacification role in 1967 and leave major fighting to American troops.' This did not appear to worry the long line made up of Presidents, Secretaries of State, Generals and backroom computer boys who had warned against 'a white man's war against Asians', against 'putting American troops into a land war in Asia', and against 'making American boys do what Asian boys should be doing'. These very things were now to be done. And yet the conference at Manila was a great triumph. There was a real feeling the 'coonskins' would now soon go up on the wall. Moreover, it was not just a matter of reversing the military roles. There was to be a 'Great Society' for South Vietnam too. 'We were going to rebuild the whole political, social and economic structure of this country' said Cabot Lodge. 'Until we do this there can be no military victory,' he warned. So this line, too, had changed. Earlier, military security had been a first consideration and then political stability could be won. Now military security was supposed to depend on non-military factors. But what would the Saigon generals say about

this political, social and economic revolution? What would happen to
their power and the sources of it?

All these needed reforms had failed because those in power in
Saigon were members of, or closely associated with, mandarin families
who owned land and property which they had no intention of giving
up. Others would tenaciously cling to positions that allowed them
to make money legitimately or by corruption. Neil Sheehan, New
York Times Magazine, October 9, 1966, wrote what many knew to be
true: 'In Vietnam, only the Communists represent revolution and
social change, for better or worse according to a man's politics. The
Communist's party is the only truly national organisation that per-
meates both North and South Vietnam.' I. F. Stone, quoted in U.S.
News and World Report, December 5, 1966: 'The guerrillas' success
on the past year has been almost astonishing.' Why? The peasants
'were suffering more than before at the hands of the Communists',
but 'not only is the government security lacking, but Saigon's reform
program, so vital to the aspirations of peasants, has never really been
put in motion. In the secure areas, tenant farmers—that means 70
per cent of all farmers in the Delta—still are forced to pay up to 50
per cent and more of their rice crops to absentee landlords. . . Americans here insist that no progress will be made so long as the men at the
top in Saigon are members of mandarin families, or allied with families which have vested interests in land that they have no intention of
relinquishing.' Robert Sherwood in Life, January 27, 1967, wrote the
same theme: 'We find ourselves supporting a government of mandarins
with little basis of popular support, fighting for an army that has little
inclination to do its own fighting.' But it had to go on. Even John
Mecklin in his *Mission in Torment*, who saw through it all, was sure
'we have to go until sooner or later the Vietnamese themselves will
evolve a healthy, viable government which can survive without foreign
help.'

Towards the end of 1966, President Johnson, who earlier had
resisted the proposal, agreed to transfer control of the pacification
program to the American military command. Yet two and a half years
later, Vice-President Cao Ky would claim that the pacification program had failed because of corruption. But the decisions of the
Manila Conference meant the full and complete militarisation of the
war. This had come at a time when the Declaration of Honolulu
pledged the 'eradication of social injustice': a 'true democracy' and a
'true social revolution'. But this was not just the 'Johnson doctrine'
for South Vietnam. Vice-President Humphrey, ever the social demo-
crat, pledged the United States 'to defeat aggression, to defeat social
misery, to build viable, free political institutions and to achieve peace.'
These flights of fancy paid little regard to the years and aspirations
and plans that had already ended in tragic failure. They paid little

regard to the cost of $25,000 million a year for one small area of 16 million people. How much would it cost to apply Humphrey's version of the 'Johnson doctrine' to the whole area of non-Communist Asia? But Richard Nixon had no doubts or hesitations either. 'We can never negotiate, surrender, retreat, neutralise or partition Vietnam' he said. The only course for him was 'to end the war by winning it in South Vietnam.' For some indiscernible reasons Manila, in the middle of 1966, had produced a massive euphoria and confidence around the Administration.

But there was to be no great or sudden escalation. It was all going to be very gradual. The bombing of Hanoi and Haiphong could not yet be expected. A sudden and vast increase in American forces and firepower could not be expected. The President had his political problems too. The President liked both Ky and Thieu at once and they hit it off very well but the Vietnamese were made to understand that they had to do very much better. Ky wasn't too happy about the prospects of a Great Society in South Vietnam but it was reported that he had a 'real sense of dedication' and that he was not just an 'anti-Communist with a bank account in Geneva'. But even if Ky did possess a strong drive for reform, February 1966 was far too late. The time for reforms in South Vietnam had been from 1955 under Diem. Probably 1962, certainly 1963, was too late. Reform in 1966 was hopeless from the start. Reform would have been possible for some years after 1955 and might have prevented effectively the rise of the 'Viet Cong' and the NLF. But by 1963, or perhaps earlier, and certainly by 1966, no matter how sincere were Saigon government leaders about reform, the strength and interests of the 'Viet Cong' was great enough to block Saigon. None the less, in 1966 President Johnson sent them away all with no room for doubt—everything depended upon rural cadres (land reform?), schools, rice and medicine. 'I'm going to keep track' he warned them.

Even then, Honolulu did not seem to go deeply into reform. It seems to have stressed 'cadres', more rice, schools and medical posts. But these were not really reform. They did not touch on how the land was owned or how the rents and interest were charged. They did not touch on how the rice was bought and traded, or how the officials were put into office. The Honolulu program, as usual, seems to have been rather a plan to make the status quo more acceptable without really changing it. How could it be really changed without the 'Communists' assuming a role in the changed situation? Nowhere among the American advisers did there seem to be anyone who had any awareness of how societies must adapt if their economic processes are to change. They do not seem to have studied economic and political history or, if they had, they do not seem to have remembered what they had learned. They all appeared to be 'technical' men who believed that the computer made obsolete all those processes that had operated in history up to then. Rostow's views on economic growth had been considered an answer to Karl Marx. Could his plans be an answer to the Viet Cong?

As the Honolulu conference closed, the Senate Foreign Relations Committee opened its hearing on Vietnam policy[148] and veteran historian and diplomat George Kennan told it: 'Eventually there must be some sort of political compromise between the various factions involved in South Vietnam.' General Maxwell Taylor's 'formula' for the war given to the Committee, was summed up to mean 'essentially more of the same thing' so that the enemy would continue to suffer the 'heavy toll' of casualties. Taylor predicted: 'They will theoretically run out of troops by the end of 1966.' Fulbright said it seemed to him that the Administration was demanding 'unconditional surrender', and unless there was a change of aim it was headed for 'unlimited war'. General Taylor made it clear that if it meant 'compromising the freedom of 15 million South Vietnamese', he would accept a description of his idea of the American commitment as one 'that we use unlimited means, even if it means going into China or anywhere else, whatever that takes'. And so the debate went on, but President Johnson began to slip in the opinion polls. The year 1966 did not look as good as 1965.

But the year had registered clearly the significant change in American policy and attitude that was now openly admitted. In 1956, when French and British forces attacked Egypt at the Suez Canal, President Eisenhower told the world: 'We do not accept the use of force as a wise or proper instrument for the settlement of international disputes'. A day or so later, John Foster Dulles spoke for America: 'If we are to agree that the existence of injustices in the world means that the principle of renunciation of force is no longer respected and that there still exists the right wherever a nation feels itself subject to injustice to resort to force . . . then we would have, I fear, torn the charter (U.N.) into shreds and the world would again be a world of anarchy.'

Truman, Eisenhower, Acheson and Dulles, of course, had laid the foundations of the American policy of using force to achieve her ends. Kennedy and Johnson had done no more than logically and carefully carry it into effect. Of course, during 1965, Johnson and Rusk argued they were using force not because of any injustice to America, but because of injustice to the 'free people of South Vietnam'. America was acting in a completely unselfish way. The manifest destiny of America unavoidably involved aid to the weak all over the world who were the object of injustice. Nevertheless American policy now involved not only the use of force but depended entirely upon it. The year 1965 had decided and established that. The only question for the year 1966 was—would it be effective and successful in Vietnam? The future of President Johnson, if not the whole new American doctrine depended on the result. The year 1966 began with an official statement of casualties for 1965, American dead totalled 1,350, wounded and missing 5,448. South Vietnamese dead totalled 11,100, and 30,000 wounded and missing. The American official figure for 'Viet Cong' dead was 34,585 and 5,746 captured.[149]

January 9 saw what was described as the 'largest offensive of the war' by U.S., Australian and New Zealand forces in Hobo Forest in the 'Iron Triangle'. For the first time the operation had been kept secret from the South Vietnamese command, but operations began several days before with continuous high level B52 bombing, followed by napalm, and then the troops went in. Casualties at first from snipers were light and 21 guerrillas were killed. A 'vast tunnel system' was discovered and chemicals and gases were used. American casualties for the week were 43 killed and 202 injured, and by then it was claimed that 107 guerrillas had been killed; one Australian was dead and six others in hospital as a result of non-toxic gas and smoke used in the tunnels. The operation was completed without contact with any 'large enemy force'. The 'Iron Triangle' cut and churned up like the surface of the moon went back to the jungle and the 'Viet Cong'.

'Foreseeable war costs' were stated to be $10,300 million in the President's Budget message for the fiscal year 1967—about half of what they turned out to be.[150] U Thant continued to emphasise there could be no end to this unless the bombing of North Vietnam ceased and unless 'all elements of the South Vietnamese people were represented in the post-war government.'[151] Rusk announced his rejection of the 'Thant proposal' saying that 'the role of the National Liberation Front must be decided in free elections.'[152] Rusk also 'hoped' that 'friendly European powers would offer combat troops'.[153]

On January 26, Johnson, Rusk and McNamara, backed by Humphrey, Harriman, Ball, Wheeler, Taylor and Bundy, 'briefed' Congress leaders and left the impression that the year's 'peace drive' and 'bombing halt' had come to an end. Bombing would now be extended and intensified and American forces would take over the main attack role in South Vietnam. Fulbright, Kennedy and many other Congress leaders urged that the bombing halt be continued, but the argument that it would 'endanger American troops' prevailed against them. Congress dealt with the appropriation for Vietnam in this atmosphere. It was not, the Administration asserted, 'an open ended objective' but only a 'graduated response' controlled by McNamara, Rostow, Bundy and their computers. Congress was not able to make clear the view of about 20 Senators and 78 members of the House that their support of the Bill did not mean endorsement of a larger war, and Gruening and Morse voted against it. On January 31, the bombing of North Vietnam was resumed. The Soviet Union and China argued about assistance to Vietnam. The Soviet said China was obstructing their arms and equipment on the way to Vietnam. China answered that the shipments had begun only after Kosygin had failed in February 1965 to intimidate the government of Hanoi into submission to the imperialists, and that China provided special trains without ever charging transit fees. Hanoi stated they would maintain 'close ties' with China despite the 'aid pact' with the Soviet Union.

It is worth while, at this point, to look a little more closely at the roles of China and the Soviet Union in relation to Vietnam. It would be unwise to generalise from this about what these countries would do elsewhere. But their behaviour towards Vietnam has marked relevance. Only among the most extreme anti-Communists does the assumption remain that Communism is monolithic, possessing a force originating in Moscow, or in some other single place, and planned and directed to overcome the world. But the connection between South Vietnam and North Vietnam, and of North Vietnam and China, and China and the Soviet Union is a critical factor in the war in Vietnam. This is because a connection between these countries has been made by the United States the basic justification for intervention in Vietnam. But it is far from clear what, to American officials, this connection really is. In February 1966, in justifying the bombing of North Vietnam, Dean Rusk said that 'peace would come in almost a matter of hours if North Vietnam were prepared to call off aggression in the South.' Therefore, North Vietnam had to be bombed. But Rusk immediately went on to say that 'Peking even more than Hanoi has blocked the path to the conference table.' But China was not to be bombed.

We have heard from important men like General Maxwell Taylor that 'Communist China is fighting a war (in Vietnam) by proxy', and from others like Cao Ky that war between the 'free world' and China is 'inevitable' and 'it's better to face them right now than in five or 10 years.' For most of these spokesmen however, the Soviet Union seems to have been on the side of peace. Rusk has usually dismissed the Soviet influence as 'limited'. The State Department view is that China is dedicated to 'wars of national liberation' which is an 'essential element of (their) expansionist policy.' This technique had been adopted by Communist China, put into operation in Vietnam, and if it was allowed to succeed in Vietnam, 'we would be confirming Peking's contention that militant revolutionary struggle is a more productive Communist path than Moscow's doctrine of peaceful co-existence.' So much for the prevailing American theory—China was responsible for the war in Vietnam; Hanoi 'created' the NLF, while both were creations of Peking. The Soviet Union, on the other hand, was in favour of 'peaceful co-existence' and did not help to incite the war as China did. But as the war went on, two things happened. The first was that

American accusations against Hanoi increased, and against China diminished. The second was that North Vietnam's arms, equipment and potential (not so much the NLF) became more and more dependent on the Soviet Union and less on China. Rusk and the State Department then shifted to the view that Hanoi was the 'instrument of aggression', but 'the doctrine of aggression is from Peking'. Although it was known that a substantial aid pact between North Vietnam and the Soviet Union had been signed in 1965 and that under it the Soviet Union supplied jet fighters, surface to air missiles, ground missiles, artillery and mortars as well as a wide range of other 'hardware', the Soviet Union, to the State Department, was not the real enemy but a nation that believed in 'peaceful co-existence'. We needed the Soviet influence for peace in Vietnam. We should help their policy to succeed by making sure we did not negotiate at all but thoroughly defeat the 'war of national liberation' in Vietnam for which China was responsible, and would export to all peasant countries, until finally the world's peasants would be able to surround and overthrow Washington, New York and every other great industrial centre, just as they now threatened to overthrow Saigon and Hue. How does this view of the relations between Hanoi, Peking and Moscow measure up to the facts?

We have noticed that the Vietnamese have a deep historical antipathy towards the Chinese. Not only did this feeling remain effective in stultifying 'friendship with China' campaigns in North Vietnam but North Vietnamese attempts to follow Chinese methods proved wrong and unpopular. In his book *Communism in North Vietnam,* P. J. Honey, who is never slow to underestimate the power and integration of the Communist threat, says, 'The end of the North Vietnamese-Chinese honeymoon dates from 1957.' Ho Chi Minh made no attempt to follow China in the 'Great Leap Forward' and the creation of communes, and Vietnam has had no 'Cultural Revolution'. Honey believes that the 'dominant wing' in Hanoi swung with Ho Chi Minh to Moscow in 1960, and since then Hanoi has continued to manoeuvre between the two great Communist powers without ever giving up the historic Vietnamese policy which consists, as Honey puts it, of 'paying lip service to Chinese pretensions provided they (the Vietnamese) themselves retained the reins of power in Vietnam.' It is also clear that Ho and Giap have never considered themselves to be inferior to Mao, either as Communists or in their knowledge and understanding of revolutionary war. The generalised three-phase war put forward by Mao was fully accepted by Giap and was, in general, sound enough to fit the situation in Vietnam, but Giap sometimes chose to go contrary to Mao, and was sometimes compelled to do so, as we have seen, as a result of losses when he followed Mao too dogmatically.

How could Ho consider himself an appendage of Mao? In 1923 when Mao had not yet been heard of, Ho was one of the 158 delegates to the First International Peasants' Congress in Moscow, and in 1924 a delegate in Moscow to the Fifth Congress of the Comintern. When Ho was trying to teach the top international Communist leaders that the peasants were the key to revolution in colonial countries, and that this was a vital factor in the revolution in advanced capitalist countries, Mao at the same time could claim no more than that he was beginning to devote himself to the organisation of the peasantry in Hunan province. Ho has never been anti-Chinese as Giap has been, he has always recognised the eminence of Mao as a Communist theoretician and leader, but this has never diminished his confidence in the Vietnamese experience and achievement. Against this background of relationships the American bombing of North Vietnam may have had special significance.

On February 6, 1965, Kosygin arrived in Hanoi. It is now generally believed his visit was to encourage or pursuade Hanoi to agree to negotiations as a way to secure the independence of Vietnam. On February 7, American aircraft bombed North Vietnam. Instead now of talking about negotiations, Kosygin opened discussions which led to the 1965 aid agreement between the Soviet and North Vietnam. There could be no question now for the world Communist movement: aid for Vietnam had become a top priority. The words of praise and solidarity of the past would have to give way to something much more solid. As the strategists of the State Department had foreseen, the attack on a socialist State did not bring China and the Soviet Union together, and it did reduce the appeal and influence of China but not in the way they had expected. If Hanoi was to defend herself against American air attack, she needed the weapons and technical power she could get only from the Soviet Union. Hence, while the bombing continued to mount the significance of Soviet aid grew, and with it Soviet influence. China had to stand more and more on the sidelines. Even the aggregate of aid changed as a result. It has been estimated that total Chinese aid to North Vietnam in 1960 and 1961 was about $500 million, most of it non-military, while that from the Soviet Union and European countries was about $200 million, much more of it military. American figures in 1968 were that since 1953, when it began, Russia had supplied North Vietnam with more than $600 million in military aid, and of that total about $475 million has been since August 1964. American figures in 1968 put Chinese military aid since 1953 at $150 million with about $90 million since August 1964. Soviet military aid, according to American sources, was $100 million before 1964, $25 million in 1964, $200 million to $225 million in 1965, and $200 million in 1966. For China the figures are about $35 million in 1965 and $50 million in 1966. Most of the Chinese aid was in mortars and rifles mainly appropriate for use in the South, while most of the Soviet aid was in aircraft, missiles and artillery suitable for defence of North

Vietnam. It is generally believed that Soviet aid to Vietnam declined considerably between 1962 and 1964 while Chinese aid increased. Hence the great increase in Soviet aid, and its dominance over that of China after 1964, became even more meaningful.

During 1964 there was evidence that China was displeased by the trend of the war in Vietnam and by the increasing influence of the Soviet Union. China met the situation, as we have seen, by allegations that the Soviet had been playing the game of the American imperialists, that Kosygin had gone to Hanoi to press the government to surrender, but now at last had been forced to aid the heroic struggle in Vietnam, and China was carrying Soviet supplies without even charging freight. However it appears that China refused to grant the Russians an air corridor through to Vietnam. But it was in this pattern of events that the Chinese Minister of National Defence, Lin Piao, published on September 3, 1965 his famous article in the People's Daily in Peking. Now, was not this the blue-print, the Chinese Mein Kampf, setting out how China would incite and empower the world revolution for the overthrow of Western civilisation? This was how the State Department received and interpreted the article, which was manna from heaven for anti-Communists all over the world. Here was something that more than confirmed their most treasured fears. Here was a myth which was an exact corollary of their own myth. Speaking on October 31, no doubt after the best State Department briefing, Averell Harriman saw the 'portentous menace of Lin Piao's 18,000 words'. 'It spells out in unmistakable clarity and detail', he said, 'the Communist doctrine of world revolution. Its significance is similar to that of Mein Kampf. It states unequivocally what the intentions of the Chinese are, what sort of world they want, and how that world is to be created.' What was the intention and what was the plan?

Vietnam was the 'focus' of everything. The Chinese people would do everything in their power to support the Vietnamese people until every one of the American aggressors was driven into the sea. This would then prove that the people in every country who were denied their freedom by American imperialism would be able to rise and throw out the Americans. Finally, this would mean that American capitalism would be overthrown, and with the leadership of the Chinese people and their great Communist Party, the world revolution would triumph. Mr. Harriman made it clear that he did not like the Russians either, but they were much to be preferred to their Chinese rivals. Perhaps Mr. Harriman had not remembered that it was the *Russians who had put missiles on Cuba,* and perhaps he had not yet learned that *Russian aid to Vietnam had increased about eight times* in the year before he spoke, while there had been *no proven increase in Chinese aid.* The probability is that the timing of Lin Piao's statement and its meaning had a relevance quite different from that taken by the State Department, Mr. Harriman and most anti-Communists around the world.

Lin Piao's statement was a result of the trend in the Vietnam war and in the Soviet role in respect to it. Those who have seen the significance of the bombing in 1965, the need of Vietnam for modern weapons, the sole ability of the Soviet among Communist countries to supply them, the vast increase in Soviet supply of these weapons to Vietnam and the consequent increase in Soviet influence in Vietnam, have always emphasised a particular paragraph which follows Lin Piao's revolutionary rhetoric. The paragraph is:

'In order to make a revolution and fight a people's war and be victorious, it is imperative to adhere to the policy of self-reliance, rely on the strength of the masses in one's own country and prepare to carry on the fight independently even when all material aid from outside is cut off. If one does not operate by one's own efforts, does not independently ponder and solve the problems of the revolution in one's own country and does not rely on the strength of the masses, but leans wholly on foreign aid—even though this be aid from socialist countries which persist in revolution—no victory can be won.'

Lin Piao here gave emphasis to what we would expect from any one who knew the requirements of successful revolution and the history of the war in Vietnam—self-reliance . . . on the strength of the masses . . . operate by one's own efforts . . . independently ponder and solve problems of the revolution in one's own country. Surely this does not sound like a plan for revolution to begin in Peking or Moscow and spread relentlessly by 'aggression' from one country to another irrespective of the conditions in the country. It does not sound like the advice of a man who expected revolutionaries in other countries to accept doctrines from Peking or Moscow. But more than anything else there are other words of special significance. Why did Lin Piao warn against revolutions which lean 'wholly on foreign aid—even though this aid be from *socialist* countries.' Was it not a warning to the Vietnamese that they were wrong in leaning so much on aid from the Soviet Union since 1964? Is it not likely that this was the reason why the Lin Piao statement was made in September 1965 and that this was its main purpose? I do not propose here to make a thorough examination of the Chinese theory of world revolution, but the above shows how superficial and purely propagandist is the view of the State Department and Mr. Harriman—and also many commentators in Australia—on the Lin Piao doctrine.

I have been concerned here to show that there is not a simple, monolithic Communist view of the war in Vietnam and that assumptions of the links between the NLF, Hanoi, Peking and Moscow are wrong and misleading. So misleading were they in this instance, that America's bombing of North Vietnam—'bush Machiavellism', as one commentator called it—had the effect of increasing aid for Vietnam from a modern, powerful Communist State, the Soviet Union, which earlier had been very much dragging its feet, instead of from a poorer one unable to supply much of the 'hardware' the North Vietnamese needed to withstand what for the Americans was an attack calculated to win the war. At any rate it appears that Chinese-North Vietnamese relations have tended to be much less close in recent years, while those of the Soviet Union and North Vietnam have become closer. But it was the Chinese who urged Hanoi towards a defensive strategy, because of Chinese fears that if the war escalated China would be attacked. The Soviet Union might not have been too alarmed at an escalation of the war although it is going much too far to suggest they would have found it acceptable. This analysis suggests that there is a good deal of myth in the argument that China is the real enemy in Vietnam and the Soviet Union is on the side of peace. The truth is that the real enemy is first the NLF, supported mainly by a large number of people of South Vietnam, and then the government of North Vietnam, supported doubtless by a large number of the people of North Vietnam. Once that is realised, of course, much of the justification for the intervention in the war by America and her unthinking allies disappears. But the war went on.

On January 21, 1966, McNamara announced that America had lost 351 planes and helicopters in 1965, but expected higher losses in 1966. January 28 saw the beginning of Operation Masher in Binh Dinh province and the battle in North and South was re-joined. North Vietnamese were found to be 'among those fighting in Binh Dinh'.[154] Four 'major U.S. operations' and 42 South Vietnamese 'operations' were now under way. Thanat Khoman, Thai Foreign Minister, criticised the Mansfield Mission for absolving Cambodia of aiding the 'Viet Cong'. The troops in Operation Masher 'failed to make contact with the enemy', following an earlier report that 'enemy casualties were heavy', and at the end '500 Communists' were claimed killed and 106 captured in the operation. At the end of January 1966, 9 to 11 North Vietnamese regiments of 1,800 men each were 'identified in South Vietnam'. American military leaders were disappointed with the results of B52 strikes and, in operations of the 'Operation Masher' type, in their failure to reach 'large enemy units'. As a result the re-designed 'Operation White Wing' was sent into Anlao valley but found it almost deserted as the 'Communists' had in this case 'warned the peasants to flee'.[155]

On February 15, New York Times reports saw 'South Vietnamese peasants as the main victims of the allied offensive', and noted the 'destruction, killing and wounding of civilians in about 16 peasant hamlets'. There is no doubt that many of these civilian casualties were officially included as 'Communists' or 'Viet Cong'.[156]

At about the same time, Japanese Premier Sato deplored American bombing of North Vietnam and tactics in South Vietnam and 'hinted' that Japan may call for another pause. Vice-President Humphrey and British Prime Minister Wilson defended American recommencement of the bombing. This was the war story at the beginning of this critical year. But political events overshadowed military action in the news. In Saigon, Lieutenant General Nguyen Chan Thi was dismissed and Buddhists and students in Saigon, Hue and Da Nang began strikes and demonstrations. Again it was very much a case of Buddhist versus Catholic, with Thi and Thieu representing the conflict at the top. It seems that Ky came down on the Thieu-Catholic side and emerged determined to deal with the Buddhists and students. There were reports of 'Turmoil in Vietnam: War within a War' and the battle against the Buddhists and students went on. Events were repeating themselves—a year before it had been made clear to Khanh that he personally had American backing and he then reached for dictatorial powers. This had led to his overthrow. Ky had been embraced by Johnson at Honolulu. Would he now over-reach himself? But the rioting and demonstrations spread to so many towns and cities and created so much of a threat that it seemed it was the Buddhists and students who over-reached themselves this time, and Ky and Thieu had full American backing when they finally broke the revolt.

The final blows at political dissent were linked to large scale American military action. 'Operation Lincoln' involved thousands of American troops, helicopters and tanks in sweeps through the highlands west of Pleiku. Incoming American ship cargoes running at the rate of 125,000 tons a month a year ago were now around 750,000 tons a month, and the material was able to be used in main force actions the 'Viet Cong' could never equal. But February 17 saw official reports that 40 per cent of all cargo and 36 per cent of all postal supplies unloaded in South Vietnamese ports were stolen by the 'Viet Cong'.[157] A year before America had 29,000 troops in Vietnam; now it had 215,000. A year before the Air Force and Navy were just starting to take part in the war; now they could use 700 combat planes and 1,600 helicopters. The nature of the war had changed but the tactics of the 'Viet Cong' had not. Having reached the stage and capability for 'main force' action there could be little doubt their leaders would be slow to admit that different and lower level strategy was necessary, and it appears that while 'Viet Cong' tactics were to avoid clashes, their strategy was not to change till the campaign leading to the Tet offensive of 1968, nearly two years later. In the meantime many thousands of Vietnamese would die as the result of 'main force' clashes. Certainly

Administration confidence was maintained in American military operations, but the post-Honolulu euphoria very largely disappeared, with the realisation that the forces of the Saigon government, divided and in conflict, were needed merely to keep itself in power against its own political opposition. Not only this but the official theory that the Saigon government was supported by its own people in South Vietnam and attacked only by aggressors from North Vietnam lost much of its credibility. The Administration answer was simple—the disorders were a sign of political maturity and the reality of democracy in South Vietnam. There was no room for doubt anyway—even if a coup brought in a government that asked America to leave it would soon be followed by another one that brought a government that asked America to stay.

And the main force sweeps continued. 'Davy Crockett' and 'Operation Birmingham' came in May, the latter involving 15,000 American and Vietnamese troops, the largest number in any one action so far, and, for the first time, American weekly casualties exceeded the South Vietnamese. But the popularity of Ky did not grow. He was accused of dictating, and then of equivocating, and finally of bungling. It had been implied that he would leave office while a constitution was being drawn up by an Assembly but then he told them all he planned to stay in office at least until this time the following year. He finally emerged the winner in his contest with the Buddhists and just as much, it appeared, with his military rivals. By mid-1966 Nguyen Cao Ky was at the height of his career. His success brought South Vietnamese troops back into action, and B52s based in Guam made as many as three raids a day and fighter bombers from Thailand, South Vietnam and the American fleet continued to pound North Vietnam, and even had to limit raids because they ran out of bombs.

Ky had handled South Vietnamese politics in the first half of 1966 with considerable skill. At first he opposed the very idea of elections, then he appeared unwilling to accept them, finally he embraced the idea with enthusiasm when he learned how well they could be planned. At first Buddhist and other leaders opposed elections equally as much because they were seen to involve no effective choice. Then even the most militant Buddhist leaders, believing they could win a majority in the Senate and House, appeared to accept them, until finally, convinced again that they involved no effective choice, they boycotted them. But this equivocation allowed the Ky-Thieu forces not only to capture control of Hue and Da Nang by military means but to win for the election greater credibility and repute. The appeal of Thic Tri Quang, militant Buddhist leader, to President Johnson on May 17 to intervene against Ky fell on deaf ears—Tri Quang and his supporters now commanded no battalions. Five days later Ky was able to describe Tri Quang as a Communist. Tri Quang could do no more than blame Johnson for those Buddhists who had died to no purpose. But American casualties for the week at 966 were a record for the war, and 246 U.S. planes had been lost over North Vietnam since February 1965. It was Johnson not Ky who had to make a plea to his people to 'unite behind him'.

Late June brought U.S. bomb strikes against 'oil and gasoline storage tanks on the outskirts of Hanoi and Haiphong', which 'cut supplies by 50 per cent'. U Thant described the war as 'one of the most barbarous in history' and the situation as 'very urgent and critical'. British Prime Minister Wilson, while generally supporting U.S. policy, regretted the bombing of Hanoi. Canadian Prime Minister Pearson, too, regretted the bombing. U.S. bombs continued to fall on the 'fuel tanks' but soon extended to 'radar sites', 'barracks' and 'transport centres'. Cao Ky hailed the bomb strikes and claimed they would soon end the war. General Westmoreland said 'the allies were winning the war'.

For three years the world talked about the bombing of North Vietnam and when it did it spoke of the number of 'sorties' or the tonnage of bombs—but what did bombing North Vietnam mean? Normally each day between 100 and 500 aircraft were sent to bomb North Vietnam. They were supposed to bomb bridges, roads, railways, warehouses, ships, trucks, marshalling yards, power stations and industrial plants in a densely populated country. They were ordered not to hit civilians but how could they miss them? What meaning could the President's safeguard have had: 'American targets in North Vietnam are steel and concrete not human lives.' Harrison Salisbury of the New York Times reported: 'Almost every rural agricultural community in the area (where he was) had been hit at one time or another. One of the worst was an attack on the village of Kien Tiong in which 72 people were killed and 46 wounded. But attacks were not confined to villages. Individual peasants working in the fields or threshing in the courtyards had been straffed. There were the thousands of tons of bombs that fell on the countryside, on the fields on the villages, on the peasant huts, on the peasants in the fields and on the roads.' But it must never be forgotten that whatever the death and destruction in North Vietnam, it was far worse in the South. Five times as many bombs were dropped on the South as on the North and there was no anti-aircraft weapon able to reach the bombers and no aircraft to send up after them. Never has there been such a one-sided war. The middle of 1966 witnessed contradictions and confusions one on top of another.

China claimed that the bombing raids had freed them 'from any bounds or restrictions in helping North Vietnam', but the Chinese statement 'reinforced the Administration's (U.S.) conviction that China would not intervene'. President Johnson 'stressed' that the war 'may last a long time', but Ky forecast the early collapse of North Vietnam. The Administration 'quietly' started another 'major expansion' of the armed forces in Vietnam, now at 280,000 and 'expected' to be 375,000 by the end of the year. Ky, the Buddhist, backed by South Vietnam's Catholics and the United States, scorned his Buddhist opponents and called for a confrontation now with China rather than later. But Senator Mansfield thought it necessary on July 27 to call on the Administration to dissociate itself from proposals to invade North Vietnam. Forty-four Democrats and three Republicans in Congress backed Mansfield. Ngo Dinh Nhu, in Paris, defended the Communists as 'nationalists seeking justice'. She said the war would expand and destroy Vietnam, that her husband, in 1963, recognising this, had made 'secret contacts' with North Vietnam, and was about to sign a 'peace treaty' when the United States had launched a *coup d'etat* and had him murdered.[158]

Three days later, House of Representatives members had a 'rough session' with Rusk on why the Administration did not 'move towards with the National Liberation Front'. The same week saw a record seven U.S. planes 'downed near Hanoi and Haiphong' bringing the total to 333. Secretary of State Rusk did not 'exclude the possibility of a ground troops invasion of North Vietnam'.[159] 'Thousands' demonstrated in many places in the United States against the war. A United States Military Command study found that 'North Vietnam can continue indefinitely to absorb casualties in South Vietnam at the present rate'. Hanoi, it was claimed, had 40,000 troops in South Vietnam and could 'maintain that level' despite everything 'the allies' could do. 'The allies' now had 929,000 troops in South Vietnam —U.S. 286,000, South Vietnamese 614,000, and others 29,000—the Viet Cong was 'extensively recruiting' and no change in the balance of strength could be anticipated.[160] On August 25, U.S. planes dropped napalm on the U.S. 1st Division near Phulai and killed or wounded more than 20. General Duprey absolved the Air Force of blame and said he would ask for strikes again in similar circumstances. August brought a North Vietnam accusation that the U.S. had bombed civilian homes, schools, hospitals and churches as well as dikes and irrigation works. There was an immediate and complete American denial.[161] August 25 saw also a record 146 raids on 'storage areas and transportation centres' in North Vietnam. August saw also U.S. military commanders in South Vietnam ordered to 'minimise casualties to civilians to the maximum extent possible'. A similar order of September 1965 was 'noted' and 'doubt' was expressed by the New York Times and others of the 'value of official policy that is widely ignored.'[162]

In October, U.S. casualties for several weeks in succession were twice those of South Vietnam—600 to 700 dead each week. October also saw the House of Representatives Government Operations Committee reporting 'unconscionable mismanagement of the U.S. aid program' which made it a 'device for graft, corruption, black marketing and source of supply for the Viet Cong'. The 1966 aid program was $420 million in consumer goods alone. October, too, saw President Johnson on a visit to Hawaii, South Vietnam and Australia. In Hawaii, the President, his generals, Premiers and Prime Ministers, pledged that their troops would be out of South Vietnam within six months of North Vietnam disengaging itself from the war and issued a statement of 'goals and principles'. At Camranh Bay, the President told his troops that the war was a 'contest as far reaching and as vital as any we have ever engaged in.' In Canberra, just before an election, the President referred to the Australian Prime Minister's undertaking that he went all the way with LBJ by saying that he went all the way with Harold Holt. He did his best to help his friend to win the coming election. It was widely reported in America that the police had found that the Melbourne and Sydney anti-Johnson demonstrations were a 'co-ordinated Communist scheme'.[163] But in Sydney 'Premier Askin reported that excessive official anxiety had kept thousands of people' from seeing the President, whom he had so much pleased by saying to a police officer—when referring to demonstrators—'Run over the bastards'. And word swept round the world that green paint had been thrown over President Johnson's car in Melbourne.

Returning to America, the President held out no prospect of an early peace and said his journey had produced 'no miracle'. Richard Nixon came in at this point with a statement which may hold great significance. If the war did not end before the Presidential elections, he said, and if Johnson would be the Democratic candidate, the Republicans could be driven into a peace campaign.

But the war went on. Large-scale American operations 'Starlight', 'Lincoln', 'Davy Crockett', 'Masher', 'Birmingham', 'White Wings', 'Hastings' and 'Prairie', were followed in November by the largest operation of the war—'Attelboro'. Based on B52 bombs, fighter-bomber bombs and napalm and backed by helicopter gunships these actions proved capable of returning body counts with a 5 to 10 favourable ratio. The deciding factor was the speed, precision and power of the air strikes. But beginning with 20,000 troops, 'Attelboro' strength for some reason or other was 'quietly cut' to 11,000.[164] The operation continued through the week with claims of 965 enemy killed. The smaller operation 'Paul Revere', at the same time, brought 672 enemy killed while helicopter losses for the week at 5 raised total helicopter losses to 223. 'Viet Cong' mortar attacks were widespread and began against Saigon itself. December came with war costs being put at $20,000 million—twice the January estimates—and with U.S. troop strength at 361,000 and still rising. In December U.S. officials acknowledged bombing of 'military targets in Hanoi' and on

December 4 it was reported that eight U.S. planes and 13 crewmen were lost in one day. French correspondents made the first independent claims of civilian bombing in North Vietnam, claiming that the village of Candat, just outside Hanoi, was completely destroyed.

Cao Ky attributed the lag in the South Vietnam pacification program to 'corrupt officials'. But Generals Westmoreland and Wheeler both avowed their satisfaction with the progress of the war in 1966. At home the Harris Poll found support for the Johnson policy had dropped to 43 per cent, the same as before the conference in Manila with his Premiers and Prime Ministers, while Gallup reported that the trip had raised the President's popularity to 48 per cent.

Jean Sainteny, who had represented the French in crucial negotiations in 1945, reported that North Vietnam appeared strengthened by the bombing, while political leaders and columnists everywhere agreed that the President's failure to end the war could be the crucial issue in the 1968 Presidential elections. The term 'credibility gap' came into extensive use to describe the position of the Johnson Administration. With the U.S. five year death toll at 6,407, 'Operation Thayer', at the end of the year, brought the surrender of a 'Viet Cong' battalion. At the United Nations, U.S. Ambassador Goldberg urged U Thant to take any necessary steps to bring about a cease-fire. And on this note 1966 came to an end.

The new year was notable for a conflicting assessment of the physical costs of the war to the United States. Hanson Baldwin reported that the Pentagon 'disclosed for the first time' that the U.S. had lost 1,120 aircraft and 630 helicopters in five years of war to December 31, 1966. McNamara 'countered' these figures with a report that 2,273 U.S. planes and 987 helicopters had been lost since July 1, 1965.

The new year was notable, too, for another New York Times entry into a controversial area. Harrison Salisbury visited Hanoi. His most publicised work was perhaps the least significant—he proved that civilian casualties and damage to houses, schools, hospitals and churches were extensive. No longer could the Administration continue to claim damage only to military targets, although it successfully disputed some of Salisbury's claims and gained much by 'revealing' that he had quoted North Vietnam sources and evidence without saying so. The more important aspect of Salisbury's work was his interview with North Vietnamese Premier Phan Van Dong. This interview cleared several vital points—

1. Phan Van Dong's statement that once all bombing and other acts of war against North Vietnam were stopped 'it would be possible to speak of other things'.
2. North Vietnam's four-point program for ending the war was a 'basis of settlement', not conditions for peace talks.
3. The major obstacle to peace talks remained the U.S. refusal

to recognise the National Liberation Front. There could be no effective negotiations 'about South Vietnam' until this attitude was given up.

In Hanoi, Salisbury was told by NLF permanent representative there, Nguyen Van Tien, that NLF had a separate and distinct policy from that of Hanoi, that it directed the war in South Vietnam and must participate in any peace talks. America had a choice of either recognising the NLF in negotiations from which a settlement could come, or defeating the NLF in war. In this war, Hanoi would aid the NLF to the full extent that was necessary.

As if to illustrate his capacity to learn nothing, the American Ambassador in Saigon, Cabot Lodge, chose this moment to say that allied forces would make 'sensational gains' in 1967, that talks to end the war would never take place, and he ended with his favourite forecast—the war in Vietnam would 'fade out'. And the President, in his State of the Union message, 'vowed to persevere with the war despite more cost, more loss and more agony.' On January 14, it was reported by Dr. Martin Niemoller that Ho Chi Minh, in talks with him, had been clear and emphatic—he would discuss 'U.S. withdrawal and Vietnamese freedom after the U.S. halts bombing, but never before.' U Thant urged the extension of the New Year cease fire because talks were so close. Salisbury reported on the 'wide differences' between North Vietnam and the National Liberation Front in their economic and political platforms, regional interests and conflicts, and in differing attitudes to re-unification.[165]

The middle of January saw an equally important report from French journalist Robert Dubernat: the French government, on behalf of China, had informed the United States in 1966 that China would stay out of the war in Vietnam if the United States agreed not to invade China or North Vietnam and not to bomb the Red River dikes. American officials chose to make an equivocal reply—they knew nothing of the French message or the 'condition on the dikes'.[166] A few weeks later, Rusk was reported to have said that he 'would never have believed' that America could have carried her military action in Vietnam so far with so little Chinese and Soviet objection.

Early in February, the Vatican newspaper l'Osservatore Romano reached a significant conclusion—the war in Vietnam was a civil war and could not be ended unless this was recognised. The 'peace offensive' remained the significant event of the year. Harold Wilson told the House of Commons that peace was 'almost in our grasp last week'. But February 11 saw the end of the 'new year truce' in South Vietnam, and two days later the bombing of North Vietnam began again. Senator Robert Kennedy asserted that the Johnson Administration had refused to accept an undertaking by Kosygin, and several by Pham Van Dong, that there would be peace talks if the United States stopped bombing North Vietnam. Senator Edward Kennedy supported his brother's position and warned that a continuation of Johnson Administration policy would lead to heavy electoral losses for the Democrats.

It was claimed that Johnson had 'upped the ante' by demanding more from North Vietnam than 'reciprocal action'. Later figures in 1967 showed that there had indeed been a change in 'reciprocal action'. North Vietnamese infiltrations were claimed to have dropped as much as 90 per cent since June 1966. McNamara chose the occasion to state that the monthly averages for the first six months of 1966 were 6,950, while since October they had been only 1,600. It looked as if 'reciprocal action' might have been taken by North Vietnam. In his crucial letter to Ho Chi Minh, Johnson had added to his earlier 'reciprocal action' words about an end to North Vietnamese interference in the affairs of South Vietnam. U Thant chose to say that the 'key to peace rests with the United States'. He foresaw 'long and bloody war' unless the United States unconditionally halted the bombing, and he was emphatic that an 'unconditional halt' of the bombing 'would lead to early talks'. Confirmation of U Thant's position came from the governments of India and Canada and from several official spokesmen in Europe.

The 'peace offensive' ended with President Johnson's announcing new methods of military action 'to end the fighting in Vietnam'. Early March brought a record number of bombing missions against North Vietnam, and attacks within several miles of the Chinese border, upon 'downtown Hanoi', and upon power plants and the Thainguyen iron and steel complex. Few holds were now barred. February 24 saw the beginning of Operation Junction City, the biggest U.S. offensive of the war—25,000 men, nearly 1,000 helicopters, 500 tanks, armoured vehicles, and bulldozers and 500 bombers loaded with bombs and napalm. Official spokesmen described the first week's combat as 'very intense' and at the end of the week American casualties were 232 dead and 1381 wounded. Weekly casualties in March were an average of 507 killed and 2,960 wounded—a record equalled again in June. Australian and American forces began their 'largest operation of the war' but 'in 14 days made little contact with the enemy'.[167] In May the intensity of the war moved to the area in and around the demilitarised zone.

General Westmoreland, in Washington to address Congress, spoke of the 'increased enemy pressure in the Northern provinces and disappointing pace of operations, in the Mekong delta'. He stressed the importance of holding positions around the 'DMZ'. But within a few days, General Watt, in command of the marines in the area, gave the story a different stress. He claimed that his forces had disrupted a comprehensive enemy offensive and asked for more marines. While 'Viet

Cong' offensives began in many places—Danang, Conthieu, Duepho, Contho and Queson—it was expected that the main thrust was in the north. In June 1,000 'Viet Cong' were reported to have 'battered' large South Vietnamese forces 40 miles from Saigon and operations became so extensive that the Joint Chiefs of Staff warned that the United States would run the risk of losing ground if General Westmoreland's requests for more troops were not met. McNamara, in reply, advocated further integration of South Vietnamese and American forces, and told Westmoreland 'to get more Americans into the front lines'. Only 70,000 Americans were available for offensive operations out of 464,000 who were in Vietnam. American officials were reported 'dismayed' at this disclosure.

In July Westmoreland and Wheeler, at the White House, were told that 30,000 more troops would be going and Newsweek reported the White House conversation:

'The troops that General Westmoreland needs and requests, as we feel it necessary, will be supplied. Is that not true, General Westmoreland?'

'I agree, Mr. President.'

'General Wheeler?'

'That is correct, Mr. President.'

'Secretary McNamara?'

'Yes, Sir'.

'Touch on this "stalemate creature", General Westmoreland'.

'It is a complete fiction. The enemy has failed in achieving his objective. We have succeeded in obtaining our objectives'.

Early in June, Roger (now Professor) Hillsman startled some with his claim that the United States did not start bombing North Vietnam in retaliation for infiltration by North Vietnamese troops, but to 'try to force Hanoi to its knees'.[168] Middle-of-the-year debate concerned casualties and the nature of the war. The war went on with 'scattered clashes' in June, July and August among relatively large unit forces in which 'kill ratios' of 'Viet Cong' of between 5 and 10 to 1 were claimed. How were 'Viet Cong' distinguished from civilians, and South from North Vietnamese? In December 1967, an American survey in South Vietnamese hospitals showed casualties as a result of the war to be 2,510 civilian and 815 military killed and between 1,600 and 1,700 injured. U.S. officials 'disclosed' that civilian casualties in South Vietnam 'rise as the tempo of the war rises', and Major General Humphrey reported that 50,000 civilians might be treated for war-related injuries in 1967. Senator Edward Kennedy replied by putting civilian casualties at more than 100,000. At the end of the year, South Vietnamese government statistics showed that civilian casualties 'may reach 76,000 wounded and 24,000 killed in 1967'. Senator Kennedy then stated these figures were on the 'low side' and civilian casualties could now be seen as 150,000 for the year 1967. The truth was that civilian casualties were very much a matter of guesswork.

The very nature of the war was called into question in May when the Republican Senate Committee released a White Paper with a view of the war in direct conflict with that of the Johnson Administration. The White Paper claimed that U.S. military intervention in Vietnam was not attributable to President Eisenhower or to anything done by him. It was all a mistake by Presidents Kennedy and Johnson. It accused the Administration of refusing to negotiate when Hanoi had agreed on several occasions. It disagreed with the Administration that the NLF was at all a Hanoi puppet. It diagnosed the war not as resulting from 'aggression from the North', but as an indigenous uprising for national independence and for political and economic reasons. The problem of Vietnam could not be solved by military action but only by political developments. Many Republican members of Congress supported the case put by their committee, but Republican Congress leaders Dickson and Ford supported the Administration and rejected the committee's findings, although Dickson, then in hospital, later said in Washington that the committee's report was 'a substantial document which could not be ignored if there was to be any end to the war in Vietnam'.

In and around the demilitarised zone intense activities began in May. Close range battles for three hills near Khesanh constituted a military campaign considered vital by the Americans. The marines seized Hill 881 North after a 12-day campaign in which nearly half of the U.S. troops involved were killed or wounded. Westmoreland had linked his request for more U.S. troops to the increased enemy pressure in the northern provinces aimed at large American bases further south. In October, 3,000 marines were shifted to the area and Marine Corps forces were under the 'heaviest enemy shelling' of the campaign. The battle for Hill 875 brought extensive casualties—274 Americans killed and 939 wounded, and enemy dead put at 1,377. Newsweek reported that 'not since Ia Drang valley, two years ago, have the Americans had such a beating'. 'I have the feeling', a wounded soldier said, 'I'll be back for Hill 876 and 877'. Newsweek reported there was 'ridge after ridge stretching off into hazy distance as far as the eye could see'.

It would be reasonable to suppose that the pressures in the northern provinces against the marines, shortage of front line re-inforcements and the geographic situation described above, were the reasons for McNamara's dramatic decision to 'build a barrier of barbed wire and electronic devices along the northern border of South Vietnam below the demilitarised zone.' Westmoreland and his commanders were far from enthusiastic. The ensuing debate about the position in and around the demilitarised zone soon revealed:

1. The McNamara proposal was impractical and would never be attempted.
2. It was put forward as a desperate attempt further to reduce the military need for bombing North Vietnam.
3. The military tasks of holding positions in the mountainous areas were far beyond the capacity of the available American forces.

The capture of one hill in this complex of hills put American military and Press observers in position to see hundreds of similar heavily wooded hills, each of which could involve similar costs in men and artillery problems, if the area was to be cleared or even held. Military action in central Vietnam, along the Cambodian border and now in the Mekong delta, had brought no more decisive results although the reported casualties were much more favourable. War action by both sides swept ever increasing numbers into towns, cities and refugee camps. All these circumstances intensified reaction in America against the Administration.

It is now clear that the second half of 1967 brought a basic reappraisal of United States policy in Vietnam. There is a generally accepted view that American policy changed just after, and because of, the Tet offensive in March 1968. This, however, is a superficial view. The Tet offensive was merely one factor among many which had operated since the middle of 1967 to change American policy. It was merely the straw that broke the camel's back. In November 1967 the New York Times illustrated in six diagrams the 'major factors in the reappraisal of U.S. Vietnam policy'. The first factor was the number of American troops in South Vietnam—from 20,000 in early 1965 to 550,000 at the end of 1967. The point had been reached when no substantial increase in troop numbers could be achieved without a significant change in mobilisation procedures, if not 'general mobilisation'. The second factor was what the New York Times saw as an 'increase in enemy forces as the U.S. escalated'. 'Viet Cong' forces had risen from about 130,000 at the beginning of 1965 to 300,000 at the end of 1967. North Vietnam regulars rose from four or five hundred at the beginning of 1955 to 55,000 at the end of 1967. In the circumstances, South and North Vietnamese capacity to increase their forces was greater than that of the United States and the demands of a more extensive campaign, certainly in the northern provinces, were beyond acceptable American capacity. These two factors together were basic— they were the causes of the re-appraisal that was almost completed at the end of 1967. Another factor was the increase of air missions over North Vietnam, with rising casualties resulting from increasing anti-aircraft capacity. Raids were actually withdrawn from several areas because of these casualties. U.S. casualties reached a high level in the first half of 1967 and fell in the latter quarter of the year only as a result of the curtailment of missions and operations. American reaction to these factors was reflected in a consistent downward trend in both the Harris and Gallup polls from the end of 1965. Although there were upward moves the general trend was decisive and proved irreversible—from about 60 per cent approval of Johnson's handling of the war in December 1965 to about 25 per cent in December 1967.

Increasingly the anti-war demonstrations became bigger, more penetrating in their exposure and joined by more significant, respectable and influential people. Increasingly leading Americans came to stress the 'military stalemate' and the 'unwinnable war'. To 'maintain the initiative' had proved beyond American capacity. Victory demanded much more. By the end of the year it was widely admitted that bomb-in North Vietnam would not compel Hanoi to submit or even negotiate. At this period the 'three stage peace plan'—cessation of the bombing, recognition of the NLF, and some form of ceased or curtailed fire in South Vietnam—was widely accepted among all those at the U.N., in Europe and in the U.S. who knew the facts of the 'peace offensives'. But Johnson did not submit without a 'last hurrah', and on ground prepared by the 'greatest hawk of them all'—Rusk. He told the world that 'withdrawal would place the U.S. in mortal danger' and 'could lead to catastrophe for all mankind'. According to him, millions of Chinese armed with nuclear weapons were dedicated to the pursuit of world revolution.

At the end of the 'toughest year' when U.S. bombers swarmed like hornets over North Vietnam and the ground war in the South raged in a stalemated fury, 'candidate Johnson took to the hustings'. He claimed that the U.S. was making satisfactory progress . . . that troop levels could be held at 525,000 . . . that every American heart could swell with pride at U.S. leadership in Vietnam, that at home the U.S. has made revolutionary strides in health, education and conservation . . . that responsible dissent was welcome but more violent forms of protest should be wiped out. There must be 'law and order' in America and in Vietnam. Westmoreland arrived in Washington to say the war situation was 'very, very encouraging' and that a troop phase-out could begin in two years. But the polls showed Rockefeller, Romney, Reagan, Nixon, Percy, Lindsay all ahead of Johnson. Nixon, of course, said the U.S. must see the war through to an early conclusion and was doubtless worried most of all that if Johnson continued to campaign he himself would have to become a 'peace candidate'. In December McCarthy decided to challenge Johnson in the primaries. In August Bishop Fulton Sheen made a plea for withdrawal of American forces, and in November McNamara was nominated as President of the International Bank for Reconstruction and Development. This of course, 'had nothing to do with the war in Vietnam'; but it was well known that McNamara had serious disagreements with Administration policy, and

Johnson now had only two of his original Vietnam Secretaries and advisers left. The Administration's claim that McNamara had 'agreed with or deferred to' every decision concealed far more than it revealed and was yet another example of the Johnson technique that had given meaning to the term 'credibility gap'.

This was fertile ground for the Senate Foreign Relations Committee to publish testimony between Fulbright and Bundy in 1966 confirming that the Administration had prepared contingent drafts of the Tonkin Bay resolution *before* attacks by North Vietnamese torpedo boats on U.S. destroyers. The year ended leaving no doubt that the President's counter-attack had failed and the only point in doubt was what particular incident would fix the time when a change of policy would be announced. The stage was set for the 'Tet offensive'.

The year 1967 brought, of course, the State Department's 'tour de force'—the finest elections that had ever been held in a country at war. The first election event of the year was Nguyen Cao Ky's signature of two Acts in January providing for elections in 1,000 villages and 4,000 hamlets—elections had been abolished by Ngo Dien Diem—but 'Leftists' and 'neutralists' were barred from standing or voting.[169] During the year Ky and Thieu announced they would not stand for President, and then that they would, until finally their President-Vice President ticket emerged. The law against 'Leftists' or 'neutralists' was applied to the Presidential election but finally Phan Khac Suu and Phan Quang Dan stood in relatively independent positions and General Duong Van Minh and Au Truong Than and five other 'tickets' were not allowed to stand at all. Thieu and Ky, backed by the South Vietnamese Army, received 27 per cent of the vote and were elected. What might be called the 'negotiations' ticket of Truong Dinh Dzu was second with about 16 per cent, with Tran Van Huong and Phan Khac Suu tickets next.

Dzu claimed the election was illegal and invalid. But Johnson and Rusk hailed the election as a great step forward. Dzu claimed that two thirds of the Thieu vote was obtained by fraud and that the election was really a victory for a peace initiative. Ten unsuccessful civilian candidates for President lodged a formal protest asking the Constituent Assembly to invalidate the voting. On October 2, the Assembly confirmed the election results by 58 votes to 43, and Thieu's lead and percentage grew after votes from suspected precincts were counted. Buddhist militant leaders had advised a boycott of the election and now supported the invalidation process. Dzu had been charged before the election with issuing a bad cheque during Diem's regime and was now tried, convicted and sentenced. Au Truong Thanh, former Minister for Finance in several governments, and seeking to stand for office, was arrested on charges of being a member of a 'Viet Cong' propaganda unit.

The so-called elections of 1967 were an integral part of the establishment of the Thieu-Ky power structure in Saigon. They made no difference whatever in the exercise of power in Saigon, and the votes of the electorate simply confirmed in office those who held power already. Any candidate who appeared, on the slightest evidence, to represent a 'Left' or 'neutral' position was excluded. The development of Dzu towards a negotiating position and recognition of the NLF came as a surprise to his rivals but it proved impossible to exclude him. After the election, however, no time was lost in eliminating him from any position of influence.

It is unreasonable to claim or to expect that the 1967 Presidential election in South Vietnam could have tested or given any effective expression to the only vital issue confronting the country—was the war to be carried on or were there to be negotiations? The South Vietnamese military command, no more or less than the Johnson Administration, would not permit any election in South Vietnam to be a test of this issue. So this issue remained to be tested in the only way possible— between the military forces of the NLF and North Vietnam on the one hand, and those of the United States and her allies on the other.

The 1967 Presidential election was simply a public relations exercise during the course of a military campaign. It proved a valuable public relations gesture in South Vietnam as well as in America and elsewhere but did little to offset the accelerating decline of the Johnson Administration and it did nothing to strengthen the Saigon regime or make it any more an expression of the will of the people.

Early in January the U.S. sought through 'diplomatic channels' to ascertain North Vietnam's attitude to peace talks. The North Vietnamese mission in Paris replied with Hanoi's oft repeated offer to talk with the U.S. about 'relevant problems' provided the U.S. first unconditionally stopped the bombing and other acts of war against North Vietnam. A day later it was reported that the Administration was 'under mounting pressure' to halt the war against North Vietnam to test Hanoi's latest offer to begin talks.[170] Senator Eugene McCarthy thought that the resignation of Rusk would be necessary for them, and a week later it appeared that the President was 'determined to resist pressure for a bombing pause if North Vietnam had nothing else to offer'. As a climax, President Thieu attacked the U.S. for trying 'unilaterally to initiate peace talks with North Vietnam'.

General Westmoreland's several-months-long campaign for hot pursuit of 'Viet Cong' into Cambodia, included in January an allegation that a permanent base of 10,000 'Viet Cong' troops had been established near Dautieng. It now appeared probable that an American representative would be sent to Cambodia with a demand for Cambodian consent for American troops to enter the country.

The Australian Ambassador in Phnom Penh, representing America, along with several others, visited the area where it was alleged 'Viet Cong' troops were based. They reported no signs of troops, camps or bases.

The appointment of Indian Ambassador Chester Bowles to visit Cambodia was a surprise, as was his failure in Phnom Penh to press any claim for American access to Cambodia. Indeed the Cambodian Head of State, Norodom Sihanouk, and Bowles readily agreed that America would respect Cambodian borders and would not violate them by 'hot pursuit' or in any other way. Sihanouk restated his long-established position that his forces would continue to do all they could to prevent Vietnamese or any other forces from entering his country, and that they would seek a strengthening of the International Control Commission. Bundy, in Washington, immediately sought to give a different interpretation to the accord, but the matter ceased to be an issue when General Abrams, later to succeed Westmoreland, stated that he did not desire rights to go into Cambodia as this would extend lines of communication too far and these were difficult enough to defend as it was. Ground action in South Vietnam continued through the 'New Year truce' with official casualties listed at 27 U.S., 44 South Vietnamese and 553 'enemy'. But one 'Viet Cong' attack at Mytho was reported to have produced 19 Americans killed, 47 wounded and 30 'enemy' killed.

The end of January brought a report that 'the allies had called off the Tet cease fire because of massive enemy build-up in the northern provinces'.[171] American troops were air-lifted to the border region near Dakto, and North Vietnamese troops began a series of attacks at Khesanh, a U.S. marine held base. More than 5,000 marines were 'massed' at this base and 'one of the major battles of the war' was expected there. American officers had 'positively identified' 16,000 to 20,000 enemy troops in the area. Rusk announced that a 'major offensive' by North Vietnamese forces was expected. Now it was not a question of an American invasion of North Vietnam but a North Vietnamese invasion of the South. With the dominant feature the northern build-up and pressures, and with talk of invasion and reinforcement of the area—15,000 troops were moved on January 28—and with U.S. officers warning that the enemy's effort was far from over, the 'Viet Cong' struck in the 'Tet offensive', or 'attack at a thousand points', on January 30—two days after the allies had called off the Tet truce.

Reporting a few days later for Newsweek, Everett J. Martin wrote: 'Like most journalists familiar with Vietnam, I have long been unconvinced by the deluge of official optimism on the progress of the war. Yet when the enemy attacked last week, I was utterly taken aback by his daring and tenacity—and, most of all by his ability to co-ordinate his assaults with a precision he had never before displayed.'[172] Martin reported the offensive itself should have been no surprise because 'the situation in Vietnam's populated areas had steadily declined for three weeks'. For a long time 'the enemy had demonstrated that he retained complete initiative'. Now those in the big cities—the allies' 'sanctuaries' —who thought themselves immune 'are no longer safe'. Martin reported the 'devastating effect on the people' caused by the attacks. The Saigon Government had 'failed to provide the people with any reason to support it, and there is less likelihood that such support will be forthcoming now'.

On February 12, Walter Lippman wrote that 'all week long South Vietnam lay pinned in the grip of the bloodiest single convulsion the war has yet produced (and) Lyndon Johnson went into crisis consultations with top advisers—Hawks and doves alike lamented the 'humiliation' inflicted on the allied cause and complained that they had been misled about the Communists capability'. But the President restated his opposition to stopping the bombing. Things were bad, but then they would be worse. There would be more troops and aid from North Vietnam and the 'Viet Cong' would be stronger. 'In these long nights we pray', said the President. A few days later General Westmoreland claimed a victory. The 'Tet Offensive' had been beaten and the enemy was weaker than before. He told the troops: 'You have destroyed more of the enemy in seven days than the U.S. has lost in seven years'. Official estimates were 31,000 enemy killed for 920 Americans killed and 4,560 wounded. Senator McClellan thought it necessary to say: 'It is time to send a commander to Vietnam who is capable of plotting a winning strategy or, if there is no such thing, who is capable of telling the President so'. But Hanson Baldwin was 'confident that the situation in Vietnam is developing along lines foreseen by General Westmoreland'. And President Johnson was confident that the 'Viet Cong had suffered a complete military failure throughout South Vietnam this week'.

But the weight of evidence did not support the usual Administration optimism. Reports put it that 'the number of South Vietnamese unwilling to oppose the Viet Cong has vastly increased'; 'the damage . . . physical and psychological was almost incalculable'; 'the pacification program, long asserted by U.S. planners to be the real key to ultimate victory, had been dealt a blow from which it would recover slowly—if ever'. Both in Vietnam and America 'all this aroused searing doubts about U.S. strategy in the Vietnamese war and about the man entrusted with its execution—General Westmoreland'.[173] 'The people (in South Vietnam)', Newsweek reported, 'are in a vacuum of shock. They don't know which way to turn now.' Melbourne journalist Denis Warner, in Saigon in March[174] 1968, had no doubt about the effect of the Tet offensive, 'Although allied forces, in terms of casualties suffered and inflicted, have won every battle since the Viet Cong launched the Tet offensive, they have everywhere been forced back into defensive postures. Roads I used to drive along only a few years ago are not only unsafe—some have disappeared. The country has become a series of American and allied islands dotted on a Viet Cong and North Vietnamese sea.' And, 'Pacification' wrote Warner, 'in the sense of providing security for villages and hamlets is dead. About five per cent of the total area was under control both by day and night'.

The London Times correspondent reported on March 7 that returning to Saigon 'one is struck by the changes'. The 'South Vietnamese leaders have never genuinely agreed with Washington's sophisticated view of the war and of the best ways of winning it. The men who really rule in Saigon are soldiers and they believe the war must be won militarily—by the introduction of more American troops, by heavier bombing of the North and by a landing in the north and even the use of nuclear weapons.' They have 'paid lip service to the American doctrine that the war must be won through social reform and dynamic government but they know that nothing can save them but American troops and fire power'. The Times article continued: 'The United States has only two choices left in Vietnam: to negotiate its way out or to seek a pure military victory after which it can dictate terms to Hanoi.' Many of the military-minded men, Vietnamese and American, were now convinced—the Tet offensive would kill all these ideas about reform and economics. It would now be war and nothing but war. Newsweek of February 26 depicted Washington 'watching and waiting'. What was it to be? 'I don't know how to do anything better than we are doing it', stated the President. 'If I did, I would do it. I would take the better way. We have considered everything.'

The New York Times, at the end of the Tet week, reported that 'Western Europe was shocked at events and at apparent American failings.' America now had even less chance of military aid from elsewhere—she had to look even more to her own resources. The battle to regain Hue, Mytho and such provincial centres went well. But Saigon remained under continuous siege. Khesanh remained surrounded and America remained ready to defend it at all costs. U.S. and South Vietnamese forces were basically in a defensive position, waiting for the 'second wave', which might or might not come. They did not know. Whether it would come or not depended on them more than on the enemy. Prime Minister Wilson on February 12 thought the 'recent offensive' would 'make the road to peace harder'. But the road to negotiations was opening up and the clearing of it was taking place in Washington. President Johnson announced on February 17 that 'North Vietnam is no more ready now to negotiate than it was one, two or three years ago.' Apparently the bombing had achieved nothing. But U Thant said he was more convinced than ever that 'the end of bombing of North Vietnam could bring talks with Hanoi within two or three weeks'. However, through February, Washington reports were that the prospects of talks were slim and receding.

In fact, Washington was still tied to the melancholy alternative—to win the war. On February 23, General Wheeler and a Pentagon staff went to South Vietnam to confer with Westmoreland and inspect battle areas. February 28 brought a statement from President Johnson that 'the war stands at a turning point, and Americans at home, like those fighting in war, must not retreat.' He stated America's 'unshakable and untiring resolve' and did not believe that 'we would ever buckle'. What would be needed to back the President's stand? This was the question to which they strove to find an answer. The Gallup poll showed a drop during February of seven points in approval of Johnson's handling of the war from an already record low point. The last week of February brought 543 American deaths in Vietnam—a record weekly total for the war. U.S. officials reported 350,000 new refugees and the South Vietnamese government admitted the effects of the Tet offensive were deep, significant and impossible to estimate. The net effect of all this was that more U.S. troops were needed. How many? Could they be supplied? The end of February brought reports that Westmoreland wanted 50,000-100,000 more men, and that the request was the 'main topic of discussion between Westmoreland and Wheeler'.[175] Early reports of the discussions were that 'President Johnson would go along with the request', and the war would be stepped up. February 29 saw General Wheeler back in Washington and 'breakfasting at the White House' with 'many leading Government planners on Vietnam'. It was stressed afterwards that 'any proposal by Wheeler for reinforcements would be tentative and would not mean a formal request.' Here was the first glimmer the 'war winning choice' was losing momentum. On June 29 Senator Stennis, a good weathercock, called for a 'change in current strategy'. American historian and diplomat, George Kennan, described the 'Johnson policy' as a 'massive, unparalleled error'. James Reston, usually well in touch with Administration moves, wrote that the outlook from the Pacific command was for escalated war that included more men, more airpower, and more targets in North Vietnam. Out there, apparently, everything was under way for escalation. But in Washington the debate was not yet over.

Now it was reported that Westmoreland's request was for 206,000 more men and was said to have 'started debate within high levels of the Johnson administration'. The 206,000 was needed, apparently, *only to regain* the initiative in Vietnam. The request was opposed by several Defence Department, and some senior State Department, officials who contended that the increase would merely bring a matching North Vietnamese increase. An alternative proposal from some 'Pentagon officials' was for 'a concept of close-in defence of populated areas with more limited offensive thrusts than at present.' The President was said to be 'holding to current strategy' with 'Rusk, Rostow and other advisers projecting an air of confidence'.[176] Rusk, questioned on March 11 at the Senate Foreign Relations Committee, admitted the Administration was 're-examining its policy from A to Z and considering all alternatives'. He acknowledged that America had suffered 'serious set-backs in the recent enemy offensive', and that a large increase in American forces would be necessary to regain losses, but remained optimistic that 'the outcome depends upon which side most quickly seizes and then maintains the initiative'. The Committee informed the President that it would not 'consider the foreign aid bill until it gets some satisfactory answers on the future course of war'.

On March 13, Senator McCarthy won a 40 per cent vote in the New Hampshire primary and the following day Senator Robert Kennedy said he was reconsidering his decision not to seek Democratic Presidential selection. Senator Fulbright denounced the Tonkin Bay resolution, saying it was obtained on the basis of misrepresentation by the Administration. At the middle of March U.S. casualties in Vietnam exceeded those in Korea—19,670 killed, 120,131 wounded. The U.S. command now expected the main attack on Hue rather than Khesanh—10,000 enemy troops were in the Hue area and 8,000 to 10,000 within 15 miles of Saigon. It was becoming clear there would be a withdrawal from Khesanh because America had not enough suitable troops to maintain operations in the border areas. On March 16, Senator Robert Kennedy announced he would seek Democratic nomination because of President Johnson's 'disastrous and divisive policies in Vietnam'. March 19 saw the President apparently still on a warlike path. He called on the nation for 'austerity' and for a 'total national effort' to win the war and peace in Vietnam. 'We have set our course' he said, 'and America will prevail'. One could have guessed that more troops were going and the war was to be escalated. March 23, of all times, brought President Johnson's startling announcement of his intention to bring home General Westmoreland and appoint him Army Chief of Staff. The President stated the shift had been recommended by ex-Secretary McNamara and Secretary Clifford. What a moment to 'promote' his Vietnam commander!

CHAPTER NINE

THE AGONISING RE-APPRAISAL

By the end of the third week of March 1968, it was being generally reported that 'a basic turning point in the war had been reached'. Even Mayor Daley in Chicago called for a reversal of Johnson's policy, and Senator Robert Kennedy linked war policy to the dollar crisis. It was in this atmosphere that *the* announcement came. It had been said that the President would appear on national television to report on the war in Vietnam. On March 31, President Johnson, tired and strained, appeared and announced that he had ordered a halt in the air and naval bombardment of most of North Vietnam and invited the Hanoi government to join in a series of mutual moves toward peace. He offered to increase the number of U.S. troops in Vietnam by no more than 13,500 over the next five months, and then declared his decision not to seek re-election as President.

The debate was over. The decision was made. American policy in Vietnam since March 1950 had maintained a single purpose—to win the war. Now, 18 years later, there was at last a basic change. No longer was the purpose to win; it was to end the war as soon as possible. It was to enter into negotiations. Now the method was political. Military action would be limited to holding operations while the purpose would be to preserve the Saigon government, if that was possible, or to delay its final demise. On April 4, North Vietnam and the United States published statements in which they agreed to establish contacts between their representatives. Newsweek reported on April 15: 'Mr. Johnson spoke 20 words that shook the world. For a brief moment there seemed no limit to the national euphoria. The tensions, the bitterness and the cumulative rancour in the land seemed somehow to find a final catharsis. The stock market traded more shares in one day than at any time in its history, the Dow Jones average jumped a phenomenal 20 points. Everywhere he went the President was cheered and applauded'. America could, it seemed, never go back. The war in Vietnam was coming to an end. And where were the people who regretted the way it was happening.

South Vietnamese Foreign Minister, Tran Van Do, who had been in Geneva in 1954 and was now in Sydney on his way to a SEATO conference, said that South Vietnam could not afford to have the bombing stopped.

Vice-President Ky was more sweeping in his judgment. He

wrote:[178] 'The Americans are in Vietnam to defend their interests which do not always correspond with those of Vietnam. They are here because they want to remain in Asia to stop Communism in Asia and not because they have any particular concern about us.' Vice-President Ky went on: 'America wants to introduce its own form of democracy into South Vietnam, including respect for the law and freedom of speech. But that kind of democracy leads to colonialism.' 'But what the devil does democracy mean when you are dying of hunger? The elections here have been a loss of time and money. They are a joke. They have served to install a regime that has nothing in common with the people—a useless, corrupt regime.' And then he summed it up, 'We need a revolution. The laws we have protect the rich. We must make new laws that will give power to the poor.' And then Ky dismissed the attitude to China upon which the whole American policy was based. 'Ho Chi Minh is a Vietnamese and hates the Chinese like I do. He knows very well that he would make the biggest mistake of his life if he called them in. To chase out the Chinese we would all unite.' He concluded by saying of the Americans, 'Their time is ended.' But if this was so how could he survive?

It was, of course, still not clear what had happened.

On April 11, U.S. Defence Secretary Clifford pronounced that the Administration 'has adopted a policy aimed at gradual transfer of major responsibility of war effort to South Vietnam'.[179] The 'government of South Vietnam' and its army was not now able to carry the major responsibility for the war. How long would it need to be able to do so? Would the negotiations last long enough to allow this to happen? The President's declaration of March 31 had left many unanswered questions. Reacting to a wide wave of criticism of its peace moves, the Administration identified the 20th parallel as the line north of which it had halted bombing although the President had dropped the prepared reference to the 20th parallel in his statement on March 31. On April 4, the U.S. declared the 76-day North Vietnamese siege of Khesanh lifted. Speculation that there would be a 'pull-back' from Khesanh was denied. On April 10 began the largest allied offensive of the war, involving more than 100,000 troops, to 'clear enemy forces out of 11 provinces surrounding Saigon'. In most cases 'enemy forces' had been cleared out several times before.

Finally, on May 3 the United States and North Vietnam agreed to begin formal talks on May 10 or soon after. It must be emphasized that none of these developments meant any significant limitation of military action. The five weeks since March 31 had seen record numbers of missions against that part of Vietnam being bombed, and ground operations in South Vietnam were of record size and intensity. Rusk announced that the Viet Cong, aided by greatly increased North Vietnamese forces, were planning major offensives. In one counter-action alone on Ashau Valley, 377 enemy were killed for a cost of 63 Americans killed, 363 wounded and 50 helicopters lost. Fighting continued in and around Saigon, and the capital and other cities were constantly under mortar fire. In four days fighting it was reported that 22,000 had been driven from their homes in Saigon, and on May 12 U.S. planes spread napalm and high explosive bombs within two miles of the centre of Saigon and '104,000 more people were made homeless'.

On May 10, President Thieu declared that his government would never agree to a bombing halt unless the Viet Cong stopped fighting in South Vietnam and said further that he would never negotiate with the National Liberation Front even if America negotiated an end to the war. It seemed his government would take no part in the talks in Paris, but Ambassador Bui Diem was sent as Saigon's observer. On the same day American and North Vietnamese delegates met and completed procedural arrangements. North Vietnam made it clear that the first question to be settled, before any other could be considered, was the unconditional cessation of bombing and all other acts of war against its territory. U Thant asserted that no progress could be made until this step was taken, but Harriman, for the U.S., continued to claim that 'U.S. restraint must be matched by North Vietnamese restraint'. All the same the North Vietnamese negotiators proved willing to discuss a whole range of political issues. Yet the war went on. The second week of May saw American casualties at 562 killed and 2,255 wounded—the largest number of any week in the war, and in each week in April and May casualties were 50 per cent above those for April and May 1967. But American negotiators were confident that the talks would go on 'to the very end'.

General action continued throughout May in Kontum, Danang, Quangtri, Hue, Dongha, Dalat and Dakto, and operation Delaware aimed at clearing the enemy from Ashau Valley ended. General Westmoreland and Joint Chiefs of Staff continued to maintain that Khesanh base could and should be held and that bombing of North Vietnam should not cease unless North Vietnam stopped the movement of men and materials into South Vietnam. The U.S. command admitted that it had called for an 'all-out' offensive just before the Paris talks began, but spokesmen denied the order was linked to the talks.[180] General Westmoreland reported to President Johnson that 'the enemy seems to approach desperation point with forces that are declining in strength and quality.' The enemy has only 'propaganda victories'. 'Time', he said, 'is on our side.' The President must have hoped that he could have a few 'propaganda victories' of equal force. A New York Times editorial of May 31 thought it necessary to say that the 'Paris impasse is not all one-sided' and that it was 'time both sides recognised the futility of further efforts to achieve military victory'. In Paris Ambassador Harriman sought to move the talks into 'areas of possible common ground', but Xuan Thuy pressed North Vietnam's demand that the U.S. stop the bombing and all other acts of war. Harriman claimed that he could see 'areas of agreement between both sides'. North Vietnam replied that it would enter into talks on political settlement once American bombing and other acts of war stopped.

The middle of May had brought in Saigon the resignation of Premier Nguyen Van Loc and his replacement by Tran Van Huong. Vice-President Ky was absent and let it be known that he opposed the change which meant a 'softer line on negotiations' and more power for President Thieu. Newsweek on July 1 reported Tran Van Huong as saying: 'I'm having terrible problems.' It was reported that Huong 'was merely a pawn in President Thieu's intricate plan to checkmate Ky.' Six of Ky's closest political allies were killed in Saigon early in June by 'a U.S. rocket error', and now most of his remaining men were removed from office at the end of July. Ky had lost control of everything except one military area and the marines and the air force. These were still significant forces should America permit him to use them, but this likelihood was becoming more and more remote. It was clear now that the crucial events were in Paris rather than in North or South Vietnam and the point of most significance was whether the bombing would or would not be stopped.

The Australian Prime Minister, John Gorton, chose this occasion to say that American limitations on bombing enabled North Vietnam to build up forces in South Vietnam that would be used to co-ordinate attacks on Saigon. This 'hawkish' point of view, picked up from military briefings in Saigon, seemed to indicate feeling there that June or July could easily have produced a total cessation of bombing. But for the Saigon military men the danger passed. There was no end to the bombing.

June also brought reports of low-flying North Vietnamese helicopters detected by radar around Tiger Island. It may have been such reports that led to American rockets hitting an Australian destroyer though finally General Abrams stated there was no concrete evidence that the enemy had used helicopters. On June 26, the U.S. Marines quietly withdrew from the long-held base at Khesanh. Prominence was given to a 'peak level of infiltration from North Vietnam of 29,000 men in May', and on the same day Rusk stated that he saw no gain in substance as a result of the peace talks. Saigon Premier Huong left no doubt of his hard line when announcing his government's 'complete opposition to compromise with the Viet Cong'. Huong and Thieu apparently had reached full agreement.

Two months after 'the largest operation of the war, involving more than 100,000 troops, to clear enemy forces out of 11 provinces

surrounding Saigon', Saigon suffered the worst attacks of the war.[181]
President Thieu predicted this would be 'the last battle, the last all-
out effort of the Communists'. Each day of the second week of June,
20 civilians were reported killed and hundreds wounded—as well
as military casualties—as a result of mortar attacks, street fighting,
bombs and napalm.

Pressure mounted to resume U.S. bombing of North Vietnam
unless the attacks on Saigon came to an end. Finally, it seems, the
effect of the attacks on the peace talks atmosphere persuaded Hanoi
and the NLF to reduce the attacks. However, the American-South
Vietnamese inability, even with 100,000-man operations, to protect
Saigon was perhaps the most striking illustration in 1968 of the
balance of power of the forces. Yet, ironically, in June, Dr. Phan
Quang Dan, Saigon's most experienced, respected and democratically-
successful citizen was forced to leave the government for advocating
talks with the 'Viet Cong'.

In Washington, the silence of Rusk during the preceding five
weeks was interpreted to be a result of 'the tendency to regard Clifford
as the Johnson spokesman'. Early in July, with fighting proceeding in
hundreds of places in South Vietnam, North Vietnamese diplomats
in Paris held a reception to celebrate the 'destruction of the 3,000th
American plane in North Vietnam'. American officials claimed that
900 planes had been lost. While there existed unquestionably a
'current lull in the fighting in South Vietnam'—casualties were at a
low point—still Harriman refused to accept it as evidence of 'reciprocity', while Thieu and Clifford declared that another enemy
offensive was about to begin. James Reston wrote in July, that
few really thought the conflict would return to the levels of early
spring. The U.S. and the Soviet Union acted as if the war was in 'its
closing stages', and 'few officials believe the talks will break off'. But
the North Vietnamese position in Paris remained unchanged—as soon
as the bombing and all other acts of war stopped, they would begin
talks. And there would be no 'reciprocity'. President Thieu said the
NLF could come to Paris but as part of the North Vietnamese
delegation.

Soon after the Tet offensive, there was formed the Alliance of
National, Democratic and Peace Forces, a third force between the
Saigon regime and the NLF. On July 10 it was announced that the 10
leaders of the Alliance—apparently they were underground by now—
would be tried *in absentia* by the government. On July 12 they
were all sentenced to death after a 23-minute trial. A few days later,
President Johnson welcomed President Thieu in Honolulu and now
the pledge was to 'help South Vietnam resist aggression . . . to stand
firm against any deceptions . . . and strive for an honourable peace
through negotiations'. Thieu said he was 'confident in the future' and

Clifford denied reports that he had persuaded Thieu to agree to negotiations with the National Liberation Front. He apparently forgot to
mention that he had not tried.

President Johnson declared that the war would be continued
at the present pace until North Vietnam agreed to some form of mutual
restraint.[182] Ky, who was not at Honolulu, said the only way to win
over Communists was through military victory. Thieu had announced
his hope to get from Johnson a pledge that the U.S. would continue to bomb North Vietnam until all North Vietnamese troops were
withdrawn from South Vietnam, with South Vietnam playing a
'major role' in any future negotiations with North Vietnam. Thieu
was unsuccessful with the first, but Johnson promised South Vietnam
'a leading role' in negotiations arising from current Paris talks. Thieu
said he had 'no apprehension at all and no doubt of the United States
commitment'.

Returning to Saigon, Thieu stated he had no intention of negotiating with the NLF; the major U.S. problem was observing the existence and jurisdiction of the South Vietnamese Government while at-
tempting to settle the war; the bombing cessation, which might spur
the Paris talks, ran counter to the desires of the South Vietnamese government. The end of July brought a statement from a man who was
relatively unknown then but who had a bright future. Representative
Laird, reviewing the situation in Vietnam, advocated that the Republican platform 'contain strong criticism of Johnson' and laid out
the theme that the new Republican Administration 'unhampered by
mistakes' of the Johnson Administration would be able to achieve a
negotiated settlement.[183] Towards the end of July, the U.S. increased
its bombing missions over North Vietnam, simply, it was said, as a
result of better weather. Aircraft losses increased, and it was reported
that Clifford was assessing the value of limited raids. In South
Vietnam, American casualties—157 killed in the last week of July—
were the lowest for the year. There could be no longer any doubt—
there had been a curtailment of military action during July 1968.
The hawks alleged it was because of casualties inflicted on the enemy,
or for 'diplomatic ends', or it might merely be a prelude to 'the
offensive in the next few months' that had been spoken of by American
political and military leaders. Finally, a captured document was said
to have warned the 'Viet Cong' that the Paris peace talks would never
bring peace but only 'a general uprising of the people' would do so.
Yet a few weeks earlier we were told of extraordinary steps taken to
prevent the Viet Cong even from knowing that peace talks were
taking place.

Senator McCarthy argued that the Johnson-Thieu communique
at Honolulu proved the Administration's unwillingness to do what was

necessary to end the war at the very time when the circumstances proved that it was possible to do so.

Then, at the end of the month, Secretary of State Rusk broke his silence. He said the United States would not curtail the bombing of North Vietnam until North Vietnam went on record with a commitment to reduce its war effort.[184] He dismissed the argument that an apparent slowing of military actions in South Vietnam amounted to a response to the bombing limitation. White House spokesmen admitted that Rusk's remarks 'do harden the U.S. position'. But the U.S. position had not hardened and there were those who thought that Defence Secretary Clifford was much responsible for the change. On July 22 *Newsweek* commented: 'Clifford probably had the greatest influence in changing the President's policy on Vietnam, but he was helped by ex-Deputy Defence Secretary Cyrus Vance. What Clifford recognised in his evaluation of the war was that further military escalation . . . was futile.'[185] McNamara would not have become President of the World Bank if his position on Vietnam had been acceptable to President Johnson. He had wanted to replace Westmoreland in November 1967, but in that dispute the President chose Westmoreland. Westmoreland, and the weight of military opinion wanted in March 1968, 200,000 more troops to go into Cambodia and Laos and across the DMZ into North Vietnam, and they wanted more bombing right up to the Chinese border. *Newsweek* put it: 'Clifford had the guts and clarity of mind to face up to realities and tell the President frankly what he thought. McNamara probably would have come to the same conclusions.' Now Clifford won, yet his position in March 1968 was similar to McNamara's in 1967.

It is possible to piece together what Clifford advised the President. It was probably something like this:

1. In South Vietnam, the National Liberation Front, in relation to the Saigon regime, had so much popular support that aid from North Vietnam even in 1968 was far less than vital. So true was this that greatly increased American manpower and fire-power would continue to be necessary in South Vietnam. As American intervention increased so too would that of North Vietnam.

2. American bombing of North Vietnam would not compel North Vietnam to surrender nor to deny to the National Liberation Front whatever aid it needed. American bombing could not prevent effective application of that aid.

3. Greater American intervention as recommended by West-moreland would sooner or later necessitate invasion of North Vietnam. This would require general mobilisation in America and could certainly double the cost of the war.

4. Invasion of North Vietnam would lead to increased Russian and Chinese intervention, though not direct involvement. But at some point the North Vietnam regime would face a threat to its existence as a result of the American invasion and beyond that point an American ground war against Chinese troops could occur. The best to be hoped for then would be that Russia would do no more than aid China in what would become a war between China and the United States with gigantic losses of men and money.

5. The American people would support escalation of this type only if America became a police state, dedicated to a holy war and able to suppress by force the negroes and other dissenters in an inevitable civil war.

At the time something like this evaluation was being made, 'apprehensive doves' feared Clifford as a hawk, and confident hawks were ready to use nuclear weapons. Some of the latter seized the occasion to have Eisenhower say that the use of nuclear weapons could not be discounted. For some weeks there were confident predictions that if Khesanh fell the President would declare war and use tactical nuclear weapons. What people failed to see, said Newsweek, was that Clifford would 'not be governed by doctrine (his own or anybody's) but by the necessities of the problem at hand—in short, by logic'. While it is true that the Johnson Administration was now convicted by its own admission of a vast, cruel and unnecessary attack on Vietnam, it is also true that, in the final analysis, its critical decisions, as distinct from hundreds of uncritical ones, were 'governed by logic'. Clifford felt 'the logical step was to stop bombing North Vietnam and push forward peace talks. De-escalation was the only logical move.'[186] There could be no room for doubt—this would remain so under Johnson, probably so under a Democratic successor. But what about Nixon? Would the next logical move remain the same also for North Vietnam and the National Liberation Front?

By now most of the addicts of escalation, except Rusk and Rostow, had gone from high places, and General Abrams took over in July the direction of the war from the promoted General Westmoreland. It soon became apparent that Abrams' natural inclinations were suited to his instructions. In evaluating Westmoreland's 'mistakes' and Abrams' 'successes' it must not be forgotten that Westmoreland was supposed to win the war while Abrams was supposed to avoid losing it. Creighton William Abrams was a much more sensitive and flexible man than his looks indicated, and he had now to do what his common sense had for a long time told him was best to do. Westmoreland refused to admit that the enemy had won anything by the Tet offensive. Abrams believed the U.S. had taken a 'military licking', and while the American public had never recovered from the shock, the Army had. The fixed policy among Generals, Secretaries and Presidents of underestimating the enemy was now at an end. Clifford's 'logic' would now be coupled to Abrams' facts.

The change in strategy dictated a change in tactics, much of which would have come from Abrams even if he had been expected to 'win the war'. Large scale 'search and destroy operations'—massive sweeps through the country, living completely up to their name—were to be replaced by 'long-range patrols' associated with a slower and more careful process of identifying and eliminating 'Viet Cong'. There would be no more operations like 'Junction City' or 'Attelboro' and no more dramatic situations like Khesanh. The Westmoreland sort of general-ship was certainly flamboyant, prestige-making and romantic but what did it achieve? The war would be now fought rather to meet the needs of the situation than to meet the needs of the Generals.

In the first half of 1968, the number of multi-battalion operations by the U.S. Command had been reduced from 129 a month to 65, and a marine regiment at the Demilitarised Zone had been replaced by the Fifth Mechanised Infantry Division. There was a change, too, in bombing tactics. Defence Department figures showed that between 1965 and October 1968, 2,948,057 tons of bombs had been dropped on Vietnam—compared with 2,057,244 tons dropped on the whole of Europe and Asia during the Second World War. When one thinks of bombing Vietnam, it is North Vietnam that comes to mind, but of the 2,948,057 tons dropped from 1965 to October 1968, only about 700,000 tons were dropped on North Vietnam—the rest went on the far-less-publicised pounding of South Vietnam. With what result? In some cases great areas of South Vietnam had been converted into surfaces like that of the moon, as in the case of the 'Iron Triangle'. But still at the end of 1968, even after the massive 'search and destroy' operations in the area, a helicopter was in danger if it remained on the ground for a few minutes, and it was unsafe for troops to enter the area in less than battalion size. In other cases the mountain forests had ab-sorbed bombs with little sign visible from the air, and with little change in the balance of strength throughout the area. Abrams also changed B52 tactics. Instead of blanket bombing, the B52s became a close-support tactical weapon—flying in one month 1,800 close-support sorties. In addition, Abrams gave top priority to defence of the major population centres. During the same period the NLF reduced their attacks on the cities and increased their political hold in the villages and hamlets. There was bound to be a reduction in the extent and intensity of operations and in casualties, particularly civilian casualties. Something like a 'holding operation' or the hawk-abused Gavan 'enclaves' plan was coming into existence.

An account of operations and actions, of bombs dropped, of 'terror' and of casualties reveals only a little of the nature of the war

that continued in 1966, 1967 and 1968. During that period, and after
20 years of war, Vietnamese society was approaching disintegration
and destruction. Not only must destruction by American bombs, fire
and earth movers, and 'Viet Cong' bullets and mortars be reckoned.
The 'venal use of money eroded human values and resulted in widespread doubt and frustration among the Vietnamese. Nearly everyone
is prey to venality, so that money seems to be able to purchase women,
politicians, generals and intellectuals alike.'[187]

What did the war in Vietnam mean? It meant the arrival of
American and ARVIN soldiers at a village, the removal of the villagers
to some 'safe' area or re-settlement and then the destruction of the
village. The war in Vietnam meant the sight of a 'Viet Cong' flag in,
or near, a village, or some 'information' that the village was 'Viet
Cong'. And then came American aircraft with bombs, bullets and
napalm. The New York Times has often reported cases where this
happened on the basis of 'information' from people who did not even
live in the village. The 'information' was passed through South Vietnamese officers and then handed on to Americans.

Thic Nhat Hanh describes an experience that could not have
been uncommon: 'I was in a village with some 20 social workers the
night that the Viet Cong attacked the Saigon airport with mortars.
The mortars were not more than one kilometre from where we were
and we could hear the thump of their shells as they fired. Half an
hour after the attack had ceased, and long after the Viet Cong themselves had withdrawn into the jungle, American planes came over on
a reprisal raid. Their bombs fell on the village, and on our social
workers in the village, and the bullets with which they strafed us hit
innocent Vietnamese. There were no Viet Cong there and no Viet Cong
were killed that night, but the village was almost totally destroyed
and many of the villagers were badly wounded. At least one of the
peasants was buried in the debris of his own house. If this were an
isolated instance, it could be explained away as the kind of accident
that happens in war; the fact is, that it is far more typical than it is
isolated. Such events and more tragic ones occur every day, night and
day, throughout our country.'[188]

It may be that the NLF-Viet Cong demoralise people too, but as a
rule we hear mainly of their honesty and dedication. Thic Nhat
Hanh wrote: 'In the past 10 years anti-Communism has become Vietnam's most profitable business. The most vocal of the "anti-Communists" may well be enriching themselves by their written or spoken
contributions, but they are doing very little in fact against Communism.'[189] Moral fault and venality is by no means one sided in Vietnam,
but to most of its people destruction and death and devastation in
Vietnam mean American bombs and firepower. If you are to be bought
by money and become corrupt in Vietnam, it means to the people that

you will have gone over to the anti-Communist side and the money you will handle will be American dollars. The war in Vietnam has meant all these things, all of which are more significant to the people than the operations and actions that go on along their roads and tracks, through their villages and over their heads.

As the war dragged through 1968, American policy makers began to give greater prominence to the Saigon regime and its forces. They were to be built up and fitted into the new strategy. Even McGeorge Bundy—hawk of hawks—began to see the reality. 'This war', he said in October, 'cannot continue at its present level . . . not only because of what it means in South-East Asia [where it had killed probably 400,000 Vietnamese since 1965] but still more because of what it means in the United States. It is now plainly unacceptable that we should continue with annual costs of $30,000 million and an annual rate of sacrifice of more than 10,000 American lives. It is equally wrong to accept the increasing bitterness and polarisation of our people. There is a special pain in the growing alienation of a generation which is the best we have had.' Bundy remained able to see virtue in the crimes and errors from which, like the Administration, he was unable to divorce himself. 'My own view remains,' he declared, 'that the avoidance of defeat in South-East Asia was an object of such importance to us and the people of the area that the basic decision to stand and fight in South Vietnam was right.' But 'the contest in South Vietnam is a contest for the allegiance of the South Vietnamese. No foreign force can win the battle.' Just as it was, presumably, in 1945, 1946, 1949, 1954, 1957, 1959, 1961, 1963 and in 1965. Were the South Vietnamese people any less likely now to choose Ho Chi Minh and the NLF than when everyone agreed 80 per cent of them would? Was it easier now for America to avoid defeat? Were the dominoes less likely to fall now with Thailand's bases being used to bomb her neighbours and threaten China? Had America gained anything at all by proving she could not win a revolutionary war in Asia against the Vietnamese? And at a cost of 400,000 Vietnamese lives? Certainly, according to Bundy and the computers, annual costs for America of $30,000 million and 10,000 lives a year were of greater significance. But the cost of the lesson to the Vietnamese, Chinese and all other revolutionaries had gone far enough. 'The imperative of the future' declared Bundy, 'is to lift this burden from our national life.'[190] 'We' Americans, Australians, New Zealanders, South Koreans and Thais could not, it seems, go on helping the Vietnamese at this rate. There was a limit to our generosity.

But the Johnson Administration had 'twice seriously considered increasing the bombing of North Vietnam' during July, August or September. First it was because the 'Viet Cong' continued to attack Saigon and Danang with mortars, and then when Hanoi proved adamant and stubborn about a total cessation of bombing without reciprocity. In September Johnson declared he would never stop the bombing unless Hanoi 'offers reciprocal military restraints'. Hanoi offered not to bomb the United States.[191] For a while the casualties reflected the changed attitudes. For September's first week 408 Americans were killed and 2,513 wounded—the highest for three months, and Harriman claimed that more than 12,000 enemy had been killed since August 18. North Vietnamese representative Xuan Thuy said that 62,000 allies were killed in August. Operations had taken place at Conthieu, Danang, Dienban, Saigon, Nhatrang, Duclap, Hue, Tayminh, Ducpho and around the Mekong delta. There was an even distribution of initiative and offensive. Often it was the 'Viet Cong' with mortars and 'suicide squads', and often it was Abrams' 'long range patrols' and his 'close support sorties'. There can be no doubt the enemy casualty rate had not fallen as a result of Abrams' new tactics despite an early temporary drop. But both Americans and Vietnamese in Paris claimed 'smashing battle field victories'. The middle of September brought reports that 'some Americans', in Paris, were optimistic 'that North Vietnam will tire and give Johnson a clear sign of reciprocity'. But September dragged through, and October was almost gone, when reports came that it was to happen—before the election Johnson would order a permanent halt to the bombing.

It seemed obvious that President Johnson would order an end to the bombing before he lost power to do so—even if he was not influenced by a desire to help Democratic candidate Humphrey before the election in November. It was clear that Johnson was not the sort of man who would give a new President a 'blank cheque' about a war which had caused him so much trouble and anguish. Johnson would act in such a way that his mark would be left on the course of the war. He had to act before election day, and act he did. Not only did he call a permanent halt to the bombing but he opened the way for the National Liberation Front to come to Paris and he did it all without first reaching agreement with President Thieu. He had no time for that. President Johnson may well have had some promise of reciprocity from North Vietnam, although many in a position to know, like the Australian Ministers, spoke of the President's decision 'as a great act of faith'. On November 2, American Defence Secretary Clifford while speaking indicated some 'reciprocity' had been received. He said that General Abrams had authority to retaliate if North Vietnam violated any of the conditions agreed to: cessation of infiltration of the demilitarised zone, and cessation of shelling and rocket attacks on South Vietnamese cities.[192] Agreed to by whom?

What appears to have happened is this: as it was officially stated at the White House, President Johnson had informed the North Vietnamese government that he was prepared to halt the bombing as

part of a 'package deal' to get serious peace talks under way. What was
the 'package deal' and how was it arrived at? It appears that early in
October Cyrus Vance, American negotiator in Paris, returned to
Washington to argue that there was no chance whatever of peace until
the United States took a more flexible stance on the bombing of
North Vietnam. He returned to Paris and was able to give Hanoi's
representative a promise by the President to stop the bombing of
North Vietnam, provided North Vietnam *afterwards* would re-establish
the Demilitarised Zone; cease attacks against South Vietnam's cities;
accept the Saigon regime in the peace talks, and start full negotiations.
Secret meetings between both sides then began in the villa on the
outskirts of Paris occupied by the North Vietnamese delegation. A
'final break-through' is reported to have come on October 26 or 27,
with the Soviet Union guaranteeing that North Vietnam would do
what was expected of it. And the President added the new condition—acceptance of the National Liberation Front in Paris. Before
giving the order, General Abrams was told to go to Washington,
arrived at 2.30 a.m. and went to the White House where it was reported President Johnson said to him 'You have all the information I
have. In the light of what you know, do you have any reservations
about stopping the bombing now?' Abrams is reported to have replied,
'No, sir, I have absolutely no reservations'. And so the President announced: 'I have now ordered that all air, naval and artillery bombardment of North Vietnam cease as of 8 a.m. Washington time, Friday
morning. I have reached this decision on the basis of the development
in the Paris talks. And I have reached it in the belief that this action
can lead to progress toward a peaceful settlement of the Vietnamese
war.'

There was to be no prior act of reciprocity by North Vietnam.
There was a Soviet assurance that if the bombing was completely
halted Hanoi would do what was expected. If they didn't, all General
Abrams could do was resume bombing missions in the Demilitarised
Zone. There is sufficient weight of evidence that Hanoi and the NLF
would have negotiated *before* February 9, 1965, but *after* that date
only upon a bombing halt. The factor that had prevented negotiations
—President Johnson's intransigence—had now been removed. The
President had all along been advised by many who claimed to be
experts that bombs would quickly force Hanoi to give up support for
the NLF and call off the war. Instead the bombing had stiffened the
resolve of Hanoi 'ton by destructive ton' and 'created a formidable
new obstacle to settlement of the conflict'.[193]

What was the cost to the United States of this experiment? I. F.
Stone gives an estimate.[194] Between February 1965 and October 1968
about 700,000 tons of bombs were dropped on North Vietnam. The
cost of these bombs was about $700 million. To drop these bombs 914

fixed-wing aircraft and 10 helicopters were lost. Assuming a cost of $2 million per aircraft and $250,000 per helicopter, the cost is $2,000 million for planes and helicopters. I. F. Stone includes also a proportion of planes and helicopters hit by mortar fire, damaged in accidents or lost in Vietnam through other causes. The grand total of these losses for both North and South Vietnam is 1,198 fixed-wing aircraft and 1,214 helicopters. Allocating one quarter of this to the air-war over North Vietnam we arrive at a progressive total cost for the North Vietnam air-war of $3,275 million. To this must be added the cost of the pilots lost. Official figures are that 'more than 450 pilots' have been killed or are missing in the air war over North Vietnam. Stone estimates the cost of training a pilot at $450,000 or an addition of $202 million, bringing the total cost to the United States of the main items to bomb North Vietnam from February 9, 1965 to November 1, 1968 to nearly $3,500 million. 'Never' says I. F. Stone, 'was more money blown away in a more wicked cause.'

But this is merely the money cost to the United States of the main items of the bombing campaign. North Vietnam lost civilian and military lives we cannot yet estimate. That country had become the 'third largest industrial complex in Asia'. The bombing destroyed most of her steel, power, fuel and heavy industry capacity. No city or large town, and hardly a village, escaped a pounding during the three years of almost continuous bombing. To what end? So that the 'strategists' in America, Australia and elsewhere could claim that the bombing had forced North Vietnam to agree to negotiate. This is the kind of claim made by Prime Ministers and Ministers in Australia. But such a claim has not been made by President Johnson. The probability is that it is untrue and that negotiations were actually delayed by the bombing. And so the enormous costs of a piece of war strategy disappear into history with no room for a reasonable belief that it achieved any benefit for the United States or her allies.

The bombing halt, North Vietnam's response, the presence in Paris of the National Liberation Front—quick, co-operative and colourful—left the Administration's main problem as far from solution as ever. In Saigon Ambassador Bunker had worked for days on President Thieu to get him to agree to the bombing halt, and perhaps he did, but his 'colleagues' did not. Nor did they agree to the presence of the NLF. It seems that Thieu and his colleagues did eventually agree to the bombing halt provided Hanoi had, in fact, agreed to deal directly with the Saigon regime. Hanoi had not agreed to this but merely that Saigon could go to Paris. Just as Hanoi could not fail to back the NLF, Saigon could not recognise them. 'The moment we do', Thieu is reported to have said, 'half our forces will go over to them.' Doubtless Thieu had not been told about the NLF position in Paris and perhaps it was not until October 29 that he learnt from a cable from South Vietnamese Ambassador Pham Dong Lam that Harriman was 'not able to promise that the NLF would not attend as a separate delegation'. Saigon's response was to refuse to attend in Paris at all. Clifford's response was that America would have to proceed without them. However, the events of January seem to show that Saigon and its supporters in America and in Paris achieved their aim—America would not accept the NLF as a separate delegation. Hence the argument about the shape of the tables. The vital problem—the role of the NLF—remained unsolved at the end of 1968.

The central fact of the war in Vietnam at the end of 1968 was the future of American ground forces in South Vietnam. The primary object of Hanoi, and the National Liberation Front even more so, was to get them out. The primary and vital interest of the Saigon regime was to keep them in. The central question was how and when were American forces to be withdrawn. America, in fact, wanted to withdraw without appearing to lose face. The essence of this problem was how could a government that was known to be acceptable to America be expected to survive if American forces were withdrawn. In no such circumstances could it be expected that the Saigon regime could survive. What kind of government could survive? The answer was: Only a government acceptable to the National Liberation Front. What was needed, therefore, was a government acceptable to both America and the National Liberation Front. The only form such a government could take was a coalition government with significant non-NLF components which would remain as a coalition government for a considerable time. If this problem was related to what the previous three years had proved, namely, that the American army and airforce could not impose a government upon South Vietnam by military force, then there was no alternative but to accept the National Liberation Front in a government. The decisive problem for the Paris negotiators would, therefore, be how to arrive at a compromise government, including the NLF and significant non-NLF members. Such a composite government would be acceptable to the United States only if that country felt certain that the NLF would sincerely allow it to work, at least for a considerable time, and that re-unification of North and South Vietnam would take also a considerable time and be the result of genuine negotiations and adjustments. At the beginning of 1969 this seemed to be the best result the United States could expect from the long and costly commitment to this war-without-end.

As we have seen, the Johnson Administration began a basic re-assessment of policy in Vietnam about the middle of 1967. The re-assessment did not begin or end with the Tet offensive of February 1968. The Tet offensive was no more than one of many significant events which, for a year or so, had been moving policy relentlessly

towards de-escalation. This, we have seen, was because the war could
not be won militarily in South Vietnam, nor by bombing North Vietnam, nor by a combination of both actions, unless perhaps escalated
to a point beyond which the America of 1968 was not prepared
to let it go. By March 1968, President Johnson's advisers also saw that
even if America was prepared to go further, this would be only one
more point in the onward escalation. If the 'Viet Cong' forces of South
Vietnam were defeated and destroyed, then North Vietnamese forces
would become involved to the extent necessary to carry on the war. If
the North Vietnamese forces and government were threatened to the
point of defeat then Chinese forces would become involved. Then if
China was threatened with defeat, could the Soviet Union fail to act?

American policy had assumed that a single, monolithic Communist world force was being fought. There was only this much to sustain
the assumption: each Communist line of force had taken a very cautious position, but each section had increased its participation as the
need for it became necessary or unavoidable. North Vietnam had,
until 1960, sought to impose political action on the National Liberation Front in South Vietnam. Hanoi had, until 1960, opposed and
criticised military action. From 1960 to 1964 Hanoi's aid had been
reluctant, marginal and indirect. Then from 1965 North Vietnam became increasingly involved in a war that now filled the whole of Vietnam. China and the Soviet Union had incited the Vietnamese to action
from about 1960, but no Chinese or Russian had become directly involved until after the American bombing of North Vietnam was well
under way and then only in a most cautious manner. Soviet and
Chinese aid became significant for the Vietnamese after 1964 but even
in 1968 the great bulk of the war effort in South Vietnam fell on the
South Vietnamese people who fought for the National Liberation
Front.

American intervention and aid has always been vastly more significant than Russian and Chinese. The New York Times on March
23, 1964, reported: 'No capture of North Vietnamese in the South has
come to light.' The American White Paper, 'Aggression from the
North,' issued in February 1965, gave the names of only five North
Vietnamese up to then who had been captured in South Vietnam.
Secretary of State Dean Rusk admitted under questioning by the
Senate Foreign Relations Committee in 1966 that '80 per cent of those
who are called Viet Cong are, or have been, Southerners.' Even at the
end of 1968, official American estimates of North Vietnamese actually
operating in South Vietnam were never more than 55,000. At times
official figures of more than 100,000 were given but they always
included North Vietnamese units which operated in or south of the
Demilitarised Zone and which normally moved in or out of South
Vietnam to suit the technical requirements of the defence of North

Vietnam. Early in 1965 Secretary of Defence Robert McNamara stated that North Vietnamese forces in South Vietnam consisted, in their entirety, of '400 to 500 men of the Second Battalion of the 325th Division.' And on March 2, 1966, he admitted that the total amount of supplies North Vietnam was shipping into South Vietnam was between 12 and 30 tons a day against the total American shipments into South Vietnam of more than 27,000 tons a day. (New York Times, March 9, 1966.)

Transformed now into the facts, the theory of 'Communist world revolution' or 'aggression from a Communist country' in support of a revolution, meant a number of distinct propositions, each of which has been demonstrated in the case of Vietnam:

1. The revolution depended mainly on the people living in the area or country concerned.
2. Aid from Communist countries came, but it came slowly and cautiously, and the interests of the aiding area or country were always put well ahead of the aided revolution in South Vietnam.
3. As the need arose the aid increased and probably the adjacent Communist governments, and the Soviet Union, would not permit the defeat of the aided revolution without their own very full involvement.

But the National Liberation forces in South Vietnam were so strong and the North Vietnamese government demonstrably so able to survive the bombing, given the aid that reached them from Communist countries, with the prospect of more to come, that the Johnson Administration on March 31, 1968, announced a change in the direction of the war from escalation to de-escalation and negotiations.

Now it is essential to try to explain much more fully why this change of direction took place. It appears that the causes of this change of direction can be discussed under the following headings:

1. The strength of the aided National Liberation Front-Viet Cong.
2. The non- or anti-revolutionary nature of the Saigon regime and its corruption and unrepresentativeness.
3. The damage and destruction caused by the American and allied forces.
4. The international nature of the war.
5. Mistakes made by the several American Administrations.

First, let us look at the strength of the aided National Liberation Front-Viet Cong. To understand this we need no less than an accurate understanding of revolutionary war in Vietnam. Since 1954 much thought has been given to the subject in the United States but even now the American interpretation is inadequate. This American interpretation may be summarised as follows:

(a) A revolutionary war is designed and carried out by a small group of revolutionaries and involves essentially a technical problem—one of plotting, subversion and terror on the one hand, and of intelligence and suppression on the other.

(b) The revolutionaries are not strong or popular in their own country and obtain what support they do have mainly by terror against the people, many of whom they compel to support them against the legitimate government. According to W. W. Rostow, a supposed American expert on the subject, 'its task is merely to destroy while the government must build and protect what it is building.' Dean Rusk, himself no expert but presumably well 'advised', declared that the 'Viet Cong' had 'no significant popular following . . . it relies heavily on terror.'

(c) Lacking, as it is assumed to do, indigenous support and strength, the revolutionary war is taken to be directed, inspired, supplied and maintained from abroad. It relies on 'sanctuaries' from which the guerrillas can smuggle supplies and obtain their orders and leadership, and train their troops in safety. This external support is considered to be the primary factor in success, so much so that the revolutionary war is regarded as merely another case of attack by one country on another just like that of Nazi Germany or of Japan. President Johnson, in his Johns Hopkins Speech of April 1965, called it 'the heartbeat of the war.' 'In reality,' he said, 'North Vietnam has attacked the independent nation of South Vietnam . . . It is an attack by one country upon another.'

The history of the war in Vietnam has shown that this American interpretation is inadequate and misleading, and false in substance and in particular. The 'heartbeat' of the war in Vietnam was a Vietnamese heartbeat. What was Chinese and Russian had only marginal significance at any time, and for the greater part of the war the 'heartbeat' was a South Vietnamese one. Unless this is recognised and put into effect in a settlement, the war cannot ever be ended, except by total destruction of South Vietnam.

The true nature of revolutionary war can better be summarised in the following way:

(a) If revolutionaries are to be successful in any circumstances, they must consider that popular support is essential, and winning and maintaining it must be their primary objective. Castro was able to win in Cuba without widespread popular support, but once the United States enters the struggle with its sophisticated and massive fire power nothing less than a very high degree of popular support can allow the revolutionaries to survive, let alone win. The fact that 575,000

Americans, 65,000 allied troops, and immense fire power, indicated by the dropping of 2,948,057 tons of bombs on Vietnam between 1965 and 1968 (it was reported in 1969 that in
one attack 250,000 tons of bombs were dropped) could win
no more than a mere stale-mate, proves beyond doubt that
the National Liberation Front must have won and maintained a high level of popular support. In affluent societies
it is hard enough to induce people even to vote with any
perspicacity. In revolutionary societies the revolutionaries
need to induce people to risk their lives every minute of the
day. In the latter case, therefore, a far higher level of involvement is needed. Unless it is won, the struggle will never
extend beyond a flutter or an heroic expedition into the
mountains led by a Che Guevara. The national revolution
in Vietnam was not like this. It was historically more than a
century old, it was strong and it went deep into the lives and
experience of the people. It was unique. One cannot possibly
deduce any dominoes theory from it.

(b) The nature of a successful revolutionary war, as well as its
history, particularly in Vietnam, establshes pre-eminence of
political factors and political methods and the importance
of avoiding war. This, I believe, is confirmed by the details
provided in earlier chapters of this book.

(c) Mass support for the guerrillas depends upon the *moral
alienation* (no better term has so far been used) of the people
from the existing government. Moral alienation can result,
as in Cuba before 1958, from the corruption of the government over a long period and its dependence upon foreign
indulgence; but it may require, as in Vietnam, a more positive and conscious effort on the part of the indigenous revolutionary forces over a long period. This is not to lessen the
significance of Castro and the July 26 movement as a political
force in Cuba, but merely to say that in Vietnam the revolutionary movement from 1857 to 1968, had more powerful and
comprehensive opposition from the French and the Americans
than did the movement in Cuba. Once a high degree of moral
alienation has been achieved, no military power can 'win the
war'. Even 'complete military victory' would then leave a
situation in which the military victor would be quite unable
to govern politically. Such was the situation at the end of the
war in Algeria.

(d) It is important to realise that the conditions producing a
strong revolutionary war are not created by any conspiracy
or by any foreign intervention or assistance. They are
always inherent in the historical conditions of the country,

as we have seen they were in the case of Vietnam. But they are mainly dependent upon the failure or refusal of the ruling class to respond to the needs of the situation. Revolutions are always strengthened and extended by foreign intervention on the side of the ruling class as they were in Vietnam.

(e)   A revolutionary guerrilla movement, if it is to be successful against great odds, as it was in Vietnam, must concentrate on governing, on politics, and on 'out-administering', not on 'out-fighting' its enemy. This is a constructive task, requiring great care about 'terror' and the burdens it imposes on the people. The use of 'terror' has to be selective, following from the knowledge that the official killed is recognised by the people as corrupt or oppressive. 'Terror' is not the main or even an important factor in securing support for the guerrillas; it is successful and effective only if the guerrillas have won popular support *before* using terror. Furthermore, the external 'sanctuary' or aid from a Communist country, is not basic, but of secondary psychological and diplomatic value. If it has to be basic, in the sense that the guerrillas are dependent upon it, and therefore follow its line, then such external Communist aid will undermine and weaken the essential nationalism of the movement. The only Communist parties that can dogmatically follow the Peking or Moscow line are those which have no power or influence in their own country and therefore can't lose any. The Vietnamese revolutionary movement has essentially retained its own mind and soul although it has made some of the usual obeisances to Moscow or Peking in exchange for aid.

Each of these five requirements of successful and effective revolutionary war have been fully carried out and demonstrated in Vietnam. It is true that in some cases what appears to be a revolutionary movement may depend upon a Communist country. It may be directed, inspired, supplied and maintained by one or more Communist countries (although there does not appear to have been even one case so far) but it will not be successful if it is. Up to as late as 1962, the main theme of American doctrine about revolutionary or guerrilla war, was precisely that it did depend on the support of the people. [See 'Modern Guerrilla Warfare', ed. Mark Osanka.] We found repeated statements by Communist leaders, like this one of Mao Tse Tung: 'Because guerrilla warfare basically derives from the masses and is supported by them, it can neither exist nor flourish if it separates itself from their sympathies and co-operation.' Marshal Tito was often quoted: 'What a first class example it is (the unfavourable terrain around Srem) of the relative unimportance of geographical factors in an uprising. The basic factors are studious political work, the attitude of the masses of the population and the fighting leadership—if these are present the people will fight to the last man.' They will win too, no matter how militarily powerful the enemy, once a sufficient degree of moral alienation of the people from the government and the foreign imperialists is achieved. If the enemy military force is powerful, there is no other way to win but through these three factors.

This was recognised, as we have seen, by the Eisenhower Administration, when aid was guaranteed to the Diem Government in 1954. The French had to go to get rid of foreign imperialism. They did go. The Diem government had to carry out basic political and economic reforms and win the support of the people. They did not. They were overthrown, with American acquiescence. Their 10 successors did not carry out these reforms. All except the last were overthrown. Why have sufficient Vietnamese been prepared to back the National Liberation Front, to bring the American-supported Saigon government to the point of defeat in January 1965, and then to compel America to bring in 575,000 men and drop more bombs than were dropped on the whole of Europe and Asia during the Second World War only to 'stalemate' the war? How did the National Liberation Front get the support that enabled it to do that? Why were Americans so often complaining, 'If only our Vietnamese would fight like theirs?'

The answer is that the time was 'ripe' for a revolutionary war in Vietnam. For a century in Vietnam, as we have seen, there was resistance to the French and to their Vietnamese collaborators. There was a 50-year-long guerrilla war in the 19th century. There were uprisings in the villages and cities through the 20th century. But these were not enough for a national revolutionary war. Revolutionary war requires more than discontent. It requires more than spontaneous and periodic disturbances. It requires a 'sense of desperation and a grim determination to end injustice and humiliation. It demands patience with prolonged suffering, and a determined conspiracy of silence and militancy.' [See 'Revolutionary War', by Eqbal Ahmad, in 'Vietnam, History Documents and Opinion on a Major World Crisis', Gettleman. This is the best summary of the nature and meaning of revolutionary war.] Further, revolutionary war is a response to a systematic and ruthless counter-revolutionary action by the government like that carried on by Diem between 1956 and 1959. [See Chapter Seven for the story of XB village and how vital was the attack on the village by the ARVIN forces in turning it from a village conscious of its own interests, but prepared to risk little, into a 'combat village'.]

People have to risk their lives if they are to take up arms in a revolutionary war. Perhaps as many as a million of them have been killed in the war in Vietnam. People don't easily choose to risk their lives. They can be forced to do so only by extreme circumstances. They were forced to do so in Vietnam—first by the French, then by the succession of Saigon governments and finally by the United States and her allies. Bombs, napalm and helicopter gunships were simply the final architects of revolutionary war in Vietnam.

The extent and depth of the revolutionary war in South Vietnam can be seen from official statements about the National Liberation Front. The Front has successfully undermined the authority of the Saigon government in many areas of South Vietnam. Indeed, in many areas the authority of the government has never been exercised at all. In many areas the NLF has established an effective government and in many other areas 'a parallel hierarchy' to that of the government and the Americans. Official reports show that about four million people in South Vietnam live in NLF territory. In 'Liberation' territory the NLF is the sole government. Allied forces enter these areas on 'search and destroy missions' or 'long range patrols', or bomb or shoot from the air, and then depart, leaving damage and destruction behind. (Indeed, these areas are often designated 'free bombing areas' which can be bombed at any time.) But there is a total absence of Saigon government authority in 'Liberation' territory. In these areas American or allied operations are never carried out at less than battalion strength and often much greater, and contact is rarely made with large scale NLF forces. Sometimes Special Forces are put down in these areas to carry on a civic action program, but remain 'walled out' from the people and operate within the limits of their camps. In addition to about four million people who live in 'Liberation' territory, about six and a half million people live in areas of nominal Saigon government authority, which are under varying degrees of NLF control. It is estimated that about two million of these six and a half million pay taxes to the NLF. In these areas the NLF has what is called an 'infrastructure' or 'parallel hierarchy' or simply a government. In some areas the Saigon government representatives accept an arrangement with the NLF infrastructure. The Christian Science Monitor correspondent, Beverly Deepe, summed up the situation in a way differing only in emphasis and degree from reports most unfavourable to the NLF. This correspondent wrote: 'In the government areas, 70 per cent of the hamlet and village officials operate in exile, refusing to live in their areas, particularly at night. Some have set up their village offices several miles away from the district headquarters.'

By May 1968 all six major roads leading into Saigon were 'choked off' by the NLF and an effective economic blockade of the capital city from the country was set up. The same was done for every other city or district in South Vietnam. More than 100,000 allied troops had been sent out to 'clear the Viet Cong' from the 11 provinces around Saigon, yet two months later Saigon was receiving its most severe mortar attacks of the war. Dozens of areas 'controlled by the government' had been cleared in 1966, in 1967 and again in 1968, only to remain subject to the same degree of direct or indirect NLF power. The only certainty one had of security was the presence of a large American or allied force. It must not be imagined that 'Liberation' territory is geographically separated from other areas. It is mixed up with areas under government control and at dusk in Saigon-controlled areas, hamlet chiefs do leave their offices, and with armed escort, drive to the town or city, and for the night the area goes over to the NLF. About 10,500 hamlets, or five out of six, are without a Saigon hamlet chief at night.

The 'Viet Cong' are not men who come in from outside in the case of many villages, but they are there in the day time and take over at night. Where necessary, of course, 'terror' is used to prevent their exposure to the government authorities or the Americans. In many villages young and middle-aged men are rare, and one sees only children and old people. The young and middle-aged men are either killed or are elsewhere with the 'Viet Cong'. It is in the main cities and bases that Saigon government and allied authority is strongest. Indeed in such areas are several million people, many of whom live by jobs with the armies or administrations. These, in effect, are 'sanctuaries' for the government and allies and one purpose of the NLF 'generalised offensive', before and after Tet in February 1968, was to destroy the 'security' of these 'sanctuaries' for those Vietnamese who were serving Saigon and the allies. But the NLF exercises considerable influence even in the cities. A high proportion of businesses pay taxes to the NLF, including, of course, some American ones. Newsweek's Senior Editor, Arnaud de Borchgrave, recently recorded the opinion that in Saigon the NLF has a more effective tax collecting system than the government. According to an official American report, Saigon government control is 'acceptably effective in only 13 per cent of the South's provinces.' Clare Hollingworth of the London Daily Telegraph, on November 2, 1968, reported: 'The government in Hanoi and the political arm of the Viet Cong—the National Liberation Front— today administer more than 1,800 of the 2,500 villages and more than 8,000 of the 11,650 hamlets inside South Vietnam. Indeed, Saigon administers less than eight million of the total population of 17 million and of this 8 million some four and a half million are soldiers and civil servants paid by the State.'

We have noted the effect of mistakes made by the American Administration on the course of the war (not that Hanoi and the NLF did not make many mistakes, too); but the basic mistake of the United States was nothing less than about the nature of the war in Vietnam. We have seen that this mistake occurred with a change in American view of the nature of the war which came about in 1962. It was no longer a 'civil war'—it was something inspired, directed, supplied and carried on from 'outside the country.' It was 'aggression from the north.' It was 'an attack by one country on another.' We have seen too, that this meant that 'political and economic reform' no longer had the importance at first attributed to it. We have seen also that this meant that military action would be given greater importance in American calculations. We have seen that military escalation of the war, and keeping in office a junta of generals was an inevitable outcome of this 'mistake'. We have seen that in turn de-escalation and negotiations became an outcome of this 'mistake'. At this point I will quote two statements by Eqbal Ahmad, to whom reference has already been made. I believe that our survey of the war, made elsewhere in this book, will make the reader immediately aware of the relevance and significance of Ahmad's opinions: 'The defending army's pressure for conventional attack on an external sanctuary is yet another sign that a revolutionary war has been lost on the home grounds. In revolutionary warfare, armies trained for conventional combat follow a vicious logic of escalation, which derives from acute frustration over an elusive war that puts in question not only their effectiveness but the very validity of their training and organisation.' And, of course, it puts in question their assessment of the war itself. Is this not an accurate view of the American Administration and General Staff in their increasing frustrations between 1962 and 1968?

And then Ahmad makes reference to a final point. 'The assumption,' he writes, 'that a guerrilla outfit, like a conventional army, can be controlled and commanded by a foreign or externally based government, ignores the organisational, psychological, and political facts of revolutionary warfare. The distrust of the "home-based" guerrillas, even for their own government in exile, cannot be over-stated. The resourceful and tough "interior" leaders and cadres who face the enemy daily, collect taxes, administer, make promises, and give hopes to the population are not easily controlled from abroad and make suspicious, exacting and hard-to-please allies. Therefore, zone commanders and political commissars are, for the most part, monarchs of all they survey. As a group, they are joined together by shared experiences, by a common mood which is defiant and insular, by a shared suspicion of "politicians and diplomats over there" selling them out, and by a collective will to defy a settlement that is not of their making.'

In one sense, as we have seen, it is unimportant to debate whether it was 'aggression from the north' or an indigenous South Vietnamese national, revolutionary movement supported by large numbers of people. There is only one Vietnam. The NLF is thoroughly Vietnamese. North Vietnam would finally do what it could, and perhaps what was necessary, to aid the NLF. But in another sense it is vital to decide the truth of this question. That is because the foundation of American policy in Vietnam was false. Much of the death and destruction resulting from action by both sides since 1962 were the consequences of that false foundation. Unless we resolve to arrive at a more correct view of the nature of revolutionary war, it will be difficult to adopt the essentially political methods required to deal with the situation in Vietnam in 1969. It will be difficult also to avoid the extension of a similar American counter-revolutionary policy to many other areas in the economically 'under-developed' world.

CHAPTER TEN

WE'RE ALL NEGOTIATORS NOW

They are all in Paris now. The beginning of 1969 saw the world's greatest military power, the United States of America, involved in a *political* struggle against half of one of the smallest countries in the world.

The parties are at the conference table for one reason only—that the war could not be won militarily. They have turned to political methods because they were compelled by costs and casualties to give up military methods. If they return to military methods the costs and casualties may be far greater, and there could then be even less certainty of victory than before. Unless the new Nixon Administration needs to learn these lessons for itself, we can expect the parties will want to stay at the conference table. But it must not be forgotten that the conference table was not chosen by the United States and Saigon. The evidence shows that by 1964, at the latest, the NLF and Hanoi had proved they could win the struggle against Saigon if it was political or military, and it was equally apparent that if Saigon was to have a chance the struggle had to be military and it had to be fought by America. The evidence shows that Hanoi and the NLF preferred political methods, and adopted military methods as they were forced to do so by an escalating war, conducted at first by Diem and his successors, and then by the United States. The NLF could not win that kind of war, although they could 'stalemate' it. But they can still win a political struggle. The United States and her allies could not win that kind of war either and like Hanoi and the NLF they could 'stalemate' it. But unlike Hanoi and the NLF they may not be able to win a political struggle. It is now necessary to look at the extent and limitations of power in the situation. It is essential to recognise the facts.

The truth is that up to 1965, Hanoi and the NLF were winning and, more or less, were ready to negotiate. The United States and Saigon were not winning and they were not ready to negotiate. After the bombing of North Vietnam began Hanoi was not ready to negotiate and neither was the United States. As soon as the bombing and other acts of war against North Vietnam ended, Hanoi was prepared to negotiate and did so. Hanoi, and the NLF, are now prepared to negotiate, as they were before 1965, because they do not want to accept the costs and casualties of further war and because they believe they can win in the negotiations—that is, they believe they can win the political struggle. Saigon is now prepared to negotiate because they know the United States will not support them in war, but they are prepared to negotiate only with North Vietnam. These negotiations would not be about anything in South Vietnam but only about the cessation of North Vietnamese involvement in South Vietnam. The Saigon position now is that South Vietnam is a separate, sovereign country and in this they have been backed by the United States. Saigon wants to negotiate this position into final acceptance by Hanoi. Then they want to go on, of course with American assistance, in fighting the NLF until they win. It is at this point where some uncertainty remains. Perhaps the United States under the Johnson Administration had accepted negotiations with the NLF, facing the fact that this would lead to a 'composite' government in Saigon including the NLF. The real question here is who else would appear in that government? Thieu? Ky? Huong? Who? It is hardly likely that the Nixon Administration will as readily go that far. It is more likely the new President will support Saigon in resisting the NLF and in carrying on the fight in South Vietnam while negotiations go on in Paris. Indeed this will provide the shape of the immediate future.

It appears, therefore, that at this point we should consider two questions—who could enter a composite government with the NLF (should that course be chosen) and what would be the likely future of such a composite government? On the other hand, should that course be rejected what are the chances of Saigon carrying on the fight against the NLF and what kind of war would that involve? The Nixon Administration, of course, must be weighing up each of these alternatives for it seems that they are the only ones available for it. In this debate there will be those, of course, who say that the allied war situation was not really bad in 1968, that the effect of the Tet offensive was exaggerated and that America and Saigon were militarily stronger at the end of 1968 than at any other time. There will be those who will say that Saigon's military strength has greatly increased and that with American weapons and money Saigon can defeat the NLF, perhaps, with one proviso—that aid from North Vietnam can be cut off. The Nixon Administration will fully explore this alternative, at least while negotiations are protracted in Paris. What, however, appears beyond doubt is that this is just the old war all over again. And in that war Saigon had no hope of beating the NLF. Increasing American military action had been proved essential even for a 'stalemate'. What is more, the kind of American action that had proved essential was peculiarly American and, probably, could not be taken over by Saigon. The critical factor in 'stalemating' the war in 1967-68, and in 1969, has been American air power. Not only does this mean the largest helicopter force ever assembled, but it means a bomber fleet capable of dropping the greatest bomb loads ever carried and it needs air fields in Thailand and it needs the Seventh Fleet—the world's greatest single strike force—just off the coast. These are all 'sanctuaries'. How can Saigon duplicate American air and fire power? Even on the ground Saigon remains a very doubtful quantity. Of 10 divisions in operations recently, only one has proved capable of handling in full combat a comparable enemy force.

It hardly seems likely that even the Nixon Administration will long continue the alternative of a war by Saigon against the NLF even if Hanoi could be kept out. But can Hanoi be kept out? This seems very unlikely. Although Hanoi may keep much of her future intervention 'under wraps' and very limited, as was the case before 1965, we can be certain it will continue as long as the war does and it will always remain much more significant than it was when Saigon carried the main burden of the war, as it did before 1965. It seems probable that sooner or later the first alternative—a 'coalition' government including the NLF—will have to be faced. It would, of course, be far better to realise this now and prepare for it. It would have been far better to have realised this before the South Vietnamese elections in 1966 and prepared for it then. But this was not done and the chance has gone. Equally it seems probable that a 'coalition' government including the NLF requires the speedy development of a 'third force' in Saigon. The term 'third force' is attributable to the Buddhist leader Thic Nat Hanh and is set out in 'Vietnam: Matters for the Agenda', a publication of the Center for the Study of Democratic Institutions, Santa Barbara, California, dated June 1968.

Thic Nat Hanh defined the 'third force' as follows: The formation of a government in Saigon 'capable of representing the considerable number of Vietnamese who reject the NLF but who also oppose the present policy of Saigon.' This government must be able to prove two things: first, that 'it is not an instrument of Washington'; and, second that 'it is committed to peace not war.' 'Unless' says Thic Nat Hanh, 'it satisfies these two conditions, no government in Vietnam can gain genuine support. At this point let us face the facts—the Saigon regime does not have sufficient 'genuine support' and cannot get it. Does such a 'third force' exist? Before looking at that question, there is another feature of the 'third force'. The 'third force' does not imply withdrawal of American forces, without which there can be little chance of a government of any kind in Saigon but an NLF one; but it does mean an end to offensive military actions. If a government in Saigon is to have 'genuine support', Thic Nat Hanh believes that it must bring about an end to the 'terrible suffering inflicted by offensive operations.' 'In Vietnam,' he says, 'suffering and hardship are equated with bombing and military destruction.' This must end. 'Any government committed to halting military operations would attract wide support,' says Thic Nat Hanh, 'including the allegiance of many non-Communist (NLF) front members concerned primarily with independence.' This Buddhist leader makes the vital point that 'the Front' would have to accept this government and deal with it politically. 'If it refused, it would belie its own claim that it is fighting for peace and independence.'

Now the question is: does such a 'third force' exist in South Vietnam? It must be admitted that the matter is in doubt. There can be no doubt South Vietnam did possess such a 'third force' but American policy has weakened and reduced it. There was strong and effective 'third force' resistance to the Diem regime. On April 26, 1960, as we have seen, the 'Manifesto of Eighteen' was presented to Ngo Dinh Diem as Premier of South Vietnam. [A copy of the Manifesto can be read in Bernard Fall's 'The Two Vietnams', p. 442 and will repay study.]

The manifesto showed that Vietnam had passed through French colonialism and Japanese occupation. The strength of its nationalism, associated with but not controlled by Communism, had won independence. The Geneva Agreements had recorded this with international recognition and authority. But now all that South Vietnam had was 'pseudo-independence covering up for colonialism'. To continue this situation would strengthen Communism and may even give it control of the nationalist forces. The Manifesto argued that the only answer provided by the Diem government was to collaborate with a foreign power, the United States, until it had become dependent upon that power, and to 'fill the gaols and prisons to the rafters, silence the press, eliminate the political parties and religious sects and make every man fearful in the night of the secret police.' Fifteen of the Eighteen were former Ministers or Secretaries of State, one was a Governor of a Province, two were Professors and one was an M.D. Within three days of the presentation of the petition all except one, who was a relation of Madame Nhu, were arrested and detained. In November 1960, an influential and anti-Communist but nationalist journal, 'Pour le Viet-Nam', examined the insurrection against Diem and wrote of it: 'The rising is justified: in a country where the most elementary rights of the people are ignored, where the legality of the actions of the government has become an empty expression, the will of the people can only make itself felt by means of force, that is to say, by means of a revolution and taking over of the government. . . We nationalists, all of us, know that there is a race against the clock taking place between the Vietminh and ourselves.' Every nationalist who was imprisoned, every act of support for Diem aided the Vietminh. Every reduction of the power of nationalists, under Diem and later— and to reduce this power became American policy—was to weaken the 'third force'.

In November 1963 many of the 'third force' leaders arrived in Saigon from imprisonment on the island of Paolo Condore. Some of them, like Phan Khac Suu, an old revolutionary, emerged later among Saigon government leadership. Others like Dr. Phan Quan Dan have the best democratic record of any in South Vietnam. Others like Duong Van Minh have military prestige as well as political accept-ability. There are several among the leadership of the Buddhists who would qualify. It must be remembered that each time there was a real change of government in Saigon, between 1963 and 1967, the deter-mining factor was not the 'Viet Cong' but the 'third force' in the streets of Saigon, Hue and Danang. As we have seen there was a high degree of democratic participation in these 'coups' and enough power among the people to compel one general after another to toe the line. It is unfortunate that the American Administration, and the Australian Government too, for what that was worth, invariably came down on the side of the most military alternative and swung the balance against the 'third force'. Finally they installed the military junta in power by securing an arrangement between Thieu—the Catholic leader—and Ky.

This arrangement meant an end to all Buddhist power near the top, and the final elimination of Buddhist generals like Nguyen Chanh Tri.

One of the critical factors in the formation of the 'third force' is the position of the Roman Catholic community in South Vietnam. As we have seen, the co-ordinated Roman Catholic community around Saigon, many of whom had come from North Vietnam in 1954-55, per-haps 800,000 in all, had formed the main base of Diem's military power and remained thereafter the most militant, uncompromising war-like section of the South Vietnamese people. It was this Roman Catholic section who most supported the war and swung the balance to the military junta whenever the issue was in doubt. Consequently it is this community whose role in the future is most difficult to provide for or foresee. It is certain that their leaders will play a part in the future government of South Vietnam, although there is doubt whether they would take a place in any 'coalition' government. It may even be that their present leader, President Thieu, may play a significant part in the future. The Catholics in Vietnam are a minority and they have had a record of foreign collaboration. They cannot expect to impose any doctrine of absolute divine authority. They can expect no more than toleration and a fair share of influence in affairs.

We can probably say that it is possible that some South Vietnamese leaders, except the purely militarist ones like Ky, would be acceptable in future government of South Vietnam. This statement begs the ques-tion of what is 'acceptable'. Acceptable to whom? We can be sure that the United States will back the most anti-Communist leaders and groups in arriving at a governing arrangement. But this is a political not a military question. American power will, therefore, necessarily be limited. As it is a political question the power of the NLF will be greater. Not only will the future of a 'coalition' government be much in the hands of the NLF but its actual composition will also be.

This is the point at which the paralysing simplications of American foreign policy have been most starkly caught up with by events. The utter nonsense of the American attitude to the NLF is now fully exposed. The United States *recognised* the National Liberation Front by sending to South Vietnam to fight it 575,000 men, thousands of bombers, helicopters and army equipment, artillery, mortars and the most sophisticated firepower so far devised, as well as the world's most powerful fleet and some aid from 'the free world'. This was the form of recognition made by the United States and her allies. But there was to be no political recognition. Why? Because there was a realisation in American policy, not clearly recognised, that the United States and her allies would not win politically against the NLF. And so the military method of dealing with it was deliberately chosen. But the confrontation of the United States and her allies with the National Liberation Front is now a political one. It is political only because America could not win the war militarily. And since the confrontation is now political, it demands a 'front' by America and her allies very different from the one they have so far maintained. Where do men like Ky find justification to be part of the American team? This military adventurer was brought into power by the skill with which he could manipulate American aircraft to swing the balance between contending Vietnamese generals who were using tanks. This Vietnamese citizen had no greater appreciation of national independence for his people than to establish a 20-year-long record of collaboration, first with the French, recognised by the Americans as a colonial power, and then with the Americans themselves.

There have always been a few who discovered that a foreign power in Vietnam would give them positions of authority, provide them with a luxurious life, allow them to keep their land and their grip on money and trade, permit them to be corrupt even with the occupying power's own supply of goods and money for the supported regime, and to channel much of their gains into foreign bank accounts. Many of those who have held high positions during the American occupation have been able to behave more in this fashion than had any of their predecessors under the French. It was money or power, sometimes both. Those like Ky who strutted around with gun on hip and fighter aircraft idling on the airstrip could not have saved themselves for more than a few hours but for the screen of power provided by the American occupation. The government in Saigon consequently came more and more to function purely as a military organisation using almost armed force alone to maintain its position. But the 'third force' in South Vietnam has never employed armed force and functions alone as a political movement.

All those factors which relentlessly escalated the war operated also to give more and more power to the military junta and cause them to rely more and more on armed force. Now with less stress on military methods, most of the relevance and effectiveness of the generals have been destroyed. The situation in South Vietnam now demands the men and methods of the 'third force'. It is a political situation and demands political methods. However the whole direction and experience of the American occupation of South Vietnam has operated to deprive America and her allies, first of an understanding of the situation, second of a method to handle it, and third, of men equipped to do it. It is in the interests of South Vietnam that the power and influence of the dogmatic, inflexible Communists be reduced to the barest possible amount. But Communism as such was not strong in South Vietnam or even in North Vietnam. As Thic Nat Hanh points out: 'Now there are Catholic intellectuals and young people who realise that real Communist sentiment is not strong in Vietnam. Consequently they are going beyond their one-time simplistic anti-Communism and are beginning to discuss the kind of political and economic life Vietnam must have if we are to know peace.' The havoc and destruction worked in Vietnam by the American intervention has, not surprisingly, turned many people away from the dogmatic 'simplistic anti-Communism' that has no answer to Communism except armed force and suppression. The essential point here is not whether this form of anti-Communism with its armed force and suppression can work (and the experience in Vietnam shows that it cannot work) but what kind of policy and method can work to eliminate the influence of the dogmatic and relentless Communist? An answer to this question is needed or else so many other parts of the world that are dominated by poverty and injustice will either, like Vietnam, become devastated by armed American firepower, or will be won by the dogmatic and relentless Communists.

The first point to notice is that each extreme tends to produce its opposite. The greater the influence of dogmatic anti-Communists in the formation of policy the more will dogmatic Communists be produced on the other side. It operates the other way, too. The more that armed force is used by one side the more it has to be used by the other. As we have seen, the movement to 'escalation' of armed force in Vietnam was led by Diem, his successors and by America. This was basically because they were not able effectively to use political methods because political methods would have so changed the power and wealth structure of South Vietnam that all 'our' Vietnamese would have lost their positions in it. They were naturally opposed to change in the effort to maintain the status quo of power and wealth. And in this stand they were opposed by dogmatic Communists. But they were opposed, too, by liberals, by socialists, by nationalists, and by tens of thousands of others who could not be classified at all. But sooner or later most of these, who constituted the most experienced and effective *political* people in South Vietnam, were described as 'Communists' or 'neutralists' and forced into gaol or isolation or into actual association with the dogmatic Communists. Each of these moves gave the dogmatic Communists more power and diminished the power of the 'third force'. The American Administration sometimes protested against these attacks, arrests and deportations, but never backed up its protest. Finally the American Administration continually allowed the military junta to have its way, because 'effective waging of the war had to come first.' Who could wage the war? Not Dzu who came second in the Presidential election and who now is in gaol; not Au Troung Thanh, who was a minister in several governments, and who is now in gaol; not Dr. Phan Quang Dan who has won more genuine votes than any other man in the history of Vietnam, and who has now been thrown out of the Assembly for advocating negotiations with the NLF; not Buddhist monk Thic Tri Quang, perhaps a more powerful figure for the 'third force' than any other, who on being branded as a Communist by Ky was put into 'protective custody'. Not one of these men was ever backed by the American Administration. Instead it was always some pistol-packing militarist who was backed. They were the ones who could 'win' the war. They were chosen. They have not won the war. It is now admitted that they cannot ever win the war.

What is left? The answer is that the 'third force' and the NLF are left. The answer is that the policy of peace and neutralisation is left. The probability is that Ho Chi Minh and his colleagues, in Hanoi and the NLF, would have been wise enough to accept not only peace but neutralisation and the 'third force'. There can be no doubt—the havoc and destruction wrought by the United States in Vietnam must have influenced many on the Communist side towards accepting peace and neutralisation now. The death of Ho Chi Minh does not alter the basic situation. The probability is that a better result could have been achieved by elections in 1956 or by negotiations between 1963 and 1965. I hope those in Thailand, Malaya, Singapore and Australia who feel more secure in their positions of power, privilege and wealth can find some evidence, convincing for them, that the havoc they have wrought in Vietnam has been really worthwhile.

What then might be the factors in finally clearing war, havoc and destruction from Vietnam? I think they can now be listed as follows:

1. Full recognition of the National Liberation Front as a principal party in the negotiations in Paris.
2. Achievement of a cease fire in Vietnam, each side holding its

existing positions and territories.

3. Formation of an acceptable 'third force' in Saigon to speak for those opposed to the NLF.

4. Formation of a 'composite' government made up of representatives of the NLF and the 'third force'.

5. Agreed withdrawal of all American and allied troops, and North Vietnamese troops, from South Vietnam.

6. Holding of general elections in South Vietnam in which any candidate who desires to stand and any voter who desires to vote may do so. The elections to be subject to international inspection.

7. The relations between North and South Vietnam to be a matter for the government of North Vietnam and the elected government of South Vietnam.

8. The achieved conditions to be placed before a conference of the United States of America, the People's Republic of China, and Soviet Union, so that Vietnam, Laos and Cambodia may by agreement among these three powers become 'neutral' in relations and conflicts of these powers.

It may be practicable to achieve the aim of point eight by a re-convening of the 1954-1962 Geneva Conference, even though Britain now has little relevance, standing or power in the area. The points above, of course, are the contemporary requirements to achieve for Vietnam, Laos and Cambodia what have been properly called the 'sacred principles' of Geneva—that the sovereignty and the territorial integrity of Vietnam, and of Laos and Cambodia, should be determined by elections. A return to the application of these Geneva principles is essential for peace and progress of the area. This is a feasible, realistic objective consistent with the stated programs (see in particular the Political Program of the South Vietnam National Front for Liberation, August 1967) of the National Liberation Front, and of the Republic of North Vietnam. It must become, too, the program of the United States of America and whatever governing body there is to be in Saigon.

CHAPTER ELEVEN

IN SEARCH OF AN ENEMY

There has never been a time when we did not have an enemy; when we did not feel threatened. Before 1939 we had to choose between Hitler, Stalin and Tojo. For a long time we were not sure who was our enemy and in the end the decision wasn't made by us. It did not go the way we might have expected.

From first moment of the Communist revolution in Russia in 1917, until late in the nineteen thirties, it was Russian Communism that was most feared and most expected to be the enemy. It is now notorious that Hitler was 'appeased' all the way through the 'thirties. Whether or not this was a genuine mistake of men who wanted peace, or whether economic, political and other interests made many powerful people in Europe, Britain, America and elsewhere tolerant of Hitler is a question we will not discuss here. But the fact remains that before World War II Stalin's Russia looked like being the enemy and it was alone Hitler's decision to enter into a pact with the Soviet Union in 1939 (following our similar pact with him at Munich in 1938) that finally allowed Hitler a free hand to attack Poland and then to attack Holland, Belgium and France. He left little choice for us. We could come to terms with him or fight. We chose to fight. There were some then who thought it wrong. They thought Communist Russia was the main enemy and that we should either give Hitler a free hand or stand aside and watch Russians and Germans kill each other. But it was too late for that choice in 1940.

It seems sometimes inconceivable that Hitler did not give the British and French pre-war governments some assurance that he had no designs on them, and then move directly into attack against the Soviet Union. If this had been done and there been no preceding Nazi-Soviet Pact, European attitudes towards a German invasion of Poland would have been different. But this was not the plan that Hitler adopted. He chose to become our enemy. But then Hitler made another strange decision. Although he had control of Europe he had not defeated England and instead of making that his sole objective he turned off in June 1941 and began his gargantuan task of invading the Soviet Union. Some of his advisors may have told him the Soviet Union would collapse. This view was certainly held in Europe and in America by influential people, but there were others who warned him of the massive task he was undertaking.

At first, of course, Hitler made great advances, and if the Nazis had been wiser perhaps they would have made greater advances still. But finally the German armies came to a stand-still and the Russian skies were empty of German aircraft. And then came the great roll-back. General Douglas MacArthur then beseiged in Corregidor said what so many felt: 'The world situation at the present time indicates that the hopes of civilization rest on the worthy banners of the coura-geous Russian Army. During my lifetime I have participated in a number of wars and have watched others, as well as studying in great detail the campaigns of outstanding leaders of the past. In none have I observed such effective resistance to the heaviest blows of a hitherto undefeated enemy, followed by a smashing counter-attack which is driving the enemy back to his own land. The scale and grandeur of this effort marks it as the greatest achievement in all history.'

We were all soon pro-Russian. There were Supreme Court Judges in the Australian-Soviet Friendship Society. Toorak ladies were collect-ing money to buy sheepskins for Russia. Those who were Communists, or supported them, almost won a majority on the ACTU. No longer did it appear that Soviet Communism would ever be our enemy again. The new euphoria outlasted the Soviet race to Berlin and the collapse of the Nazi regime and the suicide of Hitler. But soon it was apparent that Communist Russia would emerge again as our enemy.

The agreements between the Allies and the Soviet Union at Yalta and Potsdam had the effect of recognising that the Soviet Union would have the right to influence the governments in Bulgaria and Rumania and Britain would have a similar right in Greece. Both countries ex-ercised these rights and the Soviet, if anything, with less bloodshed. But the 'spheres of influence' extended more widely. What was to happen to Poland, Hungary, Czecho-Slovakia and Austria on the one hand and Germany, France and the other European countries on the other? The end result was that the Soviet Union made sure that Com-munist governments came to power in the Eastern European countries and in Eastern Germany, while America and Britain made sure that capitalist governments came to power in Western Germany and the rest of Europe. It was an easier task in the West. It was natural that we would again become opposed to Communist Russia. Her system in-volved getting rid of private ownership. It was foreign, tough and atheistic. Hitler's remarkable choices had temporarily postponed this natural opposition. With the Soviet Union a powerful force in Europe, and engaged in an operation to install and maintain Communist governments in Eastern European countries, it was inevitable that this opposition would soon return.

The North Atlantic Treaty Organisation and the Marshall Plan were the means by which this opposition was first expressed. Policy became one of 'containment of Communism'. And Communism was contained in Europe.

It would be impossible to prove that NATO was not of some importance. Whilst the combined American-British-European armed forces and the American nuclear bomb may have had significance, there is no evidence that the Soviet Union ever considered, or would ever have thought it feasible, to take military action in western Europe. If the Soviet Union had any plans at all they were political and even then they were not militant or radical plans. Perhaps Soviet tanks and aircraft helped them. The Soviet Union had suffered enormously from a Germany the world regarded as militarist and led by insane men. There could be a resurgence of Nazism. The Soviet leaders would have been irresponsible idiots had they not at least carried into effect what had been agreed at Yalta. It is worth noting what was done there and how it was done.

But what was agreed at Yalta had been agreed much earlier. Churchill himself records how the agreement was first reached. When he met Stalin he proposed a 'ninety per cent predominance in Rumania for Russia', the same for Britain in Greece, and fifty-fifty in Yugoslavia. While this was being translated, Churchill set down on a piece of paper a proposed split in the five Balkan countries which added Hungary 50-50 and Bulgaria 75 per cent for Russia. Stalin scrutinized the paper, made a large blue tick on it and passed it back. It was Churchill, not so much Roosevelt, who had prepared to make agreements of this kind. He was so prepared because he knew the intensity of the feelings of Stalin and Molotov to protect Russia, even at the expense of the democratic rights of Eastern Europeans, of which no Western politico-religionist had ever, in the past been solicitous, when their own interests were at stake. They all agreed then, and the world then agreed with them, that the most vital factor was the 'inflexible purpose to destroy German militarism'; and, for this purpose, to divide and break up Germany and make it as difficult as possible for any militaristic resurgence to impose itself on Europe and Russia, should it ever rise again. Memories are short but the smoke of Nazi gas ovens and the sound of Nazi jack-boots could still be heard when it was agreed that the Soviet Union was entitled to impose her power in the formation of East European governments to ensure that they were not unfavourable to her. How did the world in 1944-45 think this would be done? Did it think that the Russians would stop short and leave anything in doubt?

Churchill returned from Yalta with a very convinced view. He reported to the House of Commons on February 27, 1945, 'The impression I brought back from the Crimea, and from all other contacts, is that Marshal Stalin and the Soviet Leaders wish to live in honorable friendship and equity with the Western democracies. I feel also their word is their bond. I know of no government that stands to its obligations even in its own despite, more solidly than the Russian Soviet Government. I decline absolutely to embark here on a discussion about Russian good faith.' There was no question that the Soviet Union would run any risks to her interests in the formation of governments to the east of the East German frontier. But Austria and the rest of Europe were a different matter.

At the same time that Stalin showed he would run no risk in East Europe he pressed Mao Tse Tung to enter an unfavourable coalition with Chiang Kai Shek on a basis put forward by American General Patrick Hurley; he gave no aid or encouragement to the Greek rebel nationalists movement when they were being killed in the streets of Athens by British troops and by Greeks who had worked with Hitler. He even tried to stop Tito from aiding them. In the case of Tito himself, Stalin pressed him to bring back King Peter and sought to bring about the 50 per cent British say in Yugoslavia that he had accepted in Moscow. About a year later he left the Azerbaijani Communist Party on the Russian border, to its fate before firing squads and on the gallows in Persia, when that country, with American backing and arms, took over Azerbaijani. Stalin's policy in Europe was defensive from the start. The blockage of Berlin was not to seize more of Europe but an attempt to hold what he had. Communist Europe the rigorous, austere, class-police state was under pressure. It was not expanding. It had to defend itself from penetration by ideas and agents secret and otherwise. The Berlin wall is not a springboard for movement from East to West but a barrier against penetration from the West. The Communist Parties of Western Europe, then predominantly on the Stalin line, were not encouraged to take a revolutionary or militant stand. Whenever were they? They were encouraged by the Soviet Union to support De Gaulle and to support coalition attempts in Italy. Spanish Communists, few and weak as they were, never saw any signs of Soviet aid. According to Isaac Deutscher all this by Stalin was 'to damp down the revolutionary spirit of the Western European working class in the aftermath of the second world war.' If, of course, this was the reason, it was not an end in itself. Stalin knew that he would have been less likely to have been able to get away with the establishment of Communist governments in Bulgaria, Hungary, Poland, Rumania and Czecho-Slovakia, if, at the same time, he had been inciting revolution in France and Italy. Not only were the Stalinist Communist parties working on a line in Europe that contributed little to radicalism and militancy but this was the position too in other parts of the world.

The key to orthodox Communist line policy from 1945 was not any design for world revolution or conquest but the establishment of secure, pro-Soviet regimes in eastern Europe. Hardly had this phase completed when there was the emergence under Kruschev of the more deliberate and overt line of 'peaceful co-existence'. This has led to American acceptance of the Soviet Union as a kind of working partner for 'peace'. Of course, under Kruschev, the Soviet Union was far more 'adventurous' than Stalin or Mao's China has ever been. Cuba was an example. As far as 1960 the Cuban Communist Party made a very conservative evaluation of what was attainable in Cuba and worked within, if not with, the conditions set by Batista. It regarded Castro as an irresponsible, middle-class visionary. This was consistent with the Stalinist line. But when Kruschev decided to put missiles, although they were probably short range ones, in Cuba, he committed an act of 'adventurism' Stalin and Mao would never have tolerated. Kruschev's act may however have obtained an undertaking or a de facto result which prevented America from undertaking any further invasions of Cuba.

Not only was the Soviet Union seriously handicapped because of her World War II losses in embarking on world conquest, or even that of Europe, but war was hated by the Russian people and no more of it was wanted. A people's attitude to war is always more permissive, if, as in the case of America or Australia, it has never been waged around their own homes. Not only did Russia need an un-revolutionary world to establish her own power in Eastern Europe but later on, it appears, the Russian bureaucracy, upon which even Stalin, and more so Kruschev and Kosygin, had to rely, wanted conservatism in foreign policy. As a rule bureaucrats are never radical or enterprising. There is little reason to believe that Communist bureaucrats are different and there are plenty of them in the Soviet Union. There is perhaps more need for anti-establishment youth dissenters in the Soviet Union than in Western countries. What emerged overtly with Kruschev and Kosygin as 'peaceful co-existence' had already come into force under Stalin. (It probably originated with Stalin's victory over Trotsky whose theoretical position was that the revolution was 'continuous' and should be pushed on into the rest of the world. Stalin's position was that socialism should first be securely established in the Soviet Union.) At any rate, the Soviet line continued. Nothing was to endanger Soviet influence in Eastern Europe, as the Hungarians found in 1956 and the Czechs in 1968. And little was to be done elsewhere to incite, or aid revolutionaries, if that committed or tied the Soviet Union to a position which may react to her cost or embarrass her own territorial security. This, we have seen, was the case in Vietnam. The Soviet Union seriously aided North Vietnam when she had to—and the compulsion lay in the rapidly increasing American threat to the very existence of Communist North Vietnam and in the propaganda battering the Soviet Union was getting from China as an 'Imperialist agent and

stooge' ready to sell out the 'heroic comrades in Vietnam'. Certainly
the Soviet attitude was always bellicose and confident that the Soviet
led world revolution would 'bury' capitalism and all its hangers-on.
Indeed the fantasy and extremism of the Communist line about the
overthrow of capitalism by the consciously planned and directed revolution is matched only by the fantasy and extremism with which
anti-communists allege it. Indeed this is not surprising for almost the
only evidence that anti-communists ever produce consists are claims,
assertions and boasts made by Communists themselves. But in most
places Stalinism and most of its successors so offended nationalism that
it never had a chance either in a revolutionary situation or in the
politically listless affluent social democracies.

It has been said that the Soviet leaders were dominated inexorably
by some Marxian dialectic to conquer the world for Communism, but
to explain world events since 1945 by such a proposition would be to
ignore most of the facts, and talk in language acceptable only to the
fanatic or to his victims. There were too many cases of normal human
disagreement arising from pride and prejudice, too much that was the
outcome of the clash of two very different ways of life, too much that
resulted from the obvious force of nationalism and religion to put
everything down to political ideology.

Roosevelt was everlastingly right in his gallant and sustained
effort to break out of the ancient cycle of national rivalries—arms
race—and war. The contributions of Communists to the cold war and
the arms race are immense but we of the West are primarily responsible
only for our own conduct. We are responsible for the radical, analyti-
cal, human tradition. We may resolve to go back to Roosevelt and
forget the nightmare of Truman, Acheson, Eisenhower, Dulles, even
Kennedy, Rusk and Johnson. It was not Roosevelt who failed it *was*
his successors who were unable to rise above the old prejudices, humbug and their own brand of credibility gap. But Communism was contained in Europe. We must take with us something of value from this
experience. There was a strong tendency to treat Communism solely
as a military force, and whilst NATO may have had some value in
stabilising Europe, its military aspect was kept in bounds. There was
some resurgence of Nazism in Western Europe, but the striking thing
was not that there was some, but that there was so little. The main
stabilising force in Europe was not military; it was political and
economic. Western Europe (except Spain and Portugal and had they
not been protected by Western Europe, doubtless they would not have
withstood the indigenous pressure for revolution small though it is)
possessed more or less sophisticated social democratic systems and a
long political tradition and experience. This was the place where
there was the real strength to handle stresses and strain which may
otherwise have turned into armed combat. But the purely economic

force was also powerful. The Marshall Plan was far more significant than all the guns, tanks, aircraft, tactical nuclears, Generals, computers and backroom boys in preventing people from turning to revolution, and the way that Communists actually behaved was probably a main factor in preventing people from turning to Communism. It is this emphasis on political and economic factors in the 'solution' of the European problem we should carry with us when we turn to Asia. From 1945, for several years, European and American leaders had been European minded. They had feared and contained Communism in Europe. It was in a social democratic Europe with its relatively highly developed economic system, self-governing tradition and long political experience. It was a Europe that had already had, for the most part, its anti-feudal revolution and its native capitalists were wealthy and knew how to invest and control their parliaments. This was a Europe that had undergone its nationalist revolution and was able to use the power of science and industry protected from foreign interference, to provide the goods that would make their people 'affluent' and disdainful of the untidy, long haired students who told them they were powerless. And after Europe the American leaders turned to Asia.

America's attitude to Asia had been anti-colonialist. There had been sympathy for the Chinese Communists and an ability to see the facts about Chiang Kai Shek. There had been just enough truth in this for Joe McCarthy to be able to terrorise liberal America by hinting at it. There was just enough in it for this evil faced Senator to say that the State Department had handed China to the Communists and thereby have many people believe that they could ignore all the forces in the vast history and geography of China and her six hundred millions of people in deciding how a revolution had taken place. Americans had been sympathetic to Ho Chi Minh and had air-dropped aid to him and they had said that France must never be allowed to get back into Indochina. But this was to change. Truman had carried America into a war in Korea which did not come about because of any revolution whatever. There was no revolution in South Korea. There were no guerrillas and no National Liberation Front. There were two armies, conventional armies, facing one another across the 47th Parallel. When fighting really started, everybody on the American side assumed that it would be Sighman Rhea on their side who had started it. It may not have been him, although he was responsible for more pin-pricking than the North Koreans. But the North Koreans meant business and had enough fast armour to make their business effective. It was the North Koreans who were powerful enough to sweep into enemy territory and penetrate nearly three hundred miles to Pyonyang within a few weeks. They were not aided by a 'fifth column' because there was insufficient political development in South Korea to produce any. Theirs was a conventional expedition. If the Russians had given the signal to move they were extraordinarily careless for it coincided with the time they had chosen to boycott the United Nations because that body would not admit China. This allowed the United Nations, free of Soviet veto, to authorise American resistance to the conventional invasion of South Korea as a United Nations action. There were many influential Americans who wanted to fight the North Koreans and to take China on too, for the very obvious reason that China would always get stronger than now. But there were many other Americans who did not want to fight North Korea and they were so influential to make it a reasonable judgment for the North Koreans to think they would not be resisted by America. But they were resisted, and the American trend to withdraw from Asia was abruptly changed. McCarthyism was installed for a while as the dominant political institution in America.

It was President Truman who first began to apply the European doctrine of 'containment' to Asia. It was President Truman who sent American troops into South Korea and later into North Korea. It was President Truman who sacked General McArthur for pushing the American advance so far and fast that he caused Chinese intervention. It was President Truman who got American troops 'bogged down' in a land war in Asia. And it was President Eisenhower, a Republican, supported by the Republican McArthur who had brought much of it about, who said, 'elect me, and I will get us out of Korea.'

But having got elected and having got America out of Korea, it was President Eisenhower who campaigned for a 'mandate for change' —a mandate to change American policy and begin to push America back into Asia. But to push America back into Asia on European assumptions. This became the stated policy of John Foster Dulles. And so the involvement in Vietnam began.

Everything that has happened in Vietnam was implicit in the first word ever uttered by John Foster Dulles, Secretary of State, and backed with some continuing trepidation by Eisenhower. Indeed war against China was implicit in Dulles' first word. John Foster Dulles 'first word' was written before he became Secretary of State. In an article written in 1952 he asserted that America would put an end to the 'Asia last' policy. The hang-over from Europe in 1942-43 of sacrificing the 'far East' to give time for 'the West' was to be brought to an end. There would be an end also to 'defensive containment' said Dulles, now must come 'a firm will to defeat Communism and roll it back into Russia.' It should be noted that it was *Russia* into which everything was to be 'rolled back'. John Foster Dulles was going into Asia but he was going in with European assumptions and experience. He was calling in the old world to redress the balance of the new. Here then was the problem: '20 odd non-Western nations next door to the Soviet world [and where in relation to China?] live close to despair because the U.S., the historic leader of the forces of freedom, seems dedicated to the negative policy of "containment and stalemate".' Dulles ended it all by saying: 'I venture to be dogmatic . . . (we will) commit our offensive military power to the deterring of aggression and the preservation of peace.'

For several years Dulles appeared to think that his nuclear weapons were enough for this purpose. It was to be 'massive retaliation at times and places of our own choosing.' But even in the case of confrontation with China over the offshore islands nuclear weapons could not be used or waived effectively. However, something was effective enough— China accepted an American presence about three miles off her coast, when, and for years, little North Korea didn't. However, it was inability to use nuclear weapons in 'massive retaliation' that led to the first 'agonising reappraisal'. (Dr. Henry Kissinger, President Nixon's 'right arm' became famous for writing a long book to show that 'thermo-nuclears' could not be used in little wars, therefore you needed 'tacticals'. Then after the book he discovered you may not be able to use 'tacticals' without having to use bigger and bigger bombs until you ended up using 'thermo-nuclears' of full power. Therefore, said Dr. Kissinger, you should build up 'conventional capacity' and he became so famous he was in 1968 appointed Presidential adviser.) And so the United States under Eisenhower and Dulles began to use America's offensive military power to roll back Communism in Vietnam.

It has been said that Eisenhower and Dulles brought into United States foreign policy the ideology that Communists were the source of all evil and with them there was no possibility of agreement or settlement on anything and they must be 'rolled back' by a great 'free world crusade'. Compromise, concession, or even recognition, are not virtues but futile, cowardly appeasement and moral treason. Even neutrality was immoral. This was the Dulles doctrine, but his notability lies in the fact that it was through him that it was expounded. It was more appropriate than the crude empiricism of Truman, and it remained American doctrine until 1968 when a rudimentary industrial North Vietnam and the peasant NLF compelled the world's most powerful nation to talk to communism and seek a political settlement. The basic reason for this is that for a powerful Vietnamese minority— and the majority is never committed to anything—Communism was not the source of all evil. It was, in fact, more appropriate to the needs of Vietnam than any other doctrine and in respect to the struggle for national independence and economic and political reform the communists in Vietnam had the best record. If this had not been so the Dulles doctrine would not have been overthrown by events.

At the time of Dien Bien Phu we can see all the essentials of the Dulles doctrine. Dulles allaged that what was happening in Indochina did not have much to do with Indochina. On April 15, 1954, at the height of the crisis, Dulles announced the thesis no part of which was new: 'Under the conditions of today the imposition on South East Asia of the political system of Communist Russia and its Chinese Communist ally, by whatever means, would be a grave threat . . . to the Philippines . . . Australia . . . New Zealand . . . and the entire West Pacific.' Not only was the threat to Indochina a Russian threat, strengthened by China, but it would spread around the world as much irrespective of conditions in Indochina, the Philippines, Australia and New Zealand as the waters of the Pacific were irrespective to the movement of the Japanese fleet that attacked Pearl Harbour in 1941 or sank the British battleships Prince of Wales and Repulse near Singapore in 1942. The people of Vietnam, their history, traditions and problems were as irrelevant to what was happening as the waves and winds of the Pacific were to the Japanese military expendition. They could be used just as much, and as easily, by the navigators and engineers in Moscow; or was it Peking? The spread of Communism was something that came from outside and took control of your own country. It was, in this, exactly the same as Hitler, Mussolini and Tojo. 'We failed to halt Hirohito, Mussolini and Hitler . . .' said Dulles. 'We must not fail again.'

And so American globalism was set to oppose Communist globalism. And they both looked at things in the same way. No one more than the Communist ideologists argued that Communism was all powerful. No one more than Kruschev, in telling the Americans that he would bury them, helped the American people to accept the Dulles doctrine. No one more than the North Koreans in 1950, when they drove their conventional expedition to Pyonyang, helped to install Joe McCarthy in America.

The problem was so comprehensive and so serious to Dulles that for him what was needed was not a single strike, like that proposed by Admiral Radford at Dien Bien Phu, or action by America alone, but a long term, far sighted, united operation. Although America might have to act alone if necessary, action by the whole 'free world', or of much of it as could be got—'the allies'—was needed. Dulles opposed the Radford plan, not because it was an aggressive military strike contrary to what is called international law and the Charter of the United Nations, but because it was far too modest. It was limited to France, a colonial power, and America. Perhaps Dulles had really decided that France was finished and that this may not be a bad thing. Serious consideration does not seem to have been given to what French General Ely wanted—that France should be given American aircraft to bomb and strafe the Vietminh.

The second fundamental of the Dulles doctrine was put by Eisenhower in a letter to Churchill on April 4, 1954, in which he asserted, '. . . there (is) no negotiated solution of the Indochina problem,' but only 'a strong coalition willing to join the fight if necessary.'

Eisenhower went on to say he was prepared to accept negotiation in principle but, 'To put much faith in the process of negotiations . . . in its application to dealings with Communists, I consider is unrealistic'.

But Dulles was not able to prevent the Geneva Conference from being accepted by the French. Defeat at Dien Bien Phu was, like the Tet Offensive in 1968, no more than the last of many substantial straws that had broken the camel's back. France in 1954, like America in 1968, could no longer reject or avoid negotiations. But Dulles tried every move he could to keep France in the war and then to sabotage the Conference when it did meet. Even Sir Robert Menzies, on April 28, 1954, had to deny Dulles' statement that Australia and New Zealand were supporting America. On May 21, Mr. Clifton Webb, New Zealand Minister for External Affairs stated he could not 'conceive of a satisfactory alliance in South East Asia which did not include Britain.' And what was Britain's position? Eden had said he would not support any action that would threaten the conference at Geneva. Returning home to tell his Government that Dulles proposed just this, Eden found that Churchill stood behind him. Churchill said, 'Great Britain (is) being urged to assist in misleading Congress into approving a military operation, which would in itself be ineffective and might well bring the world to the verge of a major war.' Although Eisenhower tried to persuade Congress to accept the increased taxes in America that were involved by telling it not to forget Vietnam's great value because of its 'tin, tungsten and rubber', it was not money or economics that drove Dulles on. For him it was a spiritual matter—it was the American, Christian way of life threatened by evil, atheistic Communism. This was consistent then with American financial and economic interests but no one ever starts, or follows through, a financially costly policy that does not pay for financial reasons only. It is always done for spiritual reasons.

Having got to Geneva, Dulles tried to stop the French from reaching any agreement with the Vietminh. Having failed he went home and left General Bedell Smith to refuse to sign the Agreement for America and to make sure that the Saigon regime of Bao Dai refused also to sign it. America's military and financial assistance, as we have seen, began in 1950, and by now it had reached a total of some 2,000 to 2,600 million dollars and represented, in 1954, about 80 per cent of the total French cost of the war and more than France had received in total Marshall aid. But France was finished. Her Premier Mendés France had to undertake to sign the agreement or he could not have survived in the Chamber of Deputies. He did sign it.

Now Dulles lost no time. Talks began in Washington to secure two things: United action by as many 'allies' as possible—the result was SEATO of America, France, England, Australia, New Zealand, Pakistan, Thailand and Philippines; and, a government in Saigon that could take the place of the French, who were obliged by Geneva to administer South Vietnam to ensure that there was an election in July 1956, and to pass on their responsibilities to any successor.

The basic aim of the Dulles doctrine was that the non-Communist half of Vietnam should become an American sponsored bastion against any further Communist advance in South East Asia. This remained the sheet anchor of American policy in Vietnam. But as the American Administration began to look more closely at the problem two other things emerged or were strengthened: that 'All traces of colonialism' must go—no government in Vietnam could survive that had not won full, complete and genuine national independence. Hence France had to go and a Vietnamese government had to come. In addition to nationalism, political, economic and social reform were recognised by Dulles as critical. Hence there had to be reform.

When once America had picked out a man to back—Ngo Dien Diem—he was told by Eisenhower that aid, and it was not military aid, was dependent upon reform. In 1965, Eisenhower said, 'We said we would help that country but we were not talking about military aid.' But he said at the same time that having gone so far as we have we should not exclude even the use of nuclear weapons. In 1954, Eisenhower also told Diem that his country was 'a country temporarily divided by an artificial military grouping.'

At this point we can sum up the Dulles doctrine which explained, justified and determined the American intervention for all succeeding Administrations:

(1) Communism was the supreme evil which spreads because of a power that originated in Moscow and spreads irrespective of people or their conditions of life. It was a political version of the doctrine of 'original sin'.

(2) South Vietnam must be maintained as a bastion against this spread of Communism. There could be no negotiations, compromise or settlement with Communism. It had to be stopped.

(3) To stop Communism a Vietnamese government was essential, such a government was one that was independent and did not rely in any way upon any foreign government.

(4) Such a government had to carry out political, economic and social reforms. Armed force could be used but it must never become dominant or even the main weapon.

'One lesson (from the French experience in Vietnam)', pronounced John Foster Dulles, 'is that resistance to Communism needs popular support, and this in turn means that the people should feel that they are defending their own National institutions.' The London Observer summed it up: 'The outcome of the war in Vietnam will depend . . . on which side wins the support of the people.' The 'support of the people' would not be won by democratic pleasantries. It would be won in a revolutionary war. Could America 'last the course'? This was the question in 1954 when Dulles unpacked his globalist doctrine. Would it work? We can be sure at this stage, and throughout, that each and every American Administration underestimated the task and did not understand what was being tackled. All the contradictions were built in, the seeds of failure were planted by John Foster Dulles.

And now in 1969 policy is to be changed. But the change may occur without recognition of the reasons for failure of the American intervention in Vietnam. We may all move to something different merely because of the failure of what was done. For a while we must become students of Vietnamese history, for it is there that the courses of the failure of the Dulles doctrine will be found. Although Vietnam is unique, what we can learn there can provide the foundation for a successful policy for much of the developing world.

CHAPTER TWELVE

DEATH OF THE DULLES DOCTRINE

What will America do now? The question must be answered if we want to know what Australia will do. For some little time after President Johnson on March 31, 1968, limited the bombing of North Vietnam, and said he would not stand again for the Presidency, and for a while after the initial shock of the Tet offensive, many people thought that America would withdraw altogether from Vietnam and South-East Asia. But it soon became apparent that this was not the case. What had come to an end was not American intervention but the Dulles doctrine; the doctrine that tied America to the escalation of a land war in Asia and to an absolute refusal to negotiate with Communists. America is now negotiating with Communists. The after-Vietnam America will be very careful not to go beyond, say, the 1961 point in Vietnam—never again to have American boys bogged down in a land war in Asia. Asian boys will have to do the fighting in future. Beyond that we cannot be sure what America will do.

What then is the Nixon Administration likely to do? First it will try to hold on to the basic Dulles doctrine and maintain South Vietnam as a bastion in South-East Asia against the advance of Communism. It will still try to link the situation in South Vietnam with that in Thailand, but opposition to that policy in Laos and Cambodia will block its application there. But how will this Dulles doctrine be pursued now? Most probably it will be pursued by continued strengthening of the armed forces of South Vietnam, and their use to replace Americans who are not in combat roles, so that more and more of these Americans can be withdrawn and, perhaps, the draft brought to an end at home. There will be a great hope that South Vietnamese armed forces will even be able to replace Americans in combat. The tragic experiences of the past eight years indicate little that would justify any hope that this can succeed now.

While this method of holding South Vietnam is being pursued, and it will take time, it will be Nixon Administration policy to demand at the peace talks that North Vietnam cut off all supplies and assistance to South Vietnam and withdraw what forces are there now. Furthermore, there will be a demand that the 'Viet Cong' stop fighting altogether in South Vietnam. If these aims could be achieved it would ease, if not eliminate, the task of the South Vietnamese armed forces in holding South Vietnam. But neither Hanoi nor the NLF will agree to these demands. On the contrary, it appears they will demand at least a 'coalition' government in South Vietnam and that after it takes over American troops be withdrawn over a period of time. Only then would they agree to withdraw North Vietnamese troops in accord with the same timetable. America will not willingly agree to these proposals but eventually she probably will, although it is possible that incidents, particularly effective or vicious 'Viet Cong' attacks, may set the whole war ablaze again as a result of provoking the American 'hawks'.

The only dependable way to ensure that this does not happen is for America to accept the Hanoi-NLF proposals and begin a phased withdrawal. The result would be a government in Saigon in which the NLF, and within that the Communists, would be by far the strongest component. Should this happen, the NLF and the Communists may be careful about reprisals against their Vietnamese enemies and in the severity and speed of their industrialisation policy and their anti-peasant land reforms. This will be easier for them, and more natural, because they will not plan to establish a forced-paced industrial nation as North Vietnam did, and they will have profited from the trouble caused by the Northern forced-pace peasant elimination program. Furthermore, they should, by now, know that extremes can begin it all over again and none but the most unreasonable among them would want to prolong or bring back the Americans. There will, of course, be a few such people among the NLF forces. Wars of the kind they have just gone through tend to produce such types. Similarly there may be a chance that re-unification with North Vietnam may be pushed too early. But the evidence suggests that neither North Vietnam nor the NLF is likely to want that. North Vietnamese leaders have spoken about re-unification in 10 or 20 years and all NLF programs have stated it as a long-term objective. What then, is the Nixon Administration likely to do outside Vietnam? First of all, it will continue to strengthen the Royal Lao Government by paying most of its bills and by continuing in Laos the CIA operation that has been at work for some years. In addition to air-drops and other supply operations, there is a kind of shadow American government and administration in Vientiane. Bombing of Pathet Lao forces by American planes from Thailand may even intensify. In recent years the Laos operation has been within the broad limits set by the nationalist Souvanaphouma. It is possible that some kind of de facto division of Laos may follow the war, with the Mekong river Laos provinces governed from Vientiane, and the Vietnamese-oriented hill and mountain regions governed by the Pathet Lao.

Cambodia is a totally different matter. Head of State Norodom Sihanouk considers alignment with either America or China is worse than the plague but will lean most to the side that leans least upon him. America will have less and less influence upon Vietnam and more and more influence with Thailand, although this latter may diminish too. It is still difficult to know what will be the attitude of the NLF and Hanoi at later stages but so far they have guaranteed non-interference with Cambodia and have not broken their word. Communist interference with Cambodia would have to depend on China but some kind of settlement of the war in Vietnam will not necessarily increase it. It is not likely the Americans will in the future encourage Thailand to oppose Cambodia. Hence, if Cambodia can continue to make good social, political and economic progress there is little reason to expect any significant shift in her neutrality.

Thailand is again completely different from both Vietnam and Cambodia. It will be Nixon Administration policy to maintain Thailand as the main American base in South-East Asia and to keep it as the bastion against the advance of Communism. American bases and installations will be maintained and extended and the number of American personnel in flying, administration and advisory roles, both military and civilian, will continue to rise. Thailand will be supplied with the most up-to-date anti-insurgency weapons—helicopters, bombs, napalm, rapid-fire guns, mortars, artillery and the whole range of sophisticated counter-insurgency hardware. Thai troops will use them with the help of American advisers. It will be policy to hit hard at all insurgents and suspected insurgents. Economic aid will also increase so that something can be done about the almost non-existent 'infrastructure' of the Northern and North-Eastern provinces. The Thai 'national liberation movement' is very rudimentary and lacks nationalism as a cause, although increasing American presence will eventually supply this and it will grow in strength more or less in proportion to the American intervention against it. It may even be possible that Thai leaders will consider the American presence all too high a price to pay for security. Only an aggressive policy by China could put their acceptance of it beyond doubt.

Malaysia and Singapore will not receive any direct American attention, partly because it is unnecessary, and partly because it is recognised at present in both places to be counter-productive to the level of security they want. Both governments want British troops, Singapore more than Malaysia, mainly for the money they bring in. The eventual withdrawal—Australian as well as British—is not likely to be followed by any program of economic aid that could bring in as much money as that spent on the military presence.

Indonesia presents different problems. The old Communist Party (PKI), was an 'elitist' organisation quite incapable of coping with the Army effectively even if Sukarno had agreed, and had been able to, supply it with arms. Indonesia will begin to develop a 'National Liberation Front' but there, as in Thailand, it will lack a foreign presence to give it its main drive. There never has been any real instalment of economic or social revolution in Indonesia—the nation is still more feudal than anything else—and it will be from political, social and economic aims that Indonesia's revolutionary movement will gain its momentum. This will be a relatively slow process although the need for it is far greater than in any other country in South-East Asia. Revolution remains dormant in Indonesia, but it is bound to come. Misjudging the nature and aim of the PKI, the American authorities had resigned themselves in 1965 to a Communist victory in Indonesia. The victory of the fanatical anti-Communist side after the inter-armed services coup of 1965 astonished and delighted the American authorities and administration. The main reason for this victory, apart from the military weakness of the PKI, was the fact that very few Americans or other foreigners were in Indonesia at the time, and that America had played on the soft pedal. For a nation so frenzied about the effect of a domino falling in Vietnam, the ease with which the United States accepted the assumption that the Indonesian domino would fall to the PKI is amazing.[195] But the post-Sukarno leaders have said that they do not want American interference or military personnel and they oppose as much as Sukarno the American policy of intervention in Vietnam. This policy of the present Indonesian leaders is likely to continue, although American investment and business power in Indonesia is likely to grow and so too will the military links. Should the new Indonesian revolutionary movement rise so quickly and significantly as to pose a threat for the Indonesian government and should the army find a problem to deal with, then it will turn more and more to an American-supplied counter-insurgency program for Indonesia. It is possible as it is with Thailand, that if the Indonesian government got into real trouble with its guerrillas, it might even accept American troops. It is difficult, though, to see the Indonesian leaders coming to this parlous state, for their nationalism is strong and the present threat to their power is weak. It is difficult to see the Nixon Administration willing to take again the first step towards that long nightmare that was the war in Vietnam, by putting the first combat troops into either Thailand or Indonesia. But the possibility cannot be dismissed.

What then is happening in these South-East Asian countries that makes likely revolutions and 'National Liberation Movements' and commands American attention? The answer lies in the insatiable demand everywhere for modernisation and greater economic power, and in the fact that it cannot be achieved without structural change, without changes in land ownership, without 'bold transformations and innovations that go deep'. These changes will be resisted by the landowners, officials, aristocracy and the generals. Communists will be active in the situation. Why cannot modernisation and economic power be achieved in 'under-developed' countries without structural

changes? Economic development is not primarily an economic process.
It is a political and social process which leads to economic results. It
is not just a matter, as it is in the United States or Australia, of new
technique, investment of money, production, income and growth. It
is not just a matter of technique and organisation as so many Western-
trained thinkers believe it to be. Nor is economic development likely
to be evolutionary as it has been in America and Australia for about
two centuries. America could never have developed economically the
way she did had she not won political independence from George
III's England and from the colonial ruling class in America. Australia
could never have developed economically had the people of England,
from whom our institutional structures were copied, not overthrown
Kings and land-owning barons and installed money-making capitalists
in power. But most of the economically 'under-developed' countries
have not yet had these political and social changes. When a society
is mainly agricultural, power tends to be located with those who
own land. Then, eventually, merchants become powerful. Then
industrial capitalists. As these changes occur the location of power
changes and those who held it before oppose those who are getting
it. Sometimes there are serious wars as a result.

Land reform is needed in economically under-developed countries;
lower rents are needed, and lower interest charges, and higher wages.
Are landowners likely to lead a campaign for land distribution and for
the lowering of rents? Are money lenders likely to lead a campaign for
lower interest charges? Are employers likely to start a campaign for
higher wages? Hence, economic development becomes associated with
taking from one class and giving to another. The wealthy and power-
holding classes always believe they have to give up far more than they
really do; the poorer classes always look as if they are going to get
much more than they do. Consequently this tends to polarise the
people: those who hold power won't give up any, and resist every
change; those who want land or money seem to want to change everything overnight. Very often there are simple economic matters that
make change essential. Take the basic matter of efficiency. China,
Indonesia, Thailand and similar countries produce mainly rice. But
they are not efficient rice producers. For 1955, the following figures
were published by the United Nations:

Rice Yield per Hectare in kilos

Australia	45,900	Thailand	14,300
United States	34,300	India	12,600
China	24,700	Vietnam	12,300
Indonesia	16,500	Philippines	11,900
Burma	14,800		

The traditional rice producers are by far the least efficient, and the
modern capitalist countries are the most efficient. This is because

land in the old traditional rice-growing countries has been subdivided into blocks sometimes a few yards in area; sometimes there is great exploitation of those who do the work so that they are not strong and fit; at all times there are few mechanical aids. Landlords will resist the changes necessary to improve these conditions and tenants have no power to introduce what is needed.

Take the balance of payments as another example. A country cannot make economic progress unless it makes appropriate use of what it earns from the outside world. It may need to use its foreign earnings to buy food, as China buys wheat, or machinery for production. But the following United Nations figures show how little of foreign earnings is available to Latin American countries for these purposes. Percentage of items in Balance of Payments:

	1955-60	1961-63
Profits and debt service paid out	16.8	29.9
Other money sent out	1.8	7.3
Freight, insurance and travel	15.0	15.4
Other services	7.1	5.6
	40.7	58.2

This is the balance of payments position not only of Latin America but of any area possessing little indigenously national power favourable to economic development. It is the balance of payments of an area in which the people have an average income per head of about $200 a year or less and in which most people are small tenant farmers, rural labourers or simply unemployed. It is a balance of payments position of an area in which the rich people are non-functional in the sense that they are not involved in production. They have a celebrity type of relationship with their own society and with the United States and Europe. A balance of payments position of this kind which cannot ever allow economic development unquestionably must change. But if it is to change then there has to be a shift of power from those who make it what it is, to those who will change it. It cannot be changed without this shift of power.

Hence one class of power holders must be changed for another. The institutions of the country, the attitudes to life and the priorities of the country must change if there is to be economic development. It appears probable that these changes will not take place smoothly. Landowners do not readily redistribute land. Merchants do not give up their monopolies. Money lenders do not lend for less. Powerful officials do not readily give up their jobs. Similarly most of those in positions of ancillary power—in the churches and universities, etc.—are rarely found on the side of change.

It seems improbable that these changes can take place smoothly and without resistance and it seems probable that they will need concentrated power and authoritarian methods. The probability is that either rule by the army or rule by civilians drawing 'support' from the 'people' is the form it will take. Generally the army is on the side of the contemporary power holders and is therefore likely to be against change. It may be possible for an army to bring about economic development when it is not drawn from, or dependent upon, the traditional class but is somewhat professional or 'middle class'. Perhaps South Korea is an example of this, but Formosa is not. Formosa may well be a special case where a ruling class was imported—from China—and exercised motives to weaken the local Taiwanese ruling class and were not themselves involved in losses that came from granting land to peasants. The choice available to under-developed countries, if they are to develop, is usually seen as a 'Right-wing' military dictatorship or a 'Left-wing' civilian dictatorship. But what we are concerned with here is not whether a 'Right-wing' military dictatorship can do it (and that is the kind America is likely to support) but how far America can go in supporting such governments. The position may be as follows: a social revolution is necessary in all under developed countries if they are to develop. A Right wing military dictatorship may achieve such a revolution with *limited* American aid. If such a case, a revolutionary war will not occur. But if the army does not achieve results with limited American aid then even America won't be able to afford to go any further. This is what the war in Vietnam seems to prove. Look at it simply in figures: if the cost of intervention had to become $30,000 million a year to stalemate a revolutionary war in half of one country with 16 million people, how much will intervention cost for Latin America, Africa and the rest of Asia?

Let us summarise then what America is likely to do in South-East Asia. First, America will try to hold South Vietnam as an anti-Communist area by persuading Hanoi to give up supporting the NLF and the NLF to stop fighting. America has been unable to force Hanoi by bombing, and the NLF by ground war, to do this; beyond doubt she will not achieve it in Paris. Bombing and the ground war might rapidly re-escalate again. Still, it seems that the limiting factors escalation will continue to be the possibility of war with China and the Soviet Union, should escalation go beyond some undefined point, to say nothing of the costs of it in Vietnam. In this sense the 'victory of the Vietnamese national revolution' (as it is put in Moscow and Peking) would be far less likely if not backed by China and the Soviet Union. But, of course, the Vietnamese do all the fighting. It appears, therefore, that America will have to accept, sooner or later, a Saigon government with NLF representation. The NLF will be the strongest part of it, but will probably follow a moderated policy towards their enemies and towards industrialisation and removing peasants from the land. Re-unification between North and South Vietnam will not come overnight.

Above all America will maintain and develop her cordon of power around Asia. Air, naval and nuclear forces will continue to be used to deter Chinese 'expansion'. So powerful is this American cordon that Chinese penetration of it is highly improbable, even if that were China's intention, for which there is no evidence at present. It is probable that there will soon be American efforts to establish and improve relations with China.

It appears likely that the Nixon Administration will seek to put into effect its proposal to get the Asian nations to accept more responsibility for their own defence. What SEATO has failed to do another arrangement of Asian nations may do better. The objective of this arrangement would be to have Asian troops, like the South Koreans and Thais, available for ground fighting in an anti-insurgency action if the host country began to face difficulties. It is not easy to see what likely members of such an arrangement could give it any real strength. Recent American evaluations suggest that Australia is too small to contribute much to Asian collective security. In addition, our troops are white, and not well suited because of that, for ground action in Asia. There have been suggestions—in Australia too at that—which would have the effect of making Australian forces into a kind of trip wire to induce American intervention in Asia. The implied argument is that if Australian forces were in Asia, and Americans were not, and if Australians were attacked, America would be much more likely to come in to aid than if the attacked troops were merely indigenous. Australia's role as a trip wire for American intervention may increase our value to America. But it is hardly likely that America will emerge from the war in Vietnam believing that Australia has any significant role to play with her own troops in Asian ground wars. Indeed, it is likely that she will conclude that she herself does not—or hopes she does not—have any significant role to play in Asia with her ground troops.

Of course an adequate view of American policy as a background to Australian policy cannot alone be obtained from looking at what is likely to happen in Asia. Australia is involved not only in following America in Asia. We are involved too in the American nuclear system. This is the result of the acceptance by the Menzies-Holt-Gorton governments of several American nuclear missile installations in Australia. These Australian governments seem to have made Australia as much a part of the American nuclear missile system as is America herself. But this has been done without any explanation or admission. Indeed on many occasions there has been a point blank denial of what is involved. The first admission of Australia's nuclear involvement came on April

23, 1969 from the Minister for Defence.[196] While we cannot be fully
certain of the nature and purposes of these American nuclear missile
bases in Australia we can now be certain, on the admission of the
Minister for Defence, that they would involve nuclear attack on
Australia in the event of a nuclear war. The exact scientific nature
of these bases and secrecy about them is now an academic question.
Once it is admitted and recognised that they are significant enough
to attract nuclear attack, the precise 'scientific reason' for them is no
longer of much significance. What is more, we can have no doubt that
the function of these bases will be well known to an enemy which
possesses advanced nuclear and missile technology. Australia has now
been made vulnerable to nuclear attack without any adequate explanation to the Australian people.

Despite the government's curtain of secrecy we can be reasonably
certain that the powerful low-frequency radio station at North West
Cape, Western Australia, will transmit signals to American submarines
in parts of the Indian Ocean and that these submarines' nuclear
missiles would be targeted on the southern parts of the Soviet Union
and China. It is known that the commanders of the submarines cannot
make decisions when to fire their nuclear missiles and that the signal
can be given only by the President of the United States. It is clear
that the North West Cape radio station is needed to transmit the
vital decision to fire. It would be in the interests of an enemy who
feared, or was under, nuclear attack, to put out of action such a vital
piece of mechanism before it could be used at all, or as soon as possible
afterwards. It is unlikely, in the event of nuclear war, or the threat of
it, that North West Cape could last more than a few minutes. Indeed
the very nature of such a station presupposes that it could not survive
an enemy attack upon it. Its very nature seems to presuppose that it is
a first-strike mechanism. Its purpose seems logical only if an American
decision to strike was made before the enemy had a chance to act. A
well-known mechanism so obviously located must be constantly targeted so that it could be knocked out before it could be used. It is
hardly likely that anything less than missiles would be used for such a
purpose and it would be certain that the missiles would carry a nuclear
warhead.

We cannot be at all sure of the nature, purpose and powers of the
other American bases in Australia. There is a station near Alice Springs
for the purpose of recording nuclear explosions in China. There is an
installation at Pine Gap and one at Woomera. This latter station
has brought the admission from the Minister for Defence that in
the event of nuclear war Australia would attract nuclear attack. It is
hardly likely that the Pine Gap station is less important than will
be the one at Woomera. The Pine Gap and Woomera stations may be
for the purpose of helping to guide American nuclear missiles on

their way to targets in China and the Soviet Union, and for the purpose of helping to detect and intercept enemy missiles on their way to targets in the United States. The location of these stations is no doubt determined by its being the most suitable for use for missiles travelling in a fractional South Polar orbit. Stations in the United States, or elsewhere, would not be able to operate as effectively in direction or give as much warning of missiles in this orbit. Now if such stations were in the United States they would be protected by the most advanced anti-ballistic-missile (ABM) system possessed by the United States. But there is so far no evidence that they will be protected at all in Australia. These installations therefore could be of no protection whatever to Australia because there are no intercepting missiles located near enough to stop missiles destined for Australia.

While many Australians take an unemotional, almost indifferent, view of the involvement of a few thousand Australian soldiers in Vietnam, with only a few hundred getting killed—less than on the roads, we are often told—and believe that there is very little risk to themselves involved in such a policy, the position is very different when one takes into account the nuclear missile aspects of the involvement of the 'American alliance'.

We may, it appears, be out on a limb. We have American bases here that would attract nuclear attack because they are a vital part of the American nuclear missile system. But we have no protection by an ABM system against this attack. The American government would never install such a base in the United States without a powerful and costly ABM system to protect it, and recently decisions have been made by the Nixon Administration to extend and intensify that system. Yet the Australian government allows the establishment of such 'lightning rod' bases in Australia with absolutely no effective protection at all. We may indeed consider ourselves a prime nuclear target unprotected by an ABM system. And all this has happened in secrecy—without any hint by the responsible governments that this was being done. We can be sure that few other governments in the world have gone so far with LBJ and his successor as has the Australian government. And probably no other government in the world would so lack respect for its people as to behave with such secrecy. It remains to examine whether such a policy is in Australia's interests, let alone whether it will be accepted by the Australian people.

CHAPTER THIRTEEN

WHAT DO WE DO NOW?

Australia today is supposed to be re-assessing her international position. The Prime Minister, Mr. Gorton, is said to be seeking a new image. He cannot appear the same as his famous predecessor, Sir Robert Menzies, 'British to the boot-heels', because Britain no longer has much power in the South Pacific. And there seemed something wrong about the convivial Harold Holt's 'all the way with LBJ'. So Mr. Gorton needs a new image. He has chosen to pass as a tough Australian, ever ready for a few beers with the boys, and this style has been linked to an image of independence . . . Australian nationalism to a faint distant theme of Waltzing Matilda—all four verses. The Prime Minister says we have to control foreign investment instead of lying like a puppy with its legs in the air having its stomach tickled. And we must have an independent defence and foreign policy. He has spoken in such a way that his position was described as that of a 'fortress Australia', an 'Israeli type defence', and 'no more troops for Vietnam'. But he has since corrected that impression and has said that he meant none of those things.

But we *have* gone all the way with LBJ. Will we continue to go all the way with his successors? What would that mean? Will a Gorton-type government make any difference? These are some of the questions that must now be answered. Going all the way with LBJ has meant, first, getting involved in the war in Vietnam . . .an immoral and unjust war. Very few people in Australia have bothered with the facts about Vietnam. Most people have been unconcerned or credulous. They have accepted the Vietnam involvement on less evidence than would be demanded by a man buying a second-hand car or by a woman buying a hat. But when the facts are examined the case for intervention in Vietnam falls down. The case consists of two parts. The first is that unjust aggression has taken place in Vietnam and we are justified in opposing it. The second part of the case is simply that Australia may be attacked in the future and America is the only country strong enough to defend us. The argument goes: we must now help America so that she will defend us if we are attacked.

The case for unjust aggression in Vietnam falls down on the facts reviewed in this book. The war in Vietnam did not originate with aggression from North Vietnam or from China or the Soviet Union. The facts show that the war originated as a civil war, first in Vietnam as a whole against the French, and then in South Vietnam between the Diem Government, backed by the United States, and Vietnamese rebelling against that very government. The evidence is that the aggression did not originate with the rebels but with the Diem Government whose main reason for being was to destroy all those who threatened its position as a bulwark against Communism in Indochina. The rebels were an indigenous national force among whom Communists were significant, but who represented a movement that was concerned with the interests of the Vietnamese people. Not only were the Vietminh no more aggressive than the French, as the record in this book shows, but the NLF were no more aggressive than the forces of Diem or of the Americans. Not only did most people who accepted the case of unjust aggression against the government of North Vietnam and the NLF pay no attention to the facts, but many of them were influenced by a dogmatic form of anti-Communism which would never allow them to recognise the facts. I have no doubt that there was as much vicious and unnecessary killing by the Hanoi and NLF forces as is claimed. Such conduct can never be justified in any situation as a means to any end. It is rather the result of action taken by people who have no regard for either the means or the ends. Indeed they probably damage their own position more than anything else. But this does little to justify the kind of anti-Communism with which it has so much in common. When one is trying to see how all this affects the people of Vietnam it is wise to look at how some who are not Communists view the situation. In his recent book, 'Vietnam, Lotus in the Sea of Fire' Thic Nhat Hanh, wrote:

'Because anti-Communism has taken on a mystical, non-rational, almost religious character in the United States and some other Western countries, I want to explain that I do not use these terms in referring to my own attitude or that of the Vietnamese Buddhist or other nationalist leaders. Communism has a basis of social and personal idealism, and recruits thousands of men and women passionately concerned to eliminate the exploitation and inequality that have characterised much of Western society (and, of course, even more Eastern society) and to create a form of social organisation whose slogan will be 'from each according to his ability, to each according to his need'. This is an objective consistent with the best in most of the world's great religions, and with which religious men have no quarrel. Moreover, the economic organisation of society in socialist terms, meaning one in which the means of production are operated for the good of the people generally rather than for the profit of a minority, is consistent with the needs of a country like Vietnam.

'Few Vietnamese Buddist or nationalist leaders could believe that their country could afford a Western-type capitalism even if they thought it was a moral form of social organisation. Vietnamese anti-Communism stems from the methods that organised Communism uses to attain its ends: the suppression of even the most sincere and committed opponents, violently if need be; the assumption of omniscience on the part of the Party, which is a form of fanaticism that is stultifying to the never ending search for truth to which, Buddhists for example, are committed; and the willingness to sacrifice the very existence of a small country like Vietnam to the 'larger' interests of the Communist powers in the cold war. This is not theorising for Vietnamese non-Communist nationalists who have found themselves and their organisations repressed with the same ruthlessness north and south of the 17th parallel, by the North Vietnamese-Viet Cong-China coalition as well as by the Diem-Ky-U.S. grouping. I do not mean to imply that all Vietnamese nationalists who are also anti-Communist shared exactly the same view. Some of them undoubtedly are far to the Right, politically. For many of us, however, for whom the stated objectives of Communism are largely acceptable, the opposition we feel grows from our conviction that when such methods are used to attain these "good" ends, the ends themselves become unattainable because the methods used corrupt the whole struggle. If humanistic religion has any meaning at all, it is that humanistic ends cannot be achieved by inhuman and depersonalising means'.

Not only do I agree with this view of Asian Communism, but I deplore each of its essential features which are features of Communism almost everywhere else. But it still remains that China under Mao Tse Tung is no worse off than would China have been under Chiang Kai-shek; North Vietnam under Ho Chi Minh no worse off than North Vietnam under the French; and South Vietnam under the National Liberation Front is no worse off than South Vietnam under Diem or his successors or under American bombs and firepower. No foreign power has a right to do to Vietnam what America has done, and what Australia has run along with, because of the difference between the Communist Vietnamese and those we have backed. At the very least the venal dictatorship of the Nhus, the corruption of their officials and the corrupting influence of the American occupation are no better than what Hanoi or the NLF can offer. The difference does not justify the million or more Vietnamese deaths resulting from French and American intervention. But Communism or anti-Communism for South Vietnam might not originally have been the only alternative. It is my belief that the increasing American escalation and support for military action made them so. The choice in South Vietnam may well have been the Lotus rather than the Eagle. It is difficult to say how significant the Lotus may have been as a contender against Communism. Certain Asian cultures faced by the poverty and helplessness of India or pre-revolutionary China can withdraw into something that adds up to nothing more than self-annihilation.[107] These cultures can lose, and have lost, relevance and influence when they have nothing to offer their own people to cure the sickness that affects them all. They succumb to Communism on the one hand, or to European power on the other. And who can say the result is worse for the people?

The robot of China or the Coca-Cola culture of the United States may not be attractive to the Western intellectual or churchman. Both offer something for the Asian people better than poverty and helplessness.

But the robot of China and the Eagle of America may not be the only choice in some places. South Vietnam may well have been one of those places. Most of those who support the devastation of Vietnam, because they think that what threatened it was so unjust, have rarely even thought of the possibility of anything else. Asia has certainly inherited an introspective approach to life, which may finally persuade its people to withdraw from a hideous, repulsive and incomprehensible world. But there is much of this in the West too—a West that does believe itself to be in a position to judge what is best for others. In Asia it is called 'mysticism'. In the West it is called 'apathy'. But Communism will have nothing to do with either. To Communism man is not powerless. He can change the world. Asia needs confidence that change can be brought about. She does not need to choose between Eastern withdrawal from life and Western support for a Diem-like status quo. We cannot be sure how much the Buddhist-nationalist Lotus of Vietnam could have done on its own. But we can be sure that at first it was stronger than the National Liberation Front, and we can equally be sure that the American commanders in Vietnam, always believing that military force was vital, weakened and divided the powers of the Lotus.

Indeed the thesis of this book is that the Eagle played a crucial and vital role not in successfully resisting Communism—for Communism is no weaker now than it was in 1954 or 1961 and may well be stronger—but in weakening the Buddhist-nationalist alternative. Now that the struggle in Vietnam is more political and social than military, the Vietnamese generals and their army are not very well equipped to handle the situation. I think it is probable that the South Vietnamese Lotus—the Buddhist-Nationalist alternative— would have handled Communism more in the interests of the Vietnamese people than did the American military intervention and its pistol-packing generals.

But it is not for me to prove such a point. Those who support the intervention and the killing of perhaps a million Vietnamese are under strong obligation to justify their action.

While many Australians are concerned with the moral aspect of the war in Vietnam, there are many more who make their decision on 'realistic' grounds. Such grounds were recently stated by that supreme realist, the Minister for Trade and Deputy Prime Minister, Mr John McEwen. His argument was that the sending of Australian troops to Vietnam was primarily to guarantee Australia's protection in the future and that it had finally and completely cemented the relationship between Australia and the United States. Morality, of course, does not enter into this argument, and for those who accept it, there is no question at all of just or unjust wars or whether the war is in the interests of the Vietnamese people or not. For Mr McEwen and the other realists the war is in Australian interests and that's the end of it.

Sending 8,000 Australians to Vietnam does not cost much financially. The cost to June 30, 1968 was $76 million and the estimated additional cost for the financial year to June 30, 1969, was a further $42 million—a total of about $120 million. Australia's policy of intervention in Vietnam has added much to the normal defence costs —over $1,300 million in 1968-69. But the argument goes that it is essential Australian dead and wounded list only those directly involved and they are much fewer than the road toll anyway. Another virtue of the intervention is that it directly affects so few people: only some permanent Army men drafted to Vietnam and a few young conscripts about 20 years of age. The majority can be very realistic about this because they are not likely to be involved at all. They can reason, too, that it is good for young men to have the discipline of military service at that time of life, and they can reason that they did their share in earlier wars. What is more, the money cost of the war has been met without any increase in tax rates. It has been paid for by governments spending less than they would have on things like education, health and social services, and to some extent, by price increases caused by the increased spending on war and defence. But the individual realist does not see the way the cost is imposed on him, and it is probably imposed less on him than it is on his parents, children and wife. If he does see the cost, he is prepared to face it because of the security gained from following a policy that has 'completely cemented the relationship between Australia and America' for ever. This is security on the cheap and the realist is attracted by anything on the cheap.

But let us examine this policy alone on realist terms. First, is it security on the cheap? Is the only cost involved that of sending a few regular servicemen and a few long-haired conscripts to Vietnam? Obviously not. This is part of the American alliance, and the American alliance involves many other things too. It involves becoming part of the American nuclear missile system. It involves, as we have seen, the establishment in Australia of vital pieces of mechanism used to direct some nuclear missiles at China or the Soviet Union and to detect some that may be directed at the United States. This aspect of policy has put Australia in the front line of nuclear war. On the admission of the Minister for Defence, it means that Australia would be the subject of nuclear attack should nuclear war occur. And it means that Australia, unlike America, would have to meet that attack without the advantage of an Anti-Ballistic-Missile system—well beyond the financial capacity of Australia—which America herself considers essential once she has installed mechanisms likely to attract nuclear missiles. But not for Australia. We can have those vital pieces of nuclear missile mechanism but we don't have an ABM defence, so it takes much more than sending a few troops to Vietnam to pay the premium on our American insurance policy. We had to become part of the American nuclear missile system with all that it involves. Is that the end of it? Suppose that China or the Soviet Union did decide to attack Australia—to knock out these American bases—can we be sure that America would then answer back? At the risk of having her own bases and cities attacked? Certainly what is involved here is speculation, and it is speculation which realists are not very good at. But how sure can we be that what we have done has completely cemented the relationship between Australia and the United States?

The American government has not been prepared to install bases at home which would be subject to nuclear attack without ABM defence, but it has proved willing to install them in Australia without ABM defence. The Australian government has been ready to accept them without telling the Australian people what it is doing. How far can you go in this kind of policy? How much security is there in it? This is a question which sooner or later the realists may have to answer. What chances then are there of a change from this policy of involvement in an unjust and immoral war in some other country and of involvement in a nuclear missile system which may bring attack which Australia would be incapable of meeting? This question is a challenge indeed but we can be fairly certain that it will be decided not on moral grounds but on very realistic grounds. It is important to realise that we do not follow America simply in the sense of finding out what America is doing and then deciding to do the same. We do not follow America just because our leaders think like American leaders. Defence Minister Fairhall could be a successful American electronics corporation manager; Treasurer McMahon a New York banker's public relations man. Even the tough critic of America, John McEwen, could be a Texan who would get on as well with LBJ as did Harold Holt. And it is not confined to obvious cases. So many of the new Australian 'establishment' are like Americans in the same sense. They think like Americans not just because they copy them, and they do, but because they live similar lives and have similar aspirations.

A country behaves as it does because of its own cultural background and the Australian cultural background has for purely Australian reasons become more and more similar to that of America. We can learn more about what to do and what not to do from America than from any other place. But the fact is that America is so big and overwhelming that we have little real choice at all but to follow. What then is this cultural background? It is not just similar homes, television programs, motor cars and sport. It is a general practical materialism. It is that we prefer material goods to personal responsibility and personal decision-making when the two appear to conflict. The affluent society has not made us more able and willing to act independently, but less willing, because we have more to lose if we do act independently. The 'conventional wisdom' is that if we have to choose between money and making a personal decision which may conflict with getting money, we come down on the side of money. Hence we are not interested in politics because we think if we are it will harm our income or social status. We are free in the sense that the police only arrest no-hopers and ratbags and book traffic offenders. But we are not free in the sense that every man tends to be his own policeman. He is afraid of what his neighbours might think if he acts independently or differently, or of what they might think if they really knew what he was thinking. We are not even much afraid of the police or 'security' or anything sinister like that because we know we are careful enough to be well beyond their reach. It is only that we do not want our neighbours, or the people at work, or at the club to think that we are a Communist or a critic or a no-hoper. You never know what might happen if they did.

Then again we tell ourselves that we 'can't do much about it anyway'. The war in Vietnam! Electronic bases! Missile attack! 'What can I do about those things?' And so from being very realistic about little things—about money as it comes to us directly—we become very unrealistic about big things. It is, of course, true that we 'can't do much about it'. We live in a kind of benevolent dictatorship in which we have only the power to resist if it goes too far and it doesn't do that very often or in a tangible way. But we can't expect to be able to do 'much about' things because we never really try. We will protest or whinge all day about trivia but on national questions or political issues we will shy away and refuse to participate in decision making. A result is that we have become involved in the war in Vietnam and in the American nuclear missile system far more deeply than has any other country in the world and we don't really know whether there was any other way or whether what we have done is in our own interests or not. Who does know? Those politicians for whom we have so little time and respect? Would we give them control of our own personal affairs? Control of our money? But we will give them control of our place in the nuclear world and of our involvement in wars.

Would it not have been a lot better if in 1965 Sir Robert Menzies had said to Mr. Cabot Lodge: 'No, we cannot send combat troops to Vietnam but we will spend as much by providing doctors and by building hospitals in Vietnam and by providing food and rehabilitation for the wounded'? Would it have been likely that the Americans would have appreciated this any the less? By making such a fuss about sending combat troops to Vietnam we tended to create our own sense of obligation from which we could not conceivably withdraw. But it was not America that created this sense of obligation, it was Sir Robert Menzies and his establishment who accepted so easily a military obligation for 'political' reasons. The American 'hawks' knew that Australia's motives were political and that we did not intend to make a significant military contribution to the war. And they do not admire Australia any more for that. The American 'doves' think even less of us. It is indeed far from certain that sending combat troops to Vietnam has 'completely cemented the relationship between Australia and America'.

It may be that Australia's acceptance of nuclear missile control and detection bases in Australia has created a greater sense of obligation among American 'hawks' than has her contribution to Vietnam. But the whole thing is so secret that few people, even among the American 'hawks', know about it. But here, as in the case of Vietnam, what was the alternative? The alternative was to say, 'No, we are unable to accept these bases in Australia because they would attract nuclear attack and we cannot possibly provide an anti-missile defence as it would cost far too much for us. You know yourself that you would not put one of these bases in America without adequate ABM defence and you know the cost of that.' It would not be impossible or even very difficult for America to find an alternative to the Australian sites. The Soviet Union undoubtedly has done so. What then would be Australia's position? The truth is that without American bases in Australia it is extremely unlikely that any part of Australia would ever have become a nuclear target for the Soviet Union or China. It seems that on purely realist terms Australia has gained little for certain but worry and risk out of sending combat troops to Vietnam and out of the establishment of American bases in Australia.

I have said that any possibility of change from this situation will depend not upon moral considerations but upon practical and realistic ones. The average Australian who has accepted Australia's position in the nuclear world and the world of wars has done so on practical and realistic grounds. He will change that position only if equally realistic and practical considerations make him change. Are there any such considerations? While it will take some time to end American intervention in Vietnam it is only time that will determine the withdrawal of all foreign forces. We can also be sure that no South-East Asian government will ever again accept a foreign intervention in the way America and her allies intervened in South Vietnam. We can be sure that the next generation of political leaders in South-East Asia will not choose to rely upon American forces to stop the political, social and economic transformation which must take place in their countries. We will not again have to make a choice like that in 1965 of sending combat troops to South Vietnam. We may, for some time, have land and air forces in South-East Asia, like those in Malaysia, and we may assist in training and supplying the armed forces of one or two South-East Asian countries, but these interventions are marginal and of no real significance. Great care will have to be taken that Australian forces in no way become involved in conflicts between South-East Asian countries like that between Malaysia and the Philippines; and equally as much care will have to be taken that Australian forces are not used in any internal disorder or insurrection whatsoever.

This being the case one is left to wonder why they will be there at all. They can help in training but the lack of purpose beyond that suggests that they are really there because their presence creates in Australia a political issue which up till now has operated in the interests of the Menzies-Holt-Gorton series of governments.

As the facts of the situation force themselves upon more and more Australian voters this situation will change and finally there will no longer be an apparent majority in Australia in favor of sending Australian forces to South-East Asia. Probably sooner, governments in Malaysia, Singapore and Thailand will come into office who will want withdrawal of Australian forces from their countries. What is difficult to predict is how long will this change take, but there can be little doubt that it will happen.

This development will allow Australians to question effectively some of their basic assumptions about Asia. We will begin to see that the vital political, social and economic transformations in economically underdeveloped countries cannot take place without some upheaval and we will come to see that the people of those countries are best able to handle these matters themselves. We will begin to see that those upheavals do not threaten Australia. On the contrary, they can benefit Australia. If Australian exports are to increase, thus keeping our balance of payments favourable enough to allow a fairly continuous rate of growth in Australia, we will need to export more and more to Asia as we have exported wheat to China. We will need in turn to be able to import from Asia. But rapid development of this constructive trading role for Australia has been delayed because of our choscn relationship with Asia—a blend of militarism over-protection-ism and muted racism.

Both because of our relations with Britain and our desperate attempt to replace her as a 'powerful friend' by the United States we have become involved in a surprising number of wars so many miles from our own shores. We sent Australian troops to the Sudan 90 years ago, to the Boer War a few years later, to the Middle East and Europe a decade and a half later, then to many points around the world 30 years later in the Second World War; to Korea in 1951 and to Vietnam in 1962. However much some Australians may feel that each of these expeditions was justified, few countries in the world have equalled our record for far-distant military expeditions to protect what we have claimed was our own security. Few countries have ever proclaimed as a national slogan that it is 'Better to fight them there than here'. Furthermore, we have always been conscious of our own high material standards of living and of the widespread poverty of Asia and it has been easily assumed, in Australia, that one of the main purposes of the Asian people was to come to Australia in large numbers and take all we have. It so happens that Asians we fear are people of a different race and so an element of racism enters into our national posture. Similarly, Australia shares that brand of anti-Communism described by Thic Nhat Hanh as 'mystical, non-rational, almost (of a) religious character'. But there is a very realistic base to these military, racist and irrational reactions. They will diminish only when Australia's military intervention in Asia is recognised as anachronistic. Then our realism can be expressed in constructive relationships with Asia and in a convincing system of continental defence for Australia. That time is not far off.

Australia must come to replace the 'forward defence' policy—under which we send a few Australian troops into other countries far distant from Australia—by a 'fortress Australia' policy. Our forward defence policy was appropriate only for a country able to follow a world power, first Britain and then the United States, to all these places around the world. It was their policy not ours. That phase has now ended. We are not big enough, nor do we have the interests, to be able to send our troops around the world alone. We will become now concerned with our own defence in and from Australia. The 'fortress Australia' policy hinted at even by the defenders of the old order will soon become the faith of Australian realists. Behind the 'bastions' of 'fortress Australia', we may be able to develop the confidence necessary to increase our trade both ways with Asia and even to accept gladly an increasing number of Asian migrants able to strengthen us in every conceivable way. We may even begin to develop an indigenous culture not alone the product of the world-wide acquisitive society of which we have remained a receptive annexe.

What then about these nuclear missile installations which destroy our sovereignty and make us into a nuclear target? Here again the realists are likely to have their way. They shudder somewhat at the realisation that these installations will attract nuclear attack in the event of war yet they may remain convinced that they are the very thing that will prevent nuclear war. But sooner or later they will become convinced by the argument that if these installations were not here there would be only a negligible chance of nuclear attack on Australia without them. As soon as the 'fortress Australia' concept becomes a reality Australian realists will oppose nuclear bases in these circumstances. It is more than time that they be given a lead.

However, accepting the fact that these American bases are here, this should make it unnecessary for Australia to acquire her own nuclear weapons. While it would be unreasonable to expect that Australia could ever develop a nuclear-missile capacity to have any effect upon the Soviet Union or China, it is much more likely that the United States would seek to prevent the acquisition of nuclear weapons by other countries which could threaten her nuclear installations in Australia. It would be wise for the Australian Government to join with the United States in this non-proliferation objective. There is enough risk in having nuclear-missile installations in Australia without adding to it by a proliferation of nuclear weapons in the South-East Asian areas in which Australia would take a leading part. What then is the future of North West Cape, Pine Gap and Woomera? It is likely that they will stay until they are outmoded by the introduction of more effective mechanisms on space platforms. This may come surprisingly quickly. Within a decade it may well be that the American and Soviet nuclear missile system may be fully in space. At least the people of Alice Springs and places east will breathe a little easier when this is achieved.

We may even have enough time to reassess our views of Communism. The practice of Communism is appropriate only for a desperate situation in which mass action is needed. But it is not a force that spreads from Moscow or Peking on a mission to conquer the world. Neither the Soviet Union nor China has shown signs of adopting the policy of military expansion similar to that of Germany in the First and Second World Wars and Japan in the Second World War. Comparisons between the Soviet Union and China on the one hand, and Hitler and Japan on the other are false. Both the Soviet Union and China, in different ways, seek to influence and control revolutionary movements wherever they are. But whether there will be a revolutionary movement depends not upon them but upon the conditions of the country or area concerned. Both the Soviet Union and China have always placed their own interests well ahead of the interests of the revolutionary movement with which they are dealing. China more than the

Soviet Union has warned revolutionary movements they must depend upon their own resources and strength and that nothing much to help them can be done from outside. The United States is much more interventionist and active in aiding the counter-revolutionary side than are China or the Soviet Union in helping the revolutionary side.

But in many countries political changes must take place if they are to have the necessary social and economic progress. Wherever this occurs there will be some American and some Chinese and Soviet interference. Neither form of interference has ever proved very helpful to those aided and American intervention has usually ended by stimulating the anti-Western side of the equation and helped to give the Communists a stronger case for their own leadership. More than one competent observer has drawn the conclusion that Western intervention actually is necessary to convert the normal form of nationalism of an underdeveloped country into Communist leadership.[198] These interventions seem more likely to retard the changes that are necessary. Some observers believe that if they are made in defence of the old order, the changes cannot take place at all.[199] But these changes must take place within some political pattern if the people are to develop the productive capacity they need to feed themselves and to trade increasingly with others.

But in these situations the collective strength of the people is not great. It is slight. This peoples' movement need cause no fear to Australians thousands of miles away. No, we in Australia should not fear these changes. We should welcome them. But to explore the possibilities of peace we do need to look beyond revolutionary situations in countries like Vietnam. Senator Fulbright has correctly pointed out that: 'As long as China and America are competitors for predominance in South-East Asia there is unlikely to be a secure peace in that part of the world.'

There will be competition, antipathy and aggression between China and the United States, between Capitalism and Communism, for a long time. The vital question is not that there will always be a struggle, but what form the struggle will take. The form of the struggle has changed between the Soviet Union and the United States. It is not long since it was predicted that war between them was inevitable and that the antipathy between them would never change. Few now still hold those views. What has happened between the Soviet Union and the United States will happen between the United States and China. It may take longer between China and the Soviet Union. No one can be certain what China will do in the future. When she is stronger she may become aggressive in deeds as well as words. But she had not yet begun to build the kind of armed forces that would be necessary for this. China has not done much, nor is able to do much, to strengthen the mainly indigenous revolutionary movements. The revolutionary movement in Vietnam, which America has been unable to stop, could not be stopped for precisely this reason—not that it was aided by China but that it was so much a part of Vietnamese history and tradition, so much a part of Vietnam's struggle for national independence and for social and economic reform. It was moved by the peasants' desire for land, the workers' desire for better wages, the women's desire for status and equality, and the desire of youth for a say in its own future.

This is where its strength came from, not from China or the Soviet Union.

If a revolutionary movement is not mainly indigenous it will not require American intervention to destroy it. If it is mainly indigenous American intervention cannot destroy it. The result of American intervention against any revolution that is mainly indigenous cannot be other than it was in Vietnam—continuous military escalation with 'victory' depending on physical destruction of the country concerned and with a rising probability of war against China or the Soviet Union as they are compelled to come to the aid of the embattled revolution.

The scale of escalation is set by the United States as it was in Vietnam, with first the revolutionary forces turning to military action only because they had to—they prefer to win without war and by political methods—and then North Vietnam, China and the Soviet Union, arguing and contending about what should be done, becoming more involved in reply to the American escalation. The truth is that the United States and some of her allies, first among them Australia, are more strongly against revolution than the Soviet Union and China are for it. I believe there is profound truth in the observation of American diplomat and historian George Kennan, who wrote: 'It may be said ... that for the Western world, the Soviet and Chinese threat is primarily an internal crisis in the West's own development. In this appreciation there lies, in my conviction, the key to the understanding of the correct approach.'

Just what does Kennan mean and what are the corollaries if he is right? He means that the threat to which the Western world has responded by military escalation is not a threat that exists in countries like Vietnam but it is a threat that exists in the Western countries themselves. He means that the fundamental cause of the over-military reaction is lack of confidence in America and Australia. In a word, those who are responsible in America and Australia for military escalation in foreign relations and for police state tendencies at home are people who lack confidence in the ability of America and Australia to hold their own politically and socially against the Soviet Union and China and against the Asians who are rising out of their years of poverty and suppression. One has to look only at the way they react to a few students who demonstrate in the streets. One would imagine they thought the students capable of bringing down the whole political, social and financial edifice upon which they depended.

And ironically, the people who react so much against those who symbolise change consider themselves realists. But the truth is they do not know the facts. They do not know how supremely difficult it is to bring about social changes in any country. Just as the poor Dorchester labourers were sentenced to seven years transportation in 1834 because a haughty and ignorant establishment, lacking confidence in itself, thought they possessed the power to cause a French-type revolution in England, so the former Victorian Minister for Education Sir John Bloomfield, seriously said in Parliament in 1969 that 'underground newspapers' in Victorian High Schools were the 'first shots in the Third World War'. Not only do those Western leaders who behave in this way have no knowledge of the facts, and of the strength or weakness of movements for change, but they have no confidence in the Western tradition. There are significant people, of course, who join them mainly for other reasons and have no better factual knowledge. All these people lack real faith in free enquiry, democratic participation and moral commitment. They have little room for these practices in Western countries because they lack confidence in their own ability to deal with what will happen if they are more widely practised. This is the core of the problem. If in Australia and America the present policy-makers continue to rule there will be little change in foreign policy. Although their policy had suffered a serious setback in Vietnam it will not become less militaristic abroad and it will become more authoritarian at home. These policies can change only if we protect free enquiry from attack and practise and extend it more widely; only if we enlarge and intensify political participation at all levels, particularly in organisations like the trade unions and the Australian Labor Party, which are capable of accepting a point of view different from that of the ruling policy-makers.

We must resolve to apply simple moral standards to a wider range of national and international questions. If this is to be done the realists must learn to see the facts and regain confidence that something can be done about them. The fault of the realists is not that they are realists but that they do not know the facts and that they have lost confidence that they can act like realists.

We can help social progress elsewhere only if we have some of it in America and in Australia. But of one thing the realists can be warned: the world cannot for ever pile up nuclear weapons without one day becoming the victims of their use. The Western world cannot for ever oppose those social revolutions that are necessary if the deprived and suppressed majority on this earth are to escape from the control imposed upon them by the wealthy minority.

The test is ours: can we respond to this challenge with less militarism and with fewer bigoted assumptions of a superiority which inwardly and basically we know we do not possess? Can we in Australia derive confidence from our own tradition of untrammelled pursuit of the truth knowing that this tradition will emerge victorious in every conflict?

CHAPTER FOURTEEN

POSTSCRIPT

In Chapter 12 I put down a few of my expectations of how events would go in South East Asia, America and Australia. That chapter was written in March 1969. Some of the events have occurred earlier and their directions have been more significant than I expected.

America withdrew troops from Vietnam sooner and in larger numbers than I thought possible. She did this not because the Saigon government forces are able to take over and deal with the 'Viet Cong'. They are not and will never be able to. If Saigon cannot evolve a 'third force' to enter a coalition with the NLF then Saigon governments and potential governing bodies will completely collapse.

Majority support in Australia for withdrawal of our men has come sooner than I thought likely, although it almost exactly coincides with an extrapolation of the points on preceding Gallup polls. No Australian government will be able to delay for long announcement of withdrawal of Australian forces from Vietnam.

America has not demanded that North Vietnam sever all connections with South Vietnam, nor that the NLF have to stop fighting and withdraw to the North. Instead the American Administration has merely called for 'responses' to their own programme of withdrawal. This represents a more thorough and open admission of NLF strength than I expected. I do not think Ho Chi Minh's death will change Hanoi's policy much, although, if anything, it will make it less inclined to compromise. It is worth noting, however, that some of those, like Le Duan, earlier classified by the so-called experts, as among the most aggressive, are now called moderate.

I certainly did not expect Thailand to call so soon for withdrawal of American forces, although clearly she could not forever allow the use of airbases for round-the-clock air bombardment of Vietnam and Laos, and her territory for CIA inspired attacks on Cambodia. It is amazing that China did not take a much stronger stand against this long ago. But Thailand probably now realises that the America Administration wants to use her territory in the interests of immediate American military requirements in ways certain to provoke China and Thailand's other neighbors, while at the same time, America will not commit herself to 'defend' Thailand with large numbers of ground troops. The recent American Senate vote for aid to Thailand, but against putting in American troops, indicates this position.

It is now clear that no American Administration will become involved in another Vietnam, and no South East Asian country wants to become another Vietnam. Furthermore those countries probably now recognise that the sort of military presence—air, and CIA 'counter-insurgency'—unless it is most subtly handled, will do no more than provoke 'the enemy' and leave them without large American backing. The day of big power military presence in South East Asian countries is now apparently over.

But it does seem that the 'counter-productive' nature of foreign interference is not yet understood clearly enough by the Americans or by the Russians. Perhaps the Chinese are more aware of it. This being so, America will remain keen to back conservative and reactionary governments with a sophisticated 'counter-insurgency' system, with 'advisers' and CIA conspiracies. Here one can say that Laos, which is an example of this method, has been much better off than South Vietnam. The Communist side has made less progress there than in South Vietnam. Souvanaphouma's nationalism has been strong enough to limit American take-over and to deprive his enemies of the claim that he is a collaborator.

Failure to realise the 'counter-productive' nature of foreign intervention will mean that the Soviet Union, and China too, will go on making dramatic expressions of solidarity with the 'heroes of the national liberation struggle'; and offering plans and predictions for the complete overthrow of capitalism. Both sides will continue to judge each other by their pretensions and boasts rather than by their achievements. Neither side will realise to what degree acceptance of their political and military advice and interference is a long-term handicap for those who do accept it. Their failure probably results more from national pride than from ideological preoccupations.

But to me the most surprising recent development has been the *admission* (in Australia even just before an election) of the acceptibility of 'practical and constructive dealings with the Soviet Union.' 'These are the words of the Australian Minister for External Affairs on August 14, 1969.) I expected that the Australian Liberal-Country Party-DLP coalition, a coalition in which the DLP wins the election but gets no seats, would fight the 1969 election on one issue—that the Russians were coming and that every other activity, education, social welfare etc., must be cut back or stabilised so that we could spend more to get ready to stop the enemy. But this has not happened. We have been told we can't do anything about the Russian advance and it may even be good for us.

This change of attitude towards the Soviet Union is not so sudden or marked as it seems. For a long time some American officials, and some people in Australia most aware of the more subtle American approach, have believed that the Soviet Union could stop the war in

Vietnam or at least induce North Vietnam to 'negotiate'. Indeed the Soviet Union, as we have seen, has often tried to do this and could have got further if the American 'hawks' had not extended or intensified bombing at precisely critical moments. And so, I think, that Nixon administration policy (the Secretary of State is said to have told Canberra about it on his recent visit) is that we must accept the Russian presence in South East Asia because the job is too big for America alone. Those Australians and Americans who fear the Russian presence are now hoping that the Soviet Union will stop aiding and encouraging national liberation movements and may even discourage them. And then, of course, there is the belief that when the Soviet Union comes into South East Asia she will be in a better position to resist and fight China.

But when the Soviet Union does come into South East Asia she will come in to secure her own interests. This may mean she will be able to supply some countries with military equipment, as she did to Indonesia, and so upset the external but especially the internal balance, and divert urgently needed funds to the repayment of a huge military debt, again as with Indonesia. It may mean that the Soviet Union will be able to get bases for her army, naval and air forces, and, for missiles as well. It is not beyond possibility to these amazing 'realist' minds that such a program may appeal to a government in Singapore.

I have for as long as anyone advocated 'peaceful co-existence' with the Soviet Union and talks and agreements about disarmament, non-aggression, non-interference and about economic and cultural relations. I have never believed that the Soviet Union has been as aggressive as have those who now advocate 'practical and constructive dealings' with her, and who, until now, have loudly and deliriously proclaimed that an inherently evil Soviet Union can never be trusted. I have supported a friendly attitude towards the Soviet Union but I have never had any doubts that the Soviet Union thought first and only of her own interests and would be ruthless in pursuing them. In this she differed from few but was more ruthless than most. And in all this the Soviet Union acted more on the normal, nationalist motives of a big power than on motives derived from Communist ideology.

But the move to accept or condone Soviet Union, big power presence in South East Asia is a different matter. It is crude and superficial. For those in Australia who have come round to it, it is merely an extension of big power subservience, always the natural choice of a so-called upper class who acquired it in Whitehall, adapted it to Washington and are capable, apparently, of adjusting it even to their 'life-long enemy'. It is apparently possible for them because they have no liking for Australian nationalism and no confidence in it, and their anti-Communism has been mainly for domestic political purposes.

The Soviet Union will doubtless move more and more into the Indian Ocean and South East Asia to fish, sail her navy, build stadiums and even steel plants and talk to diplomats and politicians and impress them with her size, strength and similar 'executive' abilities. There never has been anything very harmful in this. But to imagine the new Soviet presence will stop at that is naive. She will seek influence through agreements to supply arms as she supplied them to Indonesia at enormous cost. She will be expected to discourage or suppress national liberation movements (but she will probably not be able even to attempt it) ; she certainly will want bases so that she can better threaten China or fight if it comes to that. To believe that this policy is necessary or desirable is lunacy.

Big powers, from time immemorial, have had a shocking record in other countries and the Soviet Union will certainly not raise the standard.

It is time the Australian government gave up the policy of camp following big powers around the world. It is time we in Australia realised that justice and our own security require us to accept those changes that must take place in each and every poor nation if its people are to emerge from poverty. It is time we began to plan and build effectively to defend ourselves *from our own resources* if anything goes wrong.

Big powers may be able to deter each other with their nuclear missiles against the use of nuclear missiles, and I hope they are left to it, but they cannot deter, suppress or stop those changes that will be necessary to remove poverty in Asia, Africa, and Latin America. This is partly because there are so many decent, humane citizens in big power nations. Unless all this is soon realised and translated into policy there will be more Vietnams and the admission of the Soviet Union to the team of self-righteous aggressors will add nothing to their humane quality or to stop the emergence of the world's poor people. It would merely add frightfully to the casualties of the attempt.

September, 1969

> . . . *if a great change is to be made in human affairs, the minds of men will be fitted to it.*
>
> Burke

REFERENCE NOTES

CHAPTER 1

[1] 'The Smaller Dragon', pp. 131-2.

[2] Thic Nhat Hanh, in his 'The Lotus in the Sea of Fire', chose to use 'Tuc-Trung Thuong-Si's "The Eccentric's Song" to illustrate the way in which the spirit of Zen blends with the freedom and aloofness of Taoism and the sense of responsibility of Confucianism.' (He could equally have used it to contrast Christianity with Communism and Confucianism. Christianity and Communism are institutional and dogmatic. They *know* the truth, and the individual needs no special method for reaching truth by himself. The truth is in the past, so one has to accept one's ancestors, the Church or the Party as the special repository of truth. Hence Confucians consolidate their position in the inherited 'court', Christians in the 'Church' and Communists in the 'Party'.)

[3] Thic Nhat Hanh, op. cit., p. 57.

[4] It seems that the first Roman Catholic missionaries arrived in Vietnam in 1553 but they were Spanish Jesuits not French. It is believed that missionary work did not begin rapid growth till early in the 17th century and by then French missionaries were active.

It must not be overlooked that Christianity in Vietnam has always been looked on as a foreign faith closely associated with 'white explorers, merchants and ruling classes'. Often the missionaries made use of native merchants and politicians to assist them, who of course, were anxious to have the European power the missionaries influenced thrown on their side in their own struggles for sovereignty and territory.

[5] op. cit., see pages 174 and 392-3.

[6] See "Independence in Vietnam", Gettlemen, 'Vietnam, History Documents, and Opinions on a Major World Crisis'.

[7] This conclusion was stated by Marshal Gallieni, famous French soldier and diplomat who served in Africa, Madagascar and Indochina. He was the first to advise and use the 'oil or ink spot' method of spreading out security in all directions, from a cleared and held position. This method was dramatised again by the Americans.

[8] See P. Isoart, 'Le Phénomène National Vietnamien De L'Indépendence Unitaire à L'Indépendence', 1961, p. 149.

[9] See F. Bernard, 'L'Indochine, Erreurs et Dangers', 1901, p. 40. 'At Haidund in 1892 where our side suffered not a single victim in the uprising we had 64 people beheaded without trial'. Buttinger records De Lanessou's finding: 'Every village that has given refuge to a band of guerrillas, or not reported their passage, is declared responsible or guilty. Consequently, the chief of the village and two or three principal inhabitants are beheaded, and the village itself is set on fire and razed to the ground'.

[10] See J. Buttinger, 'Vietnam, A Dragon Embattled', Vol. 1, Ch. III. 'As soon as a patrol starts out the pirates are warned, while we', wrote the official French historian, 'walk in a hostile country as though blind.' p. 136.

[11] 'The number of lives lost during this first phase of national resistance against French rule makes the period from 1858 to 1898 one of the saddest in the history of Vietnam.' Buttinger, op. cit., p. 138.

[12] Buttinger, op. cit., p. 45.

[13] Op. cit., p. 136.

[14] Op. cit., p. 11, and see J. Chesnaux 'Contribution à l'histoire de la Nation Vietnamienne,' 1955, p. 115.

CHAPTER 2

[15] Op. cit., pp. 121-122.
[16] Op. cit., p. 159.
[17]

Population: Vietnam

	1902	1910	1950		1960
Cochinchina	2.3m.	2.9m.	5.6m.	South	
Annam	6.4m.	5.5m.	7.2m.	Vietnam	13.0m.
Tonking and Laos	7.5m.	5.9m.	9.9m.	North	
				Vietnam	15.9m.
Total	16.2m.	14.3m.	22.7m.		28.9m

[18] K. Buchanan, Professor of Geography, Victoria University, Wellington, N.Z.
[19] Op. cit., pp. 199 and 202.
[20] Op. cit., Vol. 2, p. 780.
[21] 'French Indochina,' p. 438.
[22] See James Baldwin 'Black Power', Australian, February 23, 1968.

CHAPTER 3

[23] 'Forces politiques au Viet-Nam.' See J. Buttinger, Vol. 1, p. 210.
[24] Op. cit., p. 224.
[25] Op. cit., p. 289.
[26] Op. cit., p. 297.
[27] See Kahin and Lewis, 'The United States in Vietnam', p. 23 and note p. 41.
[28] Op. cit., p. 308.

CHAPTER 4

[29] Op. cit., p. 317.
[30] 'The Struggle for Indochina', p. 16.
[31] 'Histoire du Vietnam de 1940 à 1952', 1952, p. 167.
[33] See H. Isaacs, 'New Cycle in Asia', for a translation of the treaty.
[34] In view of the closeness of interest and control by Moscow, so often assumed, it is worth while noticing the views of some Vietnamese at this time, recorded by Isaacs in 'No Peace in Asia', pp. 172-73: 'Even the most orthodox of them (the Communists) like shaggy haired Tran Van Giau, the partisan organiser, granted that the Russians went in for an excess of ideological compromise, and said he expected no help from that quarter, no matter how distant and verbal it might be. "The Russians are nationalists for Russia first and above all". Another Annamite Communist said with bitterness, "They could be interested in us only if we served some purpose of theirs. Right now, unfortunately, we do not seem to serve any such purpose".'
[35] 'Histoire du Vietnam de 1940 à 1952', p. 204.
[36] Op. cit., p. 152.
[37] Op. cit., p. 372.
[38] Op. cit., p. 412.
[39] Op. cit., p. 417.
[40] Op. cit., p. 418.
[41] See B. Fall, 'The Two Vietnams', p. 50, quoting George Kennan, 'one of America's greatest contemporary diplomats'. 'There is, let me assure you, nothing more egocentric than an embattled democracy. It soon becomes the victim of its own war propaganda. It then tends to attach to its own cause an absolute value which distorts its own vision on everything else. Its enemy becomes the embodiment of all evil. Its own side, on the other hand, is the center of all virtue.'
[42] Buttinger, op. cit., p. 427.
[43] See Hammer, op. cit., p. 183.

CHAPTER 5

[44] 'The Two Vietnams', p. 117.
[45] Op. cit., p. 114.
[46] Op. cit., p. 114.
[47] Hanoi radio frequently broadcast appeals for peace, often in speeches by Ho Chi Minh. Such occurred in 1947, 1948, 1952 and 1954. For some time before November 1953, Hanoi showed no interest in talks, but in that month Ho Chi Minh informed the Swedish newspaper Expressen that he was ready to study any proposal for a cease-fire.
[48] See Fall, op. cit., p. 128 for a map.
[49] Op. cit., p. 105.
[50] Op. cit., pp. 59-60.
[51] Buttinger, op. cit., p. 722.
[52] Op. cit., p. 104.
[53] See Gettleman, op. cit., pp. 103-112. The eight members of Congress were: Knowland, Millikin, Lyndon B. Johnson, Russell, Clements, Martin, McCormack and Priest.
[54] The Memoirs of Sir Anthony Eden, 'Full Circle', 1960, pp. 102-105.
[55] Victor Bator, 'Vietnam: A Diplomatic Tragedy', p. 50.
[56] Op. cit., p. 833.
[57] Quoted by Robert Scheer, 'How the United States got involved in Vietnam', 1965, p. 19.
[58] Kahan and Lewis, op. cit., p. 38.
[59] New York Times, May 30, 1955.

CHAPTER 6

[60] 'Viet Cong', p. 52.
[61] 'The Last Confucian'.
[62] 'A Threat to Peace', p. 3 [Emphasis provided.]
[63] Gettleman, op. cit., p. 223.
[64] See also Kahin and Lewis, op. cit., p. 87.
[65] Gettleman, op. cit., p. 229.
[66] 'The Two Vietnams', p. 146.
[67] Op. cit., p. 100. Bernard Fall states ('The Two Vietnams' pp. 153-4) that of the 860,000 who fled south, 600,000 were Catholic and 'although 65 per cent of the Catholic population left North Vietnam, more than 99.5 per cent of the non-Catholics stayed put.' Most of the other 260,000 were Vietnamese who had served in the French Army or administration.
[68] Op. cit., p. 250.
[69] Gettleman, op. cit., p. 280.
[70] Op. cit., p. 219.
[71] Op. cit., p. 154.
[72] Warner, op. cit., p. 154.
[73] Op. cit., p. 162.
[74] See 'Modern Guerrilla Warfare', Ed. F. M. Osanka, 1962.
[75] See R. Scigliano, 'South Vietnam, Nation under Stress', p. 168.
[76] See Kahin and Lewis, op. cit., p. 100.
[77] Op. cit., p. 101.
[78] Warner, op. cit., p. 107.
[79] Op. cit., pp. 136-7.
[80] 'The New Republic', December 4, 1961.
[81] Op. cit., p. 107.
[82] Gettleman, op. cit., p. 241.
[83] 'A Thousand Days', p. 545.
[84] These are the words of Cardinal Spellman.

CHAPTER 7

[85] To achieve this purpose we can draw upon the reporting by Denis Warner, op. cit., Chapter 8, 'A Village Goes Wrong'.

[86] Warner, op. cit., p. 142.

[87] Op. cit., p. 143.

[88] Warner, op. cit., p. 145.

[89] Op. cit., p. 146.

[90] Kahin and Lewis, op. cit., p. 104.

[91] Op. cit., p. 151.

[92] Op. cit., p. 153.

[93] Kahin and Lewis, op. cit., pp. 111-112.

[94] Op. cit., p. 112.

[95] Le Monde, April 15, 1965.

[96] Kahin and Lewis, op. cit., p. 114.

[97] See ibid, op. cit., p. 115.

[98] Third National Congress of the Vietnam Workers Party; Documents Vol. 3, p. 62.

[99] Op. cit., p. 119.

[100] President Eisenhower had clearly acknowledged American responsibility when he wrote: 'Our direct interest in the Geneva negotiations arose out of the assumption that the United States would be expected to act as one of the guarantors of whatever agreement should be achieved.' 'Mandate for Change', p. 357.

CHAPTER 8

[101] Warner, op. cit., p. 237.

[102] 'Vietnam, Between Two Truces', op. cit., p. 98.

[103] Lacouture, p. 131.

[104] January 2, 1964, p. 7.

[105] 'The Politics of Escalation', Schurmann, Scott and Zelnik, p. 34.

[106] Kahin and Lewis, op. cit., p. 101.

[107] Kahin and Lewis, op. cit., p. 164.

[108] Economist, January 30, 1965.

[109] New York Times, January 9, 1965.

[110] New York Times, February 15, 18 and 23, 1965.

[111] Ibid., February 20 and 26, 1965.

[112] Ibid., March 8, 10, 1965.

[113] Kahin and Lewis, op. cit., p. 171.

[114] See Jean Lacouture, op. cit.

[115] Op. cit., p. 151.

[116] New York Times, November 3, 1963 and March 9, 1965.

[117] Manchester Guardian, August 9.

[118] New York Times, February 23, 1965.

[119] London Times, April 1, 1965.

[120] Lyndon B. Johnson, 'The Exercise of Power', p. 544.

[121] State Department Bulletin, September 20, 1965.

[122] New York Times, November 19, 1965.

[123] Ibid., November 18, 1965.

[124] State Department Bulletin, December 13, 1965.

[125] 'Peace in Vietnam, A New Approach in South East Asia', p. 55.

[126] See Emmett John Hughes, Newsweek, December 12, 1966.

[127] For details see Gettleman, op. cit., pp. 450-452.

[128] See 'Peace in Vietnam', op. cit., p. 58 and Douglas Pike, op. cit., pp. 194-5-6, 344-7 and 358-9 for details.

[129] 'The Vietnam Hearings', op. cit., pp. 246-7.

[130] This was published in a letter to World Communist Leaders.

[131] State Department Bulletin, January 3, 1966.

[132] Washington Post, February 4, 1966.

[133] New York Times, May 9, 1967, article by John M. Hightower.
[134] Washington Post, February 8, 1967.
[135] Washington Post and New York Times, February 8, 1967.
[136] March 27, 1967.
[137] 'The Politics of Escalation', p. 58.
[138] 'Congressional Record', House September 1, 1965, p. 21702.
[139] 'Viet Cong', Chapter 9, pp. 154-165.
[140] Roger Hillsman, who as Under-Secretary for Far Eastern Affairs at the time may have known what happened with these estimates, quotes figures for 'infiltration' that differ from these. On page 529 of his book 'To Move a Nation', published in 1967, he states the figures:

1961	5,400
1962	12,400
1963	7,400
1964	7,400
1965	19,000

[141] See Eqbal Ahmad, Gettleman, op. cit., for a discussion of the attitude of local guerrillas to outsiders.
[142] February 22, 1965.
[143] Stanley Karnow in the Saturday Evening Post of March 27, 1965, reported that General Maxwell Taylor told him that according to President Johnson North Vietnam would be attacked on the next appropriate occasion and that 'once the decision was reached all that was required was a circumstance that justified reprisal. The Viet Cong handed us the chance at Pleiku and Quinhon.' There are reports that Taylor himself favoured an attack on North Vietnam as early as 1961.
[144] New York Times, June 6, 9 and 10, 1965.
[145] Ibid., July 8, 1965.
[146] Ibid., July 13 and 14, 1965.
[147] Ibid., August 19, 20, 23, 24 and 26, 1965.
[148] New York Times, January 8, 1966.
[149] New York Times, January 2, 1966.
[150] Ibid., January 9, 12, 15 and 25.
[151] Ibid., January 21, 1966.
[152] Ibid., January 22.
[153] Ibid., January 24.
[154] Ibid., January 31.
[155] Ibid., February 8.
[156] No one has ever really been able to speak of civilian or of Viet Cong casualties for that matter with any degree of certainty. On December 22, 1966, the Associated Press reported that the 1966 civilian death toll averaged 1,000 a month and the injured civilians were three times as many—12,000 dead and 36,000 injured for 1966. It was officially claimed for 1966 that about 50,000 'Viet Cong' were killed. Civilian casualties in 1961-63 have been elsewhere reported at about 160,000; for 1964 at 55,000; for 1965 at 75,000; for 1966 at 100,000. Official figures at first given at 100,000 for 1967 were later raised to 150,000.
[157] New York Times, ibid., February 17.
[158] New York Times, ibid., July 19.
[159] Ibid., August 6.
[160] Ibid., August 8 and 10.
[161] Ibid., August 20.
[162] Ibid., August 17.
[163] Ibid., October 22.
[164] Ibid., November 13.
[165] New York Times, January 16, for details.
[166] Ibid., January 17.
[167] Ibid., April 4.
[168] Ibid., June 5.
[169] Ibid., January 7.
[170] New York Times, January 6.
[171] Ibid., January 30.
[172] February 12.

[173] Newsweek, February 19.
[174] Melbourne Herald, March 18, 1968.
[175] New York Times, ibid., February 25.
[176] Ibid., March 10.

CHAPTER 9

[178] Melbourne Herald, April 1, 1968, reporting an article in Stern magazine.
[179] Ibid., April 12.
[180] Ibid., May 27.
[181] Newsweek, July 22.
[182] Ibid., July 21.
[183] Ibid., July 30.
[184] Ibid., July 31.
[185] In November, columnist Stewart Alsop wrote: 'Clifford . . . found a revolt bubbling close to the Pentagon's surface—a revolt of top civilian leadership in the Pentagon against continued escalation of the war by the military. At least six of the top civilians were ready to resign on principle if the Westmoreland-Joint Chief's proposal was approved, thus initiating a great public row.'
[186] Newsweek, July 22.
[187] 'The Lotus in a Sea of Fire', pp. 10, 11.
[188] Op. cit., p. 78.
[189] Op. cit., p. 80.
[190] Newsweek, ibid., October 21.
[191] New York Times, September 11.
[192] Sydney Morning Herald, November 2.
[193] Newsweek, October 28.
[194] Ibid., November 18, 1968.

CHAPTER 12

[195] See 'Facing the Brink', E. Weintal and C. Bartlet, 1967.
[196] Press conference, Canberra, April 23, 1969.
[197] See 'The Lotus and the Robot', Arthur Koestler.

CHAPTER 13

[198] See 'The Real World of Democracy', C. B. Macpherson, Massey Lectures Fourth Series, 1965.
[199] See 'The Underdeveloped Country', J. K. Galbraith, Massey Lectures Fifth Series, 1965.

INDEX